THE AMERICANIZATION SYNDROME:
A QUEST FOR CONFORMITY

CROOM HELM SERIES ON THEORY AND PRACTICE
OF ADULT EDUCATION IN NORTH AMERICA
Edited by Peter Jarvis, University of Surrey

PLANNING ADULT LEARNING: ISSUES, PRACTICES AND
DIRECTIONS
Edited by W.M. Rivera

LEARNING DEMOCRACY
Stephen Brookfield

LEARNING IN THE WORKPLACE
Edited by Victoria J. Marsick

THE AMERICANIZATION SYNDROME :
A Quest for Conformity

ROBERT A. CARLSON

CROOM HELM
London & Sydney

© 1987 Robert A. Carlson
Croom Helm Ltd, Provident House, Burrell Row,
Beckenham, Kent, BR3 1AT
Croom Helm Australia, 44-50 Waterloo Road,
North Ryde, 2113, New South Wales

British Library Cataloguing in Publication Data

Carlson, Robert A.
  The Americanization syndrome: a quest for conformity
  [Rev. and updated ed] 1. Americanization 2. Minorities —
  United States 3. Acculturation — United States
  4. United States — Emigration and immigration
  I. Title
  303.4'8273   E169.1
  ISBN 0-7099-4815-8

Printed and bound in Great Britain by Mackays of Chatham Ltd, Kent

CONTENTS

Introduction:	Educating for Liberty	1
1	The "City on a Hill"	13
2	Franklin's "Happy Mediocrity"	22
3	Americanizing the New Nation	31
4	Redefining the Ideology	45
5	Helping Immigrants Become American: The Humanitarian Americanizers	60
6	Reducing the Intake of Impurities: The Immigration Restrictionists	73
7	The Imperious Demand for Conformity: The Scientific Americanizers	82
8	Let the Professionals Do It	92
9	Broadening the Consensus	101
10	Hispanics and the Language Question	110
Conclusion:	Civil Strife or Expansion of the Consensus?	125
Important Dates in the History of Americanization		139
Bibliographical Essay		144
Index		190

Editor's Note

The Croom Helm Series on the Theory and Practice of Adult Education in North America provides students and scholars with a collection of studies by eminent scholars in all aspects of adult education in North America. It is a parallel series to the Croom Helm International Series and, like that one, it will seek to cover all aspects of the field. The books will be both theoretical and practical. Some will be symposia, while others will be single authored.

At the request of several scholars of adult education in the United States, it was agreed that a completely revised and updated edition of Professor Carlson's book on Americanization education retitled The Americanization Syndrome: A Quest for Conformity should be published in this Series. Bob Carlson has completely revised and updated his book so that it should be of interest to all people who are involved in the issues of immigration and language. The book should be of particular interest to students following graduate courses in adult education and also to all other adult educators concerned with English language education of immigrants.

Many other books are planned in this Series, including a number of historical studies, a major work on self directed learning, a study of the preparation of adult educators in North America and a symposium on adult education and work.

Peter Jarvis
Series Editor

INTRODUCTION: EDUCATING FOR LIBERTY

Cotton Mather and other leading New Englanders in the seventeenth century thanked God for their capacity to destroy, without flinching, the "heathen Tawnies" who blocked their efforts to build a model Christian commonwealth. The Puritan settlers of the country justified their harshness on the grounds that these Indians were agents of the devil, sent to torment the "chosen people" of God. Some three hundred years later, in 1968, a United States Army major reflected this traditional American view of the nation as a chosen people when he defended his order to attack a friendly Vietnamese town overrun by a force of Viet Cong soldiers. "It became necessary to destroy the town to save it," he said, assuming responsibility for the killing of the villagers. He decided it was better that they should die than live under the rule of the Communists, America's twentieth century devils. The rhetoric of the army major, associated less with military strategy than with missionary zeal, fit well into the history of a country that, from the beginning, considered itself charged with responsibilities beyond those of other nations.
 The Puritans of Massachusetts Bay set out to establish in their community the best religion, the best government, and the best society yet obtained in an imperfect world. By maintaining the purity of their settlement's way of life, they believed they could create an educational example for the entire world. Although the Puritan colony did not accomplish a global spread of its values, it had extensive influence on the history of the United States. It was largely from Puritan self-righteousness that the U.S. quite early developed a sense of

mission, a commitment to demonstrate to the world the conduct of a model Christian nation. While waiting expectantly for other countries to copy U.S. patterns, some Americans worried lest the example lose its purity. The United States was an experiment in which people of many religions, races, nationalities, political ideologies, and economic levels came by general invitation from around the world to create a new nation. Although they were proud of the policy of unrestricted immigration, these Americans wanted to ensure that such diversity would not destroy what they believed was freedom's prototype. To overcome the heterogeneity that they feared threatened the unity and example of their country, they relied on education.

These proponents of education who sought to uphold freedom by indoctrinating norms of belief in religion, politics, and economics eventually became known as Americanizers. They applied their remedy for diversity, Americanization education, to nearly all areas of life. Their quest for doctrinal orthodoxy also led them to seek for uniformity in high visibility areas like personal appearance, language, and personal habits. Conformity in these tangible respects gave evidence to the Americanizers of a person's commitment to the more vaguely defined U.S. ideology. Americanization education in the interest of liberty thus became, paradoxically, an imperious demand for individual conformity to societal norms.

This use of education to secure a homogeneous America operated through the years although modifications occurred in the ideology to which all were to give their allegiance. The religious mission of the Puritans evolved into the political mission of the United States. The goal was to serve as the exemplar to the world of the new national state based on republican, middle class, and Protestant principles. Late in the 1800s the doctrine came to include current scientific notions about race and sustained an attempt to spread Anglo-Saxon culture, law, religion, and technology to those areas of the earth that lacked them. During the 1900s "democracy" and "the Judeo-Christian heritage" became the expressions symbolizing the national consensus. This twentieth century ideology, however, encompassed most of the political, economic, racial, and religious values represented in the earlier commitments to Anglo-Saxonism, a middle class society, republicanism, and God's true Protestant religion.

Introduction

Over the course of American history one indoctrination effort after another has gathered momentum, flourished for a time, and then become institutionalized or faded away, only to break out again in a new form some years later. Americanization education entered the nation's culture early in the seventeenth century as a contribution of colonial New England. From the sermons of its pastors that urged the people to conform to the Orthodoxy of church and state, to the effort to bring the "tawny savage" into the true faith of the English, New England was the source of the American confidence in education as the best means for bringing the individual into conformity with society.

As New Englanders spread into non-Puritan colonies and settled on the western frontier, their efforts to educate for civic uniformity gained considerable support but also met opposition. The Scots-Irish Presbyterians on the frontier of the southern and middle colonies shared their faith in the value of a homogeneous society and in education as the instrument for achieving it. The Scots-Irish possessed Calvinism's missionary zeal to create right-believing, right-acting, holy communities. Those who resisted these designs were marked for special attention. While Presbyterians and Puritans alike quickly resorted to firearms with the unregenerate Indian who failed to accept their patterns of life, their solution for the nonconforming white man was usually to try to make the available education more effective.

Benjamin Franklin, himself a product of Puritan New England, was influential during the eighteenth century in educating the colonists to adopt a more secular and nationalistic mission. By encouraging members of the various Protestant sects to modify their principles in the interest of civil harmony and by working to prevent the rigid English class structure from taking hold in the colonies, Franklin promoted the development of what he termed a "happy mediocrity." He sought to educate the people to accept his vision of a secular and middle class society that would overcome what he believed was religious extremism and also would do away with both the rich and the poor, with the aristocracy and the "rabble."

Franklin's projected new society depended on an expanding frontier to provide the poor with economic opportunity. He therefore focussed much of his educational activity on gaining support for this

Introduction

prerequisite to what he hoped would be a new American political and social mission. American backing for expansion increased, but the British government opposed the territorial growth of the colonies. London's containment policy was an important factor in bringing Franklin and other prominent Americans to join in a successful rebellion against their mother country.

After the revolution, many leaders in the U.S. worked to create and inculcate a distinct national identity to replace the political and cultural ties that bound Americans to England and to Europe. As early as 1797 U.S. statesman John Jay, apologizing for his use of the word, spoke of his desire "to see our people more Americanized." Noah Webster, the lexicographer and educator, encouraged the people to reject the "King's English" and attempted to devise a uniform American English in which the new national values were to be expressed. Along with ministers, politicians, and other educators, Webster helped to spread Franklin's concept of a middle class society that undermined European notions of a rigid class structure. These Americanizers denigrated the European state church and the monarchy as decadent institutions. In differentiating Americans from Europeans, however, Webster and the others were producing a new orthodoxy, an American civic religion based on republicanism, the middle class, and nondenominational Protestantism.

This first Americanization campaign in the newly independent nation gradually evolved into more formal arrangements for transmitting the national doctrine to the next generation. By the mid-1800s Americanizers in several parts of the nation were well on their way to developing free, tax-supported public schools to further their interests. They wanted such schools to bring together children of different backgrounds, including large numbers of children of Roman Catholic immigrants, for friendly association, for training in the skills that would help them become part of America's middle class society, and for indoctrination in the Protestant republican ideology. A few years later, after the Civil War, New England school teachers and missionaries flooded into the South under Reconstruction in an attempt to bring Southerners into the republican fold. It was during this period of military occupation that Americanizers helped to spread free public schooling

4

Introduction

into the South as their remedy for nonconformity. In the aftermath of the Civil War, the American ideology narrowed more explicitly along racial lines and influenced the late nineteenth and early twentieth century effort to Americanize the newly arriving immigrants from Southern and Eastern Europe. The militant Anglo-Saxonism that had helped to reunite North and South now challenged the newcomers as a potential threat to the nation's racial purity. The lack of faith in the heritage of these people made it easy to question their loyalty when World War I and the Russian Communist revolution engendered panic in the United States. In this atmosphere, there arose an educational campaign so intensive that Americanization education came to be associated in popular thought almost exclusively with the attempted indoctrination of Eastern and Southern European immigrants.

Americanization became an all-consuming passion in the United States from about 1914 to the early 1920s. Self-styled patriots demanded that immigrants cleanse themselves of all "foreignisms." Factories established classes for the instruction of their immigrant employees in English, citizenship, and American customs. YMCAs and other community organizations offered similar programs. Under the label of citizenship education, the schools expanded and intensified the indoctrination of the immigrants and their children in Anglo-Saxon and Protestant values. Adult education developed into a profession in the U.S. at this time largely as a result of this campaign that involved large numbers of volunteers and all levels of America's burgeoning educational establishment.

In this work with the Eastern and Southern European immigrants, as with their earlier activities, Americanizers demanded an unfair exchange. Through free public schooling they promised each new group of "outsiders" or their children what Americanizers thought was the ultimate fulfillment of a resident of the United States - the opportunity for entry into the nation's middle class. In return for this and for the privileges of American citizenship, they required the recipient to give up virtually all his unique qualities of religion, culture, thought, and appearance. The schools served as indoctrination centers for the prevailing norms in America.

In light of their expressed ideal of a free society, Americanizers were forced to rationalize

5

Introduction

this demand for homogeneity. They did so by arguing that the national interest required general adherence to a common set of values. The individual gained much from America, they reasoned, and ought to be willing to sacrifice a few of his "peculiarities" to advance the cause of unity. In modern jargon, Americanizers believed it was a far greater good to socialize nonconformists to prevailing doctrinal values than to encourage the preservation of meaningful differences. These advocates of education gave higher priority to achieving a model state than to safeguarding individual uniqueness.

Throughout the years, many of the immigrants from Europe voluntarily adopted the American civic religion. With the zeal of converts they embraced the republican concept of representative government even though in many cases their native lands were steeped in feudal traditions. Many accepted the Protestant idea of lay involvement in church polity and, if their own religious organizations were operated differently, agitated for adoption of this Protestant approach. Protestant informality in the form of worship gradually infiltrated Jewish, Roman Catholic, and Eastern Orthodox services. The newcomers and their children eventually abandoned their former manners of dress and grooming for those in vogue in the U.S. They gradually gave up their native languages for English. They eagerly embraced the ideal of the middle class society. Although they usually did not become Protestants, most of the immigrants and their children developed a strong commitment to existing American religious, social, political, and economic patterns. The vast majority of these newcomers displayed a strong faith in the nation and its promise of freedom and opportunity to them and their children.

Americanization education could take little credit for the loyalty immigrants accorded their adopted homeland. The devotion to the nation of the newcomers and their descendants was more the result of the American milieu that after much struggle was made to deliver to a larger extent on its promise of freedom and economic prosperity for the immigrants. Opportunities to farm a homestead, to hold a well paying job, or to practice a minority faith were far more effective in achieving loyalty to the nation and gradual accommodation to prevailing norms than any organized program of Americanization education.

Introduction

    Americanizers showed a singular lack of confidence in this environment which was, after all, the very example they claimed to be preserving for the world. They seemed to believe that the American setting was incapable of winning loyalty and national cohesion without their ministrations. Both for his own sake and for the sake of the nation they sincerely wanted to help the outsider to become what they considered a good American. They felt that if they did not get involved in homogenizing him, the U.S. would disintegrate. These well-meaning advocates of conformity thus attempted to indoctrinate others with a faith in the United States that they themselves lacked.

    Perhaps the major accomplishment of the first 350 years of Americanization education was the pernicious indoctrination of new Americans with a hostility toward nonconformity and a desire to rid themselves of any distinctive European cultural heritage. Immigrants and their children learned in the schools, in the factories, and in other community organizations that diversity led to divisiveness. People who looked, talked, or acted differently from the majority were described as threats to the security of the nation. In the name of national unity, Americanizers discouraged cultural variety in America and promoted nativism and racism among the successive waves of European immigrants.

    Despite the reality, Americanization education came to be idealized as the process of fusing outsiders and natives into a new type of human being containing the strengths of both. Introduced by Hector St. John de Crèvecoeur, an eighteenth century French immigrant farmer and writer, this melting pot theory became popular with the orators. Very few native U.S. citizens, however, subscribed to its basic meaning. Most Americans had been too effectively Americanized to respect the cultural contributions others had to offer. Even those who relied on the U.S. environment for assimilation and rejected organized Americanization education assumed that the outsider would eventually accept their notions of the American way of life.

    One of the few Americanizers committed to the melting pot concept was the influential first generation Italian American, Gino Speranza. A lawyer active in helping Italian newcomers to the U.S., Speranza for a short time early in the twentieth century seriously advocated that immigrant Italians and native Americans blend their cultures

Introduction

to their mutual advantage. Speranza was a rare type of Americanizer, for most of the other advocates of education, some of whom used the metaphor of the melting pot, thought of it more as the dissolving of differences into a standardized American mold.

This pattern of Americanization education as an imperious quest for conformity was established by seventeenth century Puritan leaders like John Winthrop and Cotton Mather. Benjamin Franklin, Noah Webster, and Horace Mann, the latter honored by the U.S. as the founder of its public schools, were effective Americanizers in the eighteenth and early nineteenth centuries. In their path strode Congressman Thaddeus Stevens and militant Americanizer Frances Kellor. Congressman Stevens was the moving force behind the attempt to reeducate and reconstruct the South in the mid-1860s. In the early 1900s, Miss Kellor espoused the adoption of scientific management techniques by the schools and factories of the nation to reshape the immigrants from Southern and Eastern Europe to the Anglo-Saxon model.

Perhaps the most kindly of the Americanizers were the settlement house workers of the late nineteenth and early twentieth centuries. Such pioneer settlement residents as Jane Addams demanded no immediate disavowal by the immigrant of all his unique values. They were willing to mix with immigrants and to learn from them. At the same time, these social workers did expect eventual acceptance by the newcomer of the prevailing American ideology and patterns of life.

Some of the most articulate Americanizers arose from among the outsiders themselves, both from the immigrant groups and from native minorities. Booker T. Washington, a former slave, worked to Americanize blacks. Mrs. Simon Kander of Milwaukee was among the Jewish community leaders who sought the quick assimilation of Russian and Polish Jews. Archbishop John Ireland, an Irish immigrant, was a leading Americanizer in the Roman Catholic Church who worked for the acceptance of his view of the American way by coreligionists from non-English-speaking areas of the world. These advocates of conformity anticipated that Americans would accord equality to their group if most of the members accepted acculturation.

Outsiders who added their leadership to the Americanization campaigns recognized that the

Introduction

United States through the years had used much harsher means than education to impose conformity. They knew that Americans had banished or restricted immigration of unpopular groups. Up to the twentieth century the American policy toward the Indians was one of virtual genocide. In seeking uniformity through education, therefore, these Americanizers considered their approaches realistic and humanitarian.

In the 1980s a new group of Americanizers emerged with a set of policies they considered both realistic and necessary to avoid divisiveness in the country. Disturbed by evidence that some segments of the growing Hispanic and Asian populations in the country were maintaining their native languages and even demanding public services in those languages, they beheld the spectre of a linguistically fragmented nation. In response, they formed an association they named U.S.ENGLISH to sound the alarm and to build support for a constitutional amendment making English the official language of the United States. Some in this group also advocated tighter immigration restriction laws and tougher enforcement.

The leadership of U.S.ENGLISH comprised a diverse group of Americans, including a number of immigrants, who shared the conviction that national unity required a monolingual, English-speaking society. The founder, S.I. Hayakawa, had come out of Canada's Japanese minority and attained wide recognition as an English language scholar and U.S. senator. The executive director, Gerda Bikales, was an immigrant from Europe who was educated in the U.S. and whose career as a social worker led her to the position with U.S.ENGLISH in Washington, D.C. The advisory board included immigrants in academe like Jacques Barzun and Bruno Bettelheim. It also counted among its membership Walter Annenberg, a second-generation American entrepreneur, and Angier Biddle Duke, a scion of colonial stock. These and other advisory board members supported policies that would draw Hispanics, Asians, and all groups in the United States they believed were resisting linguistic acculturation into the dominant English-speaking society just as the immigrants in the U.S.ENGLISH leadership had been assimilated.

A more humanitarian approach, the acceptance or toleration of the differences manifested by nonconforming groups, had roots just as deep, if not as

9

strong, in American history as the quest for uniformity. In the early years of Puritan New England, Roger Williams, a dissenting minister, fled from Massachusetts Bay and established Rhode Island as a community more broadly based than the rest of New England. John Woolman, a leading eighteenth century Quaker, encouraged white Americans of his day to acknowledge that Indians and Negroes were their equals. Woolman and Williams helped set a precedent for the more complete expression of openness to diversity that developed in the twentieth century. Termed cultural pluralism, this alternative to Americanization called for permitting large groups to maintain their cultural identities in the U.S. without undergoing organized educational campaigns to subvert their differences.

Pluralism, epitomized by John Woolman's desire to learn from the Indians of Pennsylvania, held little fascination for most Americans. They desired homogeneity, and in order to achieve it they expected nonconformists to learn from them. Americans generally thought of themselves as the teachers, not the learners.

Throughout American history the drive for purity hit hardest at persons of darker skin. The white people of the United States considered themselves superior to the "Tawnies," the "Niggers," the "Greasers," the "Chinks," and the "Japs," as they termed their fellow citizens. Despite all his problems, the lowliest peasant from Europe - Roman Catholic, Eastern Orthodox, or Jewish - was in a better position on first landing in the United States than a Protestant Negro whose ancestors trod American soil in colonial times or a Mexican American whose forebears dwelt in the American Southwest before the settlement of New England. The native Indians experienced attempted genocide, and the Chinese faced immigration restriction. Indians who survived and Chinese who remained in the country underwent a form of banishment that kept them at a social distance from the "superior" whites. Blacks and Mexican Americans were also segregated from the majority. Such special treatment, however, did not prevent Americanization efforts aimed at helping the segregated to become as good Americans as it was thought possible for them to become.

When segregation began to break down during the 1960s under attack by blacks, especially, but also by allies such as the Hispanics, these groups experienced efforts to impose an even more intense

10

Introduction

application of Americanization education. Before according the alleged American birthright of freedom and equality to such people, white Americans were demanding their "upgrading" to uniform white standards. In the 1960s the U.S. government implemented compulsory programs of citizenship and vocational training for young and older adults as part of a new Americanization education effort intended in large measure for black people but also for Hispanics and other outsiders who allegedly needed improvement.

This study will examine the attempts through the years to educate Americans for homogeneity. Emphasis will be placed on the 1900 to 1925 period when these educational activities achieved identity as the Americanization movement. Reemergence of such efforts after 1960, directed primarily at lower income blacks and at Hispanics, will also be examined. These activities will be put into a broad historical perspective to help explain the ardor with which Americanizers and their supporters in the general public have sought to protect the purity of the U.S. example. It will show why Americans have felt justified in demanding that outsiders undergo an educational gauntlet before according them acceptance as equals. It will demonstrate, too, that many twentieth century Americans continued to feel a mission as a chosen people to maintain the purity of what they believed was the best government, the best religion, and the best society yet achieved in the world.

Although Americanization is a term often used to describe the economic and cultural penetration of other countries by U.S. values and interests, this study will deal almost exclusively with the educational struggle to preserve ideological unity at home. It will touch on the international scene in only a few instances, including the attempts by Americans to spread their values and technology to Hawaii, the Philippine Islands, and the Caribbean in the period around 1900. Direct territorial expansion beyond continental limits, although it occurred in such cases as Hawaii and Puerto Rico, seemed to deny America's self-appointed mission of serving simply as an example.

The pattern of attitudes, events, and responses identified here as the Americanization syndrome has taken similar shape through the years. After considerable struggle, a national ideology, a civic religion, emerges. The country's leadership

Introduction

attempts to maintain the consensus through Americanization education. Eventually conditions change, and a group perceived to be outsiders seems to pose a threat to national unity. Americanizers seek to alert the public to the changing situation. Public complacency tends to give way to panic. Americanizers continue to promote their educational option for bringing the outsider into conformity with the existing ideology. Often they advocate and carry out what they see as innovative programs to deal with the newly identified threat. But, in the midst of panic, their solution faces competing alternatives, alternatives that are sometimes implemented and that may be far more severe than the educational option of the Americanizers. When the public again becomes convinced that it can rely primarily on education, the panic tends to abate. Choice of the educational option provides the time necessary for the environment to assimilate the alleged threat. The "differences" that triggered the panic can eventually become perceived as so minimal as to permit a redefinition of the ideology to accept those differences. Such acceptance seems to require continued pressure by the outsiders and a growing belief by the public that the price of nonacceptance is too high. Before the change of consensus is accomplished, considerable pain is incurred by the outsiders and often a sense of guilt is experienced by the dominant group.

This study will focus on the Americanizers and their part in the Americanization syndrome. It will describe education that has sought to stamp the individual American into group norms in order to advance a U.S. mission of serving as the world's finest example of liberty. Such education will be analyzed as intellectually inconsistent with the U.S. ideal of a free society and unnecessary for national unity. The Americanizers lacked confidence in the very institutions they claimed to be upholding. The contention of some that Americanization education has been a humanitarian means of creating a harmonious society will be judged in the context of the available alternatives - immigration restriction, banishment, genocide, dependence on the environment alone, and cultural pluralism. While Americanizers did help to overcome demands for harsher measures, including genocide, their efforts for homogeneity from Puritan times to the present will be shown as no more and no less than attempts at cultural genocide.

1 THE "CITY ON A HILL"

Cotton Mather, Puritan New England's leading minister, took up his pen in 1697 to inform the world of the accomplishments of God's Israel in the wilderness. He feared that the plan of the English rulers to govern the Massachusetts Bay Colony more closely from Anglican England threatened the continued effectiveness of the Lord's model commonwealth in America. Although he could do little to change the royal decision, Mather was determined not to let the Puritan experience fade from memory. In his Magnalia Christi Americana, his history of the colony, Mather lauded Puritan New England as a rigid Orthodoxy. Yet, the potential for freedom had been considerable. The Puritans came to America trusting in the independence of their congregations and in the ability of each individual to arrive at the proper understanding of God's will with the aid of the Bible, the minister, and the rest of the congregation. But the desire to serve as an example, a "City on a Hill," soon led the Puritan authorities to establish more effective controls to eliminate diversity. The approaches these seventeenth century Puritans took toward maintaining a homogeneous community set the pattern for the Americanizers in their search for uniformity in the United States.

The history of Massachusetts Bay was an exciting story. Into a wilderness in 1630 came a weak and sickly four hundred Englishmen after a grueling voyage in rough Atlantic seas. They were a body of Puritans who disagreed with the way the king and his archbishop interpreted and administered Christianity in England. They planned to set things aright by establishing in the new land, this New England, a Christian state more in line with the

will of God. "The eies of all people are upon us," Governor John Winthrop noted, as the Puritans worked to create an example of correct Christianity that would provide a lesson to all the world.
 The English owed a debt to the Indians in the vicinity for not interfering with the establishment of the colony. If they had desired to drive the settlers out, it would have been an easy task. Instead of feeling gratitude toward the Indians for their restraint, though, the Puritans construed this favorable situation as a sign of their own status as God's chosen people.
 The Puritans were also able to take advantage of the unusual wording in their charter in organizing their unique community. The grant they held from the English king differed from most such documents in that it failed to require the corporation to hold its business meetings in England. The usual stipulation made it possible for the king to exercise surveillance over company policies and, if they displeased him, to supplant the charter with direct royal control. The leaders of the Massachusetts Bay corporation seized on this omission to remove the charter and the entire company to the New World where they could operate their holy enterprise beyond the shadow of the English crown.
 As they set about creating their new government, the Puritan authorities faced a dilemma. They wanted to establish their own version of a pure, Christian society. Yet, it was difficult for them to impose rigid codes of faith and practice when their religion placed considerable responsibility in the individual and, especially, in the individual congregation. The leaders found that their religious philosophy and church structure encouraged a diversity of opinion in the rapidly increasing population. They feared that a lack of uniformity in thought could destroy civil and ecclesiastical authority and, with it, the Christian example of New England.
 While desiring to maintain confidence in the individual conscience, the Puritan leadership sought through education to shape that conscience in the interest of the commonwealth. To ensure that the people could read the Bible, which was the foundation of New England society, the Massachusetts General Court passed a law in 1647 that encouraged townships with fifty or more householders to hire a teacher. Literacy was only part of the process. It was equally important to the

Puritan leadership that the people be educated to achieve the "proper understanding" of the Bible. The sermons of the clergy, learned and deeply theological, taught the approved faith to adults and children alike. Puritan hornbooks, spellers, and catechisms were designed to help parents and teachers to instruct children in both literacy and Orthodoxy. At a higher level, the church leaders made educational pilgrimages to "erring" congregations, arranged colony-wide ministerial meetings to keep the local pastors in line, and advised in the operation of the civil government. In the belief that the proper understanding of the Bible supported orthodoxy and that orthodoxy sustained the commonwealth, New England relied mainly on an educational approach to uphold the Puritan way of life.

This faith that the interaction of education and the individual conscience would promote allegiance to church and state differentiated the Puritans from most of the early settlers of the middle and southern colonies. Puritan clerics required an educated laity that could read the Bible and understand the case they made for the Orthodoxy. Anglicans and the tiny group of Roman Catholics in America, on the other hand, tended to rely extensively on the authority of their hierarchy and priesthood and to feel little need to read the Bible for themselves. Literacy and organized education were not so important to them as to the New Englanders. For the Quakers of Pennsylvania, God's word came from the individual's Inner Light tempered by group meditation, not from book learning. Quakers often became literate, but the motivation behind their education was more vocational than ideological. Education for loyalty and conformity was the New England way.

The Puritans soon discovered, however, that reliance on education involved a measure of uncertainty. Virtually from the beginning of the Massachusetts Bay Colony, those who educated for conformity in the name of stability found themselves in a struggle against those who argued for change. Roger Williams, an articulate young minister from Cambridge University who was involved in planning the Massachusetts Bay project as early as Governor Winthrop, joined the colony in February of 1631. An advocate of separation from the church of England, he disagreed with the majority of Massachusetts Bay colonists who believed that Puritans

15

should consider themselves a part of the English church. After Winthrop denounced such dissent as dangerous, the members of the Salem church reluctantly withdrew their offer to Williams to serve them as pastor. Within two years, however, his continuing popularity amoung the people of the colony brought Williams a call to serve as unofficial assistant pastor from the same Salem church that had earlier accepted Governor Winthrop's arguments. Williams continued to preach views that the leaders considered seditious. He questioned, among other things, the English King's right to charter the Indians' land to the colonists. Eventually another governor, Thomas Dudley, rejected pleas from Williams' fellow clergy to let them try to dissuade their colleague from his errors and banished him from the colony. The result was his establishment of the more broadly-based community of Rhode Island that for many years was a thorn in the side of Puritan New England.

To preserve their sphere of authority as Puritan, indeed as Orthodox Puritan, the leaders of Massachusetts Bay Colony resorted not only to banishment but also to immigration restriction. In 1637, they prohibited the entry of Puritan immigrants who held religious views similar to those of Anne Hutchinson and John Wheelwright, then banished both these "advocates of error." The oligarchy of elders that had taken control of Massachusetts Bay wanted to avoid any dissent that could split New England into many small bastions of holiness.

The Puritans expected all people living in their jurisdiction to adopt their way of life, even the Indians whose ancestors occupied the land for generations before the arrival of the English. Governor Winthrop made these intentions clear from the beginning. When he entertained the Indian Chickatabot one evening in 1631, he allowed him to sit at the Governor's table only because he had dressed himself in English clothing. Winthrop noted that, so clad, Chickatabot "behaved himself as soberly ... as an Englishman."

The settlers employed Christianity and English law to educate the Indians into conformity with Puritan ways. Ministers like John Eliot undertook the task of making these "heathens" into practicing Puritans. Whether heathen or Christian, Indians in New England were expected to keep the Puritan Sabbath and to conduct themselves in all other ways according to Christian principles as embodied in the laws of Massachusetts Bay. The colonists justified these demands as providing civilization to the New World. Unlike their treatment of white men, however, the colonists did not reciprocate Indian acceptance of Puritan ways by according them equality. Writing in his <u>Magnalia</u>, Cotton Mather told the story of how the earlier Plymouth Plantation, some miles from Massachusetts Bay, received God's assistance through the Indian, Squanto, who had been enslaved by an English sea captain, escaped, and lived in England for a time. Mather reported that Squanto got Massasoit and other Indian princes in the Plymouth vicinity to swear allegiance to the English king who, Squanto said, had the power to destroy the Indians with powder and plague. "Thus was the tongue of a dog made useful ...," wrote Mather in gratitude to the Indian who was crucial in the success and growth of Plymouth Colony. It was God who used "those tawny pagans" for his own ends. Indians, even friendly Indians who adopted Puritan ways and did the Englishman's bidding, could expect little gratitude from the chosen people.

In dealing with the Indians, the Puritans sensed that their cultural weapons of Christianity and English law had limitations that only the sword and the gun could offset. When members of the Pequot tribe killed the unregenerate Captain John Stone whom Massachusetts Bay had banished from the colony for being drunk and sleeping with another man's wife, the colonists determined they would have to avenge this unlawful spilling of English blood by the "savages." They felt it necessary to take vengeance even though "Captain Stone, ... for whom this war was begun, were none of ours" and even though Stone and his party gave the Indians considerable provocation. Governor Winthrop indicated in his <u>Journal</u> that the Pequots killed Stone on January 21, 1634. More than three years later, on August 31, 1637, Winthrop noted with satisfaction the receipt of the severed hand of the Pequot chief "who murdered Captain Stone." Even if provoked, the Indians could not be allowed to apply their own law. Such actions might encourage "insolence" and resistance to English control. If education failed to achieve conformity to their ways, the colonists resorted to the harshest possible methods with these non-Caucasians whom they considered savage and of a lower order than them-

selves.
The Pequots were the first of many tribes to feel the self-righteous wrath of this people with a mission. As more and more colonists arrived from England, they settled ever nearer to the Pequots who inhabited the Connecticut Valley. This tribe saw the English as a danger to all Indians and attempted to negotiate an alliance to throw the settlers out of New England. They found, however, that the enmities they had created over the years in the other tribes were too deep. Most of the Indians chose to remain neutral or to ally themselves with the colonists when the Puritans determined to teach the Pequots a terrible lesson for daring to conspire against the New Israel.

Success in their war with the Pequots enabled the English to exert authority over all the nearby Indians. Without the aid of Indian allies, the Puritans would have had difficulty in their military operations. They thanked their God, however, not their Indian friends, for their good fortune. Victory came on May 20, 1637, when, with the aid of Indian guides, the colonists surrounded and slaughtered some five hundred Pequots. They subsequently shipped off the remnant of the tribe into slavery. In his __Magnalia__ some years later Cotton Mather described how the English surprised the Pequots, put the torch to their wigwams, and "broiled unto death in the revenging flames" much of the tribe. One of the Puritan captains exulted that it was "as though the finger of God had touched both match and flint," leading to a slaughter so horrible that "if God had not fitten the hearts of men for the [military] service, it would have bred in us a commiseration towards them." When the remaining Pequots "came to see ... the bodies of so many of their countrymen terribly barbikew'd, where the Engish had been doing a good morning's work," Mather wrote in his __Magnalia__, "they howl'd, they stamp'd, they tore their hair; ... and were the pictures of so many devils in desparation." It would be more than thirty years before any Indians would again challenge the authority of the Puritans.

During these years, the colonists kept informed of developments in the nearby tribes through a number of Christian Indians like Wussausmon (John Sausaman) who studied divinity at Harvard College and then circulated among the tribes preaching the Christian Gospel to them. Wussausmon himself became a symbol for the kind of cultural change that the English were introducing into Indian life. He and Indians like him were the great hope of the settlers, the means by which the "savages" could become civilized.

But to Chief Philip, the militant Wampanoag leader, Wussausmon was a traitor and a lackey to the English. Philip ordered his arrest as a spy. While escorting him to Philip's prison, several of the Indian guards tired of Wussausmon's unsolicited exhortations on behalf of Christianity and killed him. Several months later, in the winter of 1674, the English found the body. A coroner's inquest determined that it was a case of murder. After interrogating a number of Indians, the English apprehended three tribesmen of King Philip, declared them guilty of Wussausmon's murder, and executed them. English law was triumphant again, but at a cost that would prove high for the Puritans.

Philip had complained of the treatment the Indians received from the English. According to John Easton, a Rhode Island Quaker writing in 1675, the chief accused the Puritans of favoring white men in administering justice, of using liquor to confuse and cheat the Indians, and of buying land cheaply from Indians who held no title to it when the legitimate princes would not sell to the English. The colonists, of course, knew that God intended land "to be tilled and improved" in the English fashion, not used as a hunting ground. They could therefore justify their unscrupulous land purchases as in the interest of the Lord. With the execution of the three members of his tribe by the colonists for the killing of Wussausmon, however, Philip had enough of English religion, English law, and English superiority. He believed the colonists had no right to execute any of his followers for killing another Indian. In 1675 and 1676 Philip launched actions against the English which became known as King Philip's War.

The bloody struggle destroyed Philip and his supporters and nearly exhausted the Puritans as well. Philip succeeded in laying waste some twenty English settlements and in killing more than a thousand of the English. The colonists killed many Indians in the war, executed a number of survivors, and shipped hundreds more to the West Indies for the slave trade. The English felt their actions fully justified. Cotton Mather in his __Magnalia__ reflected the Puritan attitude. "... The war was begun by a fierce nation of Indians, upon an honest, harmless, Christian generation of English, who might very truly have said unto the aggressors, ... I have not sinned against thee, but thou dost me wrong to war against me...."

In their harsh treatment of the Indians, the Puritans set a precedent for future American dealings with non-Caucasians. The estimated six hundred thousand Indians in America in 1630 were reduced to less than half that number by 1900, and they were driven into largely wasteland reservations or, as individuals, into the poorest and most disorganized areas of twentieth century cities. Americans justified this genocide and banishment by arguing that the Indians were unreasonable in trying to block the expansion of the white nation and in refusing to become acculturated to the American way.

In the seventeenth century, however, the Indian was but one impediment to the colonists' drive for dominion over the land. The Puritans emerged from the costly Indian wars to find their Orthodoxy of church and state even more seriously threatened, as King Charles II and his successors gradually reasserted royal authority over the colonists in the thirty years after 1664. In the face of stubborn Puritan efforts to continue their Orthodoxy, England finally annulled the Massachusetts Bay Company charter that enabled the colony to function as an independent City on a Hill. The British rulers were then able to exercise their power through a royal governor who resided in the colony. The Puritan leaders were required to welcome other Protestants into the settlement and accord them political rights. The power of outside forces finally overcame sixty years of education, banishment, immigration restriction, and genocide in behalf of Puritan homogeneity.

The hysterical reaction to this change found an outlet in a witch hunt within the settlement. The Puritans put to death nineteen human beings and two dogs during a series of witchcraft trials. Upstanding citizens like the Reverend George Burroughs were sentenced to be hung for refusing to cooperate in the panic.

When the acceptance of other Protestants on a more equal basis failed to engender the disasters the leaders prophesized, the colonists experienced a deep feeling of guilt over their earlier actions. The jurors who convicted their fellow citizens of witchcraft signed papers indicating their repentance. Twenty years after the trials, the legislature annulled the convictions and indemnified the heirs of the victims. In the long run, the hysteria and the resulting guilt helped to gain public acceptance of the colony's broadened consensus by discrediting the Orthodoxy and its leaders.

Cotton Mather wrote his history of New England, his <u>Magnalia Christi Americana</u>, in 1697 shortly after the old Puritan consensus gave its death rattle in the witchcraft hysteria. Mather's book provided only the glow of dying embers. Outside influences, as well as the colonists' own guilt feelings, were weakening the rigid Orthodoxy and leading Massachusetts Bay toward an early and limited version of pluralism that included most white Protestants. In trying to achieve homogeneity in their society, the Puritans had undertaken a staunch educational effort that set a precedent for future Americanization attempts. Its limitations drove them to resort to banishment, immigration restriction, and genocide - alternative approaches used by later Americans in their continuing quest for the exemplary society. None of these actions, however, was able to save Cotton Mather's New England. "But whether New England may live any where else or no," Mather wrote, "it must live in our History." He sensed an instructional potential in the example of Puritan New England even in the epitaph he was writing for it. Although their educational objectives had been largely thwarted, Mather and the other Puritans still possessed a strong faith in education as the best means for attaining a pure and homogeneous community. This commitment to education would sweep through other parts of America as New Englanders and their Presbyterian brethren settled in other colonies and in the territories to the west. From New England's education of her people in the ways of the Lord would come the United States of America's education of her people in the ways of the nation.

2 FRANKLIN'S "HAPPY MEDIOCRITY"

The evolution of the drive for a pure religious community into a more secular Americanization education was most clearly visible in the work of the influential American, Benjamin Franklin. Born and reared in a Puritan Boston home, he maintained the old New England belief that a harmonious society required homogeneity and that education was the best means to this end. But Franklin's religion was the secular state, not Puritanism. He conducted his educational efforts against diversity in the name of the general welfare, first in the Quaker colony of Pennsylvania and later on a broader scale. Ironically, Franklin's attempts to foster loyalty and stability in American society led to his participation in revolution.

Franklin was one of a large number of immigrants welcomed into Pennsylvania under the liberal immigration policy of the Religious Society of Friends, the Quakers. While some newcomers like the German pietists got along well with the Quakers, others were not prepared to cooperate with the founders of the colony. The Quaker-controlled legislature had particular difficulty with the Scots-Irish frontiersmen.

These Presbyterian settlers were disdainful of Quaker pluralism when it found expression in a respect for the Indian and for Indian culture. They vigorously dissented, too, from the colony's pacifist policies. Disregarding Quaker treaties with the Indians, the Scots-Irish moved onto Indian lands. Like the Puritans of New England, they believed God intended the earth to be farmed and developed, not used as hunting grounds. The Indians, as "heathens," failed to understand such Christian reasoning and, encouraged at times by the

French, resorted to sporadic warfare in defense of their lands. The Presbyterian frontiersmen responded by pressing the Quaker legislature for arms which they said they needed to defend themselves from Indian attack. It was the immigrant Franklin who, as an editor and legislator, gave leadership to resolving the Quaker-Presbyterian impasse in the interest of the state. Although the Scots-Irish may have brought the wrath of the Indians upon themselves, Franklin supported the frontiersmen. He sensed that Scots-Irish aggressiveness offered the state the opportunity for rapid expansion and an increased growth of population. He also worried over the alliance developing between the Indians and the French enemy of the British Empire. When the Quaker-controlled legislature balked at funding measures for war, he pointed out the possibility of its violent overthrow by disaffected frontiersmen or by the king himself. Franklin was amused to discover that the consciences of some Quaker lawmakers were less disturbed about voting funds "for the King's use" and for bread, flour, wheat, "or other grain" even though these words would clearly be interpreted as authorization for military supplies. The legislature eventually adopted a compromise based on such euphemistic phrasing, a policy encouraged by Franklin.

The educational activities of Franklin, including his influential "Plain Truth" pamphlet, brought forth in pacifist Pennsylvania an ad hoc defense organization by 1748. He called on those Quaker legislators who could not conscientiously vote funds for defense to resign during wartime. Within a decade, after the French and Indian War set the Pennsylvania frontier ablaze, Franklin achieved official Assembly enactment of his voluntary militia bill and the withdrawal of many pacifist Quakers from the legislature. He thereby met the Scots-Irish demands for defense against the Indians and by-passed the scruples of Friends against serving in the military and voting funds for war. Through education and compromise Franklin helped to undermine the pacifist and pluralist values of the colony's founders.

Franklin also conducted both educational and military efforts against the lawlessness and violence of the Scots-Irish frontiersmen. When they avenged the depredations of the warring western Indians by riding east to slaughter the remaining

Conestogas, a friendly and harmless tribe long cooperative with the English, Franklin forcefully condemned them. He met their march on Philadelphia to annihilate pacifist Moravian Indians by organizing a defense association that convinced the attackers to return to the frontier. Likening their actions to those of "idolatrous Papists," he termed these Scots-Irish vigilantes "barbarous Men" who conducted their raids "in defiance of Government, of all Laws human and divine, and to the eternal Disgrace of their Country and Colour...." He dismissed their Biblical justification from Joshua that they were commissioned by God to destroy the heathen as "Horrid Perversion of Scripture and of Religion!" While Franklin approved of Indian removal, extolling the man who "removes the Natives to give his own People Room," he preferred more subtle means than violence and resisted any action that threatened the conduct of orderly government.

Franklin would let no religious commitments interfere with the harmonious functioning of his state. He encouraged Quaker Assemblymen to vote, not on the basis of their consciences, but as "Representatives of the Whole People." He helped Friends in the Assembly to maintain the facade of pacifism and toleration while in fact enabling the Scots-Irish to drive the Indians from the land. By helping the Presbyterian frontiersmen to get military support and by attacking their excesses, he deflected their missionary drive from a holy war to the defense and expansion of the Pennsylvania frontier. Both the Quaker way and the Scots-Irish way had to adjust in the secular society Franklin was helping to create in America.

Although he was ready to work against unique or peculiar tenets of religious faith if he felt their elimination would aid the state, Franklin did not intend to destroy the Society of Friends or any other religious group. Having shed most of the Christian dogma for himself, he still favored religion for others. He believed that adherence by the people to a generalized religious faith gave the state an additional measure of control and encouraged the conformity he desired.

The compromise of Quaker values resulting from Franklin's embryonic Americanization campaign bothered the consciences of many Friends, but none more than John Woolman. Like Franklin, he had retired from business at an early age to devote his

life to service. While Franklin served his state by seeking conformity to a secular value system, Woolman worked to sensitize consciences to what he felt were the evils of that system. He sensed that the prosperity of many Pennsylvania Quakers led them to turn from spiritual values to those that motivated people like Franklin, "the improvement of our country, ... merchandize and sciences."
Concerned over the problems of conscience that the Quakers in public office were experiencing, Woolman encouraged the entire community of Friends to take leadership against war with the Indians by refusing to pay taxes. He feared that if Quakers continued to compromise their testimony against war, "by small degrees ... there might be an approach toward that of fighting" until they came so close to it "that the distinction would be little else, but the name of a peaceable people." He helped to keep alive in the Quakers the unique pacifist attitudes that Franklin was working to subvert.

Although he found that he could do little to bring peace between the Scots-Irish and the frontier tribes, Woolman demonstrated his solidarity with the Indians. With war still raging in western Pennsylvania in 1763, he braved the dangers to visit a band of Indians there. He wanted to "feel and understand their life" and discover if he "might receive some instruction from them...."

Woolman also worked to improve the lot of another hard-pressed racial group in America, the African slaves. He traveled in the southern colonies to learn more about slavery and to encourage Quakers there who held slaves to free them. In line with his religious convictions, he decided in 1762 to wear only natural colored clothing, refusing to support the dyes industry that utilized slaves. He argued that the conditions Americans imposed on non-Caucasians were the cause for the "notions of superiority" the colonists felt toward them.

John Woolman's compassion and openness to diversity were not to become the dominant American way. Like Benjamin Franklin, Americans usually insisted on uniformity, seeking it from Caucasians through education and from non-Caucasians by harsher means. The religious values of pacifism and respect for other races and religions expressed by John Woolman did continue within America, but for at least two hundred years they existed pri-

marily as troublesome aberrations from the norm.
Occasionally such religious convictions proved useful to American leaders, as Franklin showed in his support of the Quaker testimony against slavery. Franklin backed the efforts of the Friends to end the institution in America, serving as president of a Pennsylvania abolitionist society in his later years. It was not the Quaker belief in the dignity of the Negro that motivated him, however. He feared that slavery would morally weaken members of his superior English race by having others do their work. Since the English were to provide the model for all other groups in America, Franklin wanted them to adhere to a high moral and physical standard. He was also concerned that slavery promoted a rigid class society that was out of place in America. Then, too, it offended his racism to import black people. "... Why increase the Sons of Africa," Franklin asked, "by planting them in America, where we have so fair an Opportunity, by excluding all Blacks and Tawneys, of increasing the lovely White...?" He was probably disturbed, as well, over the development of an institution that flourished in only one section of the American colonies. Just as pacifism would have to give way to Franklin's view of the general welfare in Pennsylvania, so would slavery have to end in the South for the sake of a strong and harmonious American community.

It was not only the commitment to pacifism among the Quakers and to slavery among Southerners that Franklin fought on behalf of colonial and, later, national homogeneity. He was also ready to destroy the language and culture of the German settlers of Pennsylvania. He worried that the Germans of Pennsylvania were "too thick settled" in their own communities for the English language to win their children away from their traditional culture, as was happening with the Swedes in Pennsylvania and the Dutch in New York. Franklin, quite prepared to modify the values of the Quaker founders of Pennsylvania, opposed other changes in the colony. "Why should Pennsylvania, founded by the English," he asked, "become a Colony of Aliens, who will shortly be so numerous as to Germanize us instead of our Anglifying them...?" Apparently unable to conceive of two cultural groups existing cooperatively in the same community and fearful of German disloyalty to the English government, Franklin turned hopefully to schemes for schooling the children of the "Palatine Boors," as he termed them, to conform with English culture. Franklin helped to establish charity schools to teach the children of German immigrants English and the King James Bible. "By such an education, and daily converse with English children, taught in the same schools with them," Franklin wrote, "they may contract such early friendships with each other as may in time lead to those intermarriages, and create that sameness of interests, and conformity of manners, which is absolutely necessary to the forming them into one people, and bringing them to love, and peaceably submit to the same laws and government." The charity school project, had it been successful, might have eliminated German culture in Pennsylvania in the name of good citizenship.

The offer of schooling for their children led some Germans to cooperate with Franklin until they discovered that, in exchange, he expected the children to give up their cultural heritage. Christopher Saur, a publisher widely respected in the German community in Pennsylvania, helped to publicize the motives of the charity school promoters. Saur's writings and the strongly English overtones of the twelve schools that were established contributed to the termination of this Anglification project in 1763.

Franklin's definition of what constituted a problem in society helped set the pattern for future Americanizers. He was not interested in freedom for black people or in justice for the Indian. Slavery and religious fanaticism, as well as German culture and Quaker pacifism, were to be expunged because they tended toward diversity. In seeking to educate all for conformity to his own view of the American way, this immigrant Pennsylvanian and colonial leader displayed the presumption that has been endemic to Americanizers through the years.

Franklin's search for a harmonious and uniform community led, paradoxically, to his support of a new social order and a revolutionary regime in America. Although he had no specific blueprint for the good society, Franklin was convinced that the traditional class system encouraged the restiveness that continually threatened European tranquillity. He gradually became committed to the development of a one-class nation that would do away with economic and social disparities. His new mission for the "chosen people" was the creation in America of what he termed a "happy mediocrity" or middle class society, a goal that future Americanizers would vigorously promote.

Franklin worked toward his vaguely defined ideal society by attempting to educate the authorities and the public both in England and the colonies to support territorial expansion in North America. He drew up and promoted plans for new western colonies to encourage a flow of population into the Ohio and Illinois country. As a colonial representative in England, he helped gain support for those who wanted Britain to take possession of Canada after defeating the French in Quebec in 1759. Franklin believed that such expansion of the Empire would further the development of a "happy mediocrity" by furnishing opportunities for large numbers of colonists to gain access to the middle class.

Although Franklin couched this essentially American interest in the rhetoric of empire, leaders in London were suspicious of expansionist tendencies in the colonies. Franklin's arguments that expansion would increase the power of the empire were offset by British fears that settlement beyond the Appalachians would encourage independent manufacturing in the colonies. Such a development, statesmen in London argued, would weaken the imperial system of mercantilism. They were also aware of economist Adam Smith's theory that continued growth of the American colonies might result in the eventual removal of the seat of the empire from London to America. The prospect of a shift of imperial power into American hands held little appeal for British leaders.

Authorities in England frustrated the varied desires of the increasing number of expansionists in America by passing the Quebec Act in 1774. The bill catered to the interests of the conquered French of Quebec by establishing Roman Catholicism as the tax-supported state religion of Canada and by accepting, at least indirectly, their continued use of the Frengh language. It also overcame the refusal of the Americans to pay for administering the territory north of the Ohio and west of the Appalachians by ceding the area to the control of Quebec. It was a just and kindly act, the British contended. The Americans saw it, instead, as a conspiracy of the British crown with its French-Canadian subjects to cut the colonies off.

Americans reacted intensely to what many believed was the betrayal of their religious and national interests by the British. The First Continental Congress in 1774 expressed "astonishment that a British Parliament should ever consent to establish in ... [North America] a religion that has deluged ... [England] in blood, and dispersed impiety, bigotry, persecution, murder and rebellion through every part of the world." Outside forces seemed to be conspiring against Franklin's plans for America, just as they had destroyed the religious commonwealth of his Puritan ancestors.

Franklin termed the Quebec Act "dangerous to us all" and urged its repeal. "Loving Liberty ourselves," he wrote, "we wish'd it to be extended among Mankind, and to have no Foundation for future Slavery laid in America." Despite his rhetoric, Franklin was not so concerned about any menace to Protestantism as he was about the threat British policy posed for his view of America's mission. He believed that the British, by establishing Catholicism in the Northwest, were attempting to block the westward movement of America, an expansion necessary for the development of his uniform middle class society.

The Quebec Act was an important factor in driving the colonists to rebellion. From the British viewpoint, it was a necessary step to control the fanatics in America who seemed to think that the land belonged to them rather than to Britain. This act was only one of a long series of British efforts to tighten the administration of the North American colonies for the benefit of the mother country. When the colonists added up these actions, they saw a pattern of continual violation by the British crown of their rights as Englishmen. Such seditious moves by the king, Franklin and other Americans argued, justified the violent overthrow of the government.

American success in the Revolutionary War opened the way to independence and expansion, to a new social order, and to a major Americanization effort. Franklin's concept of a "happy mediocrity" became an integral part of a new civic religion that U.S. leaders promoted in behalf of nationalism. Like Franklin in Pennsylvania, Americanizers in the United States sought to develop a secular ideology that could modify and encompass the tenets of the many large groups of Protestant Europeans in the nation. Emulating Franklin again, and the

Puritans before him, the new United States relied on education to indoctrinate its people for unity through homogeneity.

3 AMERICANIZING THE NEW NATION

To establish a nation independent of European influence, the politicians, educators, ministers, and others who conducted the first Americanization campaign in the United States sought to inculcate a new doctrinal uniformity. They worked to create a national identity as a land of individual freedom based on the Protestant religion, the middle class society, and a republican form of government. The Americanizers, who were largely of New England or Presbyterian background, functioned on a modest scale at first, only later dedicating themselves to the ambitious task of founding schools to indoctrinate the homogeneity they desired. Their similar heritage undoubtedly nourished their interest in developing a model homogeneous society. They would find, however, that their allegiance to the mutually exclusive values of individual liberty and civic uniformity would prove as frustrating to them as it had to their colonial ancestors.

In developing a nationalistic doctrine, the Americanizers combined Benjamin Franklin's vision of a "happy mediocrity" with other concepts articulated as early as 1765 by New Englander John Adams. In his newspaper attack "On the Canon and the Feudal Law," Adams saw a long and continuing conspiracy between prince and priest in Europe to impose "ecclesiastical and civil tyranny" on the people, an effort gravely weakened but not as yet destroyed by the Protestant Reformation. It was this conspiracy, Adams wrote, that caused the Puritans "to fly to the wilderness for refuge" where they might more effectively carry on the struggle for freedom of conscience. In America, he explained, the Puritans sought church government consistent with "that religious liberty with which

31

Jesus had made them free" and civil government after the manner of "the ancient seats of liberty, the republics of Greece and Rome." By blending the concepts of America's middle class society and its republican form of government with the myth of its founding as a haven of liberty, Americanizers were able to differentiate the new nation from Europe as a land of freedom, equality, and opportunity.

Like the Puritans before them, Americanizers in the new United States prepared to balance their interest in freedom with education for conformity. They feared that complete trust in individual liberty might result in divisions of thought and values that could tear the nation apart. Benjamin Rush, an eminent Pennsylvania Presbyterian and a signer of the Declaration of Independence, articulated their goal when he called for educating Americans as "republican machines."

Textbook writers like Noah Webster were among the most active participants in the early years of the campaign to Americanize the new nation. "To diffuse an uniformity and purity of language in America ... to promote the ... harmony of the United States." That was the purpose Americanizer Webster ascribed to his spelling book that sold more than twenty million copies throughout the United States by 1829. Webster, a New Englander and an admirer of Franklin's ideas of society, favored cultural as well as political independence from Europe. He wanted to insulate Americans from European ideas by nationalizing the spelling and pronunciation of the English language in the U.S. Americanizing the dictionaries and school books, he thought, would overcome the influence on the new nation of British authors by making their spelling and, by association, their ideas appear foreign to Americans. He also expected that a homogeneous national language would help to eliminate sectional strife within the United States. In Webster's view, a unique American language would advance the nation's unity and its revolutionary economic, social, and political doctrine.

The school book authors joined with ministers in teaching that the revolution was the work of God who ordained the new Protestant republic to reform the world. Charles Goodrich of Vermont justified his history of America as providing "lessons upon the science of civil government, social happiness, and religious freedom of greater value than are to be found in the history of any other nation on the

Americanizing the New Nation

globe." Even the somewhat more cosmopolitan reading books of Presbyterian minister William Holmes McGuffey promoted U.S. nationalism by inculcating a common moralistic background in the rising generation of the Western frontier. Many of the school books contrasted American freedom and progress with backwardness, rigid class structures, and superstition in Roman Catholic countries. John Frost of Boston, the author of <u>The Class Book of American Literature</u>, reflected the earlier view of John Adams in attributing Italy's poverty to "the feudal and pontifical systems combined." Jedediah Morse, a New England clergyman and prolific textbook writer, stated in his <u>Geography Made Easy</u>, "The Protestant clergy are learned and exemplary in their deportment, the popish ignorant and libertine." From the pulpit Morse equated Protestantism and republicanism. Any subversion of Protestant Christianity, "our holy religion," would ultimately destroy "our political freedom and happiness," Morse asserted. "Whenever the pillars of Christianity shall be overthrown, our present republican forms of government and all the blessings which flow from them, must fall with them."

This Americanization effort, then, created a unique religio-political identity for the United States as a land of liberty. The campaign also identified America's ideological enemies as monarchy, the rigid European social class system, and Roman Catholicism, describing them as the institutions that brought Europe to the low and decadent state to which Americans believed it had sunk. This secular use of religion in behalf of nationalism would soon blur Protestantism, the middle class concept, and republicanism together into an American civic religion.

In turning a divided Protestantism to the interests of a homogeneous state, the Americanizers capitalized on the U.S. environment. The distances and sparseness of population in the West often encouraged cooperation. The different denominations found it difficult economically to sustain parochial schools or even churches on a separate basis on the frontier, much as some traditionalists wished for it. In the more populous East, as well, costs often precluded sectarian schooling. Experience taught the churches that collaboration furthered the effectiveness of churches and schools. Soon a wide range of interdenominational Protestant organizations arose nationally, including the

33

American Bible Society, the Sunday School Union, and the American Tract Society. The propaganda of the Americanizers encouraged this "nonsectarian" solution to the challenge of the U.S. environment, furthering national cooperation based on the commonalities of the Protestant denominations.

The work of the Americanizers in behalf of republicanism and a generalized Protestantism contributed to the growth of similarity in the beliefs and practices of the different Christian churches in the United States. American Lutherans, Episcopalians, and Reformed Church members had become so similar in their faith and practice early in the life of the new nation that they seriously considered merging their church organizations. The Roman Catholic Church, too, underwent a weakening of peculiar tenets similar to the earlier experience of the Quakers of Pennsylvania. The small Roman Catholic establishment in the U.S. found the American ideology infiltrating its organization. Because of a lack both of priests and of an effective organizational structure in the colonial period and the first years of the republic, Roman Catholicism in the United States depended more than in Europe upon laymen. As a result, laymen took more responsibility within the church organization than was usual in Europe, in some places even adopting the republicanism of Protestant church polity by assuming control of the church property they built. So far did Protestant republican concepts gain sway that some American Roman Catholic congregations shocked the hierarchy by appointing their own parish clergymen. Protestant republican concepts, then, seemed capable of consolidating national thought, as desired by the Americanizers, while at the same time accepting a diversity of religious organizations.

Although the U.S. ideology provided a high level of national cohesion, Americanizers found that it could not avoid all factionalism. Even the mainstream of Protestants divided theologically into orthodox, liberal, and evangelical factions. Each of these conflicting groups tacitly supported the idea of a civic religion but defined the fundamental theological content of the American doctrine differently. Each wanted the ideology to mirror its own particular view of Protestantism. Political parties, too, fought over the meaning of the American doctrine. But not even the Federalist Party could achieve conformity, despite attempts to impose its views through such repressive laws as the Alien and Sedition Acts of 1798. Divisions along religious, political, and other lines were the logical outcome of the U.S. commitment to individual liberty. Americanizers might desire "republican machines" serving the general welfare, but theoretically at least, the doctrine they advocated left even the definition of the general welfare itself to the individual's conscience.

In creating an independent identity for the nation as a land of liberty, Americanizers idealized the United States as a haven for the oppressed of Europe. In the first blush of revolutionary spirit Benjamin Rush defended the Germans of Pennsylvania from Benjamin Franklin's earlier attacks and rehabilitated them in American history as industrious, frugal, and loyal Americans. Rush chided Franklin, "otherwise an astute Statesman and a Philosopher," for allowing his "Yankee prejudices" to unite him with the anti-German "wiseacres of the times." Although Thomas Jefferson saw dangers in immigration, especially of monarchists after the French Revolution, and the Federalists feared the Irish and German immigrants who voted predominantly for the Jeffersonians, immigration to the United States remained free of restrictions. Except during the Federalist hysteria of 1798 to 1800, the legal waiting period for citizenship after 1794 was only five years. The rhetoric in behalf of free immigration was idealistic although the policy was quite practical in that it increased the nation's manpower and economic development.

Congressman John Page of Virginia reflected the victorious view that Americans ought to be generous with their immigration policy "after boasting of having opened an asylum for the oppressed of all nations, and established a Government which is the admiration of the world...." Page told Congress, "It is nothing to us, whether Jews or Roman Catholics settle amongst us; whether subjects of Kings, or citizens of free States wish to reside in the United States, they will find it their interest to be good citizens, and neither their religious nor political opinions can injure us, if we have good laws, well executed." Page, unlike Franklin and the Americanizers, assumed that the U.S. political structure could cope effectively with immigrants of diverse backgrounds.

Whether they relied on education or on the environment alone, Americans generally assumed that the newcomer would imbibe the freedom of a nation that imposed no official state religion and no hereditary aristocracy, throw off the former shackles of European church and state, and become a "true American." "Here individuals of all nations are melted into a new race of men...," wrote Hector St. John de Crèvecoeur, a French immigrant, in his popular Letters from an American Farmer. Governor De Witt Clinton of New York and others spoke glowingly of this new type of human being. In practice, though, Americans rejected Crèvecoeur's idea of blending the traits of all the nationalities. Native-born U.S. citizens had no intention of modifying their patterns of life, and they certainly were not prepared to change the newly formulated Protestant republican ideology. National commitment to the melting pot idea was a myth, for Americans expected the immigrant to discard his own patterns and adopt those prevailing at the time in the United States.

When many immigrants and even some native settlers of the frontier appeared indifferent to the civic religion, Americans feared a "return to barbarism." Easterners foresaw anarchy and chaos developing in the rough and uncontrolled frontier regions, and they anticipated a breakdown of law and order in the large cities where masses of poor Roman Catholic immigrants were settling. Between 1815 and 1860 more than three million immigrants poured into the United States from Ireland and Germany, many of them Roman Catholics of peasant background. The resulting increase in Roman Catholic institutions raised concern among the Americanized native population that anti-Protestant, thus anti-republican and un-American, ideas were infiltrating the nation. They also sensed that the poverty of the newcomers endangered the survival of the country's uniform middle class social order. The rapid demographic changes seemed to pose a threat to the U.S. ideology.

Americanizers reflected the by now traditional faith in education in seeking to develop and expand publicly controlled and supported common schooling. Horace Mann was one of many in New England who sought to strengthen that area's system of public education and to spread it to other parts of the country. On the Western frontier, New Englanders and Presbyterians led the drive for common schools that could overcome the twin perils of barbarism and Roman Catholic missionary work that they felt menaced the westward export of the American way. It was largely transplanted New Englanders like Caleb Mills in Indiana, Calvin Stowe and Samuel Lewis in Ohio, the Reverend John D. Pierce and Isaac Crary in Michigan, the Reverend George Atkinson in Oregon, the Reverend Theron Baldwin in Illinois, and John Swett in California who directed the institutionalization of public schooling in the West. Presbyterians like Samuel Galloway in Ohio and the Reverend Robert Breckinridge in Kentucky added their efforts to the struggle to maintain U.S. culture on the frontier. By 1850 Americans were well on their way to having a publicly supported, community controlled common school system available without charge to children in many parts of the North and West through which they could indoctrinate the rising generation in the civic religion.

While transplanted Easterners in the West were relatively susceptible to New England's "civilizing" influence, the immigrants offered considerable resistance. Lutherans from Germany were shocked at the modifications that had occurred over the years in American Lutheran theology. First the Germans and later the Scandinavians organized their churches separately from the native American Lutherans in order to preserve their unique tenets and their native languages. For a time the Lutheran immigrants viewed the public schools as inimical to their religious and cultural interests. Roman Catholic newcomers maintained a similar attitude toward the public schools for a much longer time. The development by the immigrants of parochial schools and other religious institutions separate from those of native Americans evoked the dread of diversity that had been so effectively instilled by the post-revolutionary churchmen, politicians, and textbook writers.

While native Americans used restraint in their treatment of the Protestant "separatist," they reacted hysterically to Roman Catholic Church leaders who challenged the Protestant aspect of the civic religion Americanizers had inculcated. People in the U.S. were alarmed at the efforts of Roman Catholic bishops to assume authority over church property that for years had been administered by lay trustees. The most publicized of these struggles was for control of St. Mary's Roman Catholic Church in Philadelphia. After ten years of contention, by 1830 the hierarchy, with the help of the pope, gained victory over the Philadelphia trustees. Americans decried the outcome as "repugnant to our republican institutions" and feared the imposition of foreign concepts on their cherished way of life. Similar hierarchical struggles with Roman Catholic laymen occurred into the 1850s in New York, New Jersey, Massachusetts, and elsewhere. This tightening of Roman Catholic church administration, Americans believed, posed a serious threat to U.S. freedom. They feared that the Protestant republican concept where the people held final authority over both church and state was in jeopardy, and they blamed "priest-ridden" Irish and German immigrants for allowing such a situation to develop.

Their fear of Roman Catholicism caused some Americans to lose faith in the capacity of education for preserving the Protestant republican ideology and to press, instead, for immigration restriction. Samuel F.B. Morse, who would later invent the telegraph, was a leader among those who urged the modification of U.S. immigration policy to slow the influx of Roman Catholics. While he had less faith in Americanization education than his father, New England pastor Jedediah Morse, the younger Morse was equally committed to maintaining a pure and uniform nation. As early as the mid-1830s, he was warning Americans of a European plot to encourage mass immigration of Roman Catholic peasants to the U.S. where they were to destroy the American example from within. Quoting an Austrian scholar and government official, Frederick Schlegel, Morse showed that some Roman Catholic monarchists in Europe viewed the Protestant Reformation and the American republic as the inspiration for opposition to the European status quo. That Austrian officials also supported the Leopoldine Society, an Austrian organization for the promotion of Roman Catholic missions in America, seemed to Morse to signify a conspiracy between church and state of a despotic Europe to destroy the American City on a Hill. The fact that most of the Roman Catholic immigrants at the time voted for the more democratic of the American political parties only attested to the "Jesuitical artifice" and cunning of the conspirators, Morse contended. He claimed that Roman Catholic immigrants were trained to obey priest and monarch as "senseless machines." Morse, who wanted "republican machines," argued for amendments to the naturalization laws that would discourage immigration and make it more difficult for the European "conspirators" to accomplish the destruction of the American way of life. Morse was undoubtedly correct in assessing the antirepublican, anti-Protestant attitudes of European monarchists and of a number of the Roman Catholic higher clergy in Europe. The European hierarchy drew much of its leadership from the aristocracy. These leaders knew that European republicans generally wanted not only to overthrow the monarchies but to disestablish the church as well. Pope Gregory XVI scandalized Americans in 1832 by terming liberty of conscience an "absurd and erroneous doctrine" and "a most venomous error." Although such antirepublicans in Europe lacked the authority to dictate their political views to the Roman Catholic immigrants and clergy in the United States, Morse and his fellow restrictionists kindled American fears of a nineteenth century return to the "Dark Ages," a period vividly described in U.S. school books and other Americanization literature of the time.

By their actions some Roman Catholics in the United States tended to give credence to Morse's position. Militant assaults on existing U.S. institutions by Roman Catholic clerics like Irish immigrant Bishop John Hughes made some Americans wonder if Americanizers could achieve conformity from Roman Catholics. Hughes rejected the Americanizers' public schooling that provided a way into the middle class for Roman Catholic immigrants and their children in exchange for giving up their "peculiar" cultural and religious commitments. He became a strong advocate of Roman Catholic parochial education. Hughes did not stop with attacking the unfair exchange in public schooling. Reacting aggressively to the conspiracy theorists, the bishop uttered grandiose statements on the inevitability of Roman Catholicism sweeping America from the feeble arms of a failing Protestantism. In his sermon on "The Decline of Protestantism and its Causes" in 1850, Hughes boasted, "Everybody should know that we have for our mission to convert the world, including the inhabitants of the United States, the people of the cities, and the people of the country, the officers of the navy and the marines, commanders of the army, the Legislatures, the Senate, the Cabinet, the President, and all!"

Roman Catholic militancy appeared subversive of U.S. institutions and of continued liberty since

Americanizers had convinced the people that the freedom of the nation depended on its Protestant heritage. Thus Americans found it disturbing when a large number of immigrants proved ungrateful to the nation that received them by refusing to honor its Protestant republican ideology. When these newcomers spurned its public schools and remained faithful to what seemed to be a disloyal, European-controlled church, the situation became intolerable.

Increasing the alienation between the two groups was the fact that native Americans most often came into contact with the generally poor Roman Catholic newcomers with their European religious and social values at the lower levels of the society where native and immigrant competed for jobs, housing, and advancement. Here Americans saw at first hand that Roman Catholics rejected American Sabbath laws and opposed public school use of the King James Bible, a symbol not only of Protestant religion and morality but also of American patriotism. They discerned, too, that many immigrants were paupers whose dependency drained the tax dollars of hard-working citizens. Substantial resort to liquor often seemed to the immigrant a means of assuaging a difficult life, but to many natives it was a sign of barbarism. Perhaps alienated by the natives' disapproving attitude toward them, foreign laborers sometimes laid claim to all the jobs in certain construction projects for their fellow countrymen and drove off American applicants by threats and violence. While Roman Catholics resented efforts of Americans to impose consensus values, many Americans saw evidence that the Roman Catholic immigrants were plotting against their Protestant religion and even against their jobs.

Americanization education was much too slow a process to satisfy these Americans. Their antipathy to the newcomers led to the rise of national anti-Catholic political parties, to rioting, to the burning and bombing of churches, to vigilante action, and to murder. In 1833 New Englanders burned down houses in the Irish section of Charlestown, Massachusetts, after a group of drunken men, identified as Irish, murdered an American there. Maryland called out troops in 1834 and 1839 to quell immigrant rioting. In New York City, street mobs stoned Bishop Hughes's home in 1842, and the Irish rioted in 1844 when the city ordered them to keep their pigs from running loose on the streets.

40

Americanizing the New Nation

In retaliation for the murder of an American, a Philadelphia mob in 1843 burned more than thirty homes in an Irish section, sparing only the Protestant Irish who displayed "Native American" signs on their doors. Roman Catholics destroyed a Protestant church in Cincinnati in 1853. Protestants blew up Roman Catholic churches in Sidney, Ohio, and in Dorchester, Massachusetts, and attacked or burned dozens of others in the mid-1850s. After 1834, elections in New York and Philadelphia regularly triggered street fighting between rival Irish factions or between natives and foreigners. Protestant-Catholic riots killed ten men in St. Louis in 1854 and twenty in Louisville in 1855. The American Party and the later American Protective Association promised political action to protect the Protestant republic from the alleged Catholic conspiracy.

The religious and economic diversity that plagued Americans found its expression in microcosm in the Ursuline convent school in Charlestown, Massachusetts. By 1830 the orderly, middle class nation envisioned by Franklin was becoming increasingly stratified economically. Many of the financially well-to-do also tended to take a liberal outlook on religion. Already the Puritans of New England had split into factions ranging from liberal Unitarians to orthodox Congregationalists. Many Unitarians hesitated to have their children attend the New England public schools that were dominated by Congregationalists. In fact, some Boston Unitarians sent their daughters to the Roman Catholic convent school operated by the Ursuline order in Charlestown. A concentration of children of the unduly prosperous Unitarian "heretics" in an institution operated by "idolatrous papists" was an outrage to Congregationalist workers who in 1834 burned the convent school to the ground.

The violent divisions in American life reflected in such incidents convinced public school proponent Horace Mann to give up a promising political career and devote full time to improving education in the United States. "The mobs, the riots, the burnings, the lynchings, perpetrated by men of the present day," he was convinced, "are perpetrated because of their vicious or defective education when children." For Mann harmony was not to be obtained by violence or by immigration restriction that slowed economic growth and rejected the U.S. tradition of serving as an asylum for the oppressed

of Europe. Horace Mann worked for more than ten years as secretary of the Massachusetts State Board of Education in an effort to create the elusive harmonious community through education.
Mann looked to the public school as the crucial agency of Americanization. He was convinced that schooling could modify "peculiar" religious tenets and overcome the growing disparity of wealth. Subscribing to Franklin's "happy mediocrity," Mann termed education "the great equalizer of the conditions of men - the balance-wheel of the social machinery." He believed that a series of fundamental values animated the nation, including Christianity, a commitment to liberty, and a love for the republic. By emphasizing these values and avoiding classroom discussions of "sectarian" political and religious creeds, Mann thought the schools could successfully indoctrinate Americans in the civic religion. He wanted to ensure that the United States had a universally available and effective educational system that would provide access to the middle class and inculcate a common morality and patriotism.
Mann's well-meaning recommendation that the schools indoctrinate morality by reading from the King James Bible without comment brought opposition from Roman Catholic churchmen. To Mann the solution was reasonable. "Is it not, indeed, too plain to require the formality of a syllogism," he wrote, "that if any man's creed is to be found in the Bible, and the Bible is in the schools, then that man's creed is in the schools?" Roman Catholic clerics argued that the Bible of the schools was a Protestant version. They claimed that the Roman Catholic Church alone had the right "to judge of the true sense and interpretation of the scriptures" and demanded that Roman Catholic children read no Bible unless it was properly authorized and interpreted by their church. Protestants, who had already compromised many of their denominational interests for the good of the nation, saw the Roman Catholic Church's position as unpatriotic and self-serving sectarianism while Roman Catholics feared the common schools would convert their children to Protestantism.
In response to the trend toward institutionalizing the use of what they viewed as a Protestant Bible in the public schools, the Roman Catholic clergy began to rely more and more on separate parochial schools in which they could propound

Catholic ideology. Despite their failure to gain public funding for such schools, the third Plenary Council of U.S. Roman Catholic churchmen stated in 1884 that no parish was complete until it had "schools adequate to the needs of its children." This separatism, of course, elicited animosity from Protestant Americans and prompted many of them, who might have preferred their own sectarian religion in the schools, to support the nondenominational Protestantism implicit in the recommendations of Horace Mann.

The increasing availability of public schools after the middle of the nineteenth century mitigated the tendency toward violence and immigration restriction and furthered a renewed confidence in Americanization education. Americans accepted the argument of Horace Mann that common schools of high quality would eventually lure away the constituencies of private and parochial schools. They tolerated parochial schools, as they earlier tolerated Quaker pacifism, as a right of conscience. But, for the sake of nationalism, they hoped that such peculiarities would gradually die out in the natural process of assimilation. Mann overlooked the possibility that religious loyalty and the opportunity for prestige might draw continuing financial support for separate parochial and private schools. He also failed to foresee the development of a form of Americanization education within the parochial schools themselves. Still, the hope that separate schools would wither away, combined with the reality of increasingly strong public schools, made Americans optimistic that eventually Americanization education would overcome both the "immigrant problem" and the "Roman Catholic problem."

The United States succeeded early in the nineteenth century in welding a national civic religion based on the middle class, a secularized Protestantism, and a republican form of government. While challenges to this doctrine resulted in violence and demands for immigration restriction, by mid-century Americans accepted the leadership of Horace Mann and the public school founders who relied on the New England solution of education to Americanize the nation. Common schools, they believed, could show the new generation the importance of the prevailing American ideology and build the long-sought harmonious community. The fact that Roman Catholics were attacking the existing

43

consensus and felt it necessary to establish parochial schools to protect their children from it did not deter the Americanizers. They believed that truly effective common schools would overcome the "peculiar" and divisive parochial school system and conserve the American way of life. Thus with the eventual solution of America's religious and class divisions in the good hands of the common schools, attention turned to another area that divided the nation, the question of slavery.

4 REDEFINING THE IDEOLOGY

With the common school system developing by the mid-1800s at least partly to instill the Protestant, middle class, and republican consensus in the North and West, the New England-Presbyterian drive for a homogeneous nation turned toward the South which possessed a peculiar and unrepublican institution. During the early years of the nineteenth century, most Americans expected that slavery, contained within a few Southern states, would gradually die out as republicanism swept into the hearts and minds of the slaveholders. But the South, for economic, psychological, and cultural reasons, perversely cherished its institution. The growth and expansion of slavery and the development of a Southern class system based upon it led to an abolitionist campaign to preserve the pure example of America as a land of freedom. The overriding motivation to end slavery was ideological, not humanitarian, as blacks would soon discover. This attempt to secure the Americanization of the South led to civil war, a modification of the national ideology, and a cooperative effort by North and South to spread the American way among non-Caucasian peoples around the world.

Most Americans sensed an inconsistency between human bondage and republicanism. The founding fathers excluded the institution of servitude from the Northwest Territory in 1787 and provided in the constitution for the cessation of U.S. participation in the international slave trade by 1808. In the Northern states, public commitment to Protestant republican ideals led by the early part of the nineteenth century to the enactment of laws that signalled the ultimate termination of slavery there. Only in the South did slavery linger on as

45

a "peculiar institution."
 The attitude exhibited by most Northerners toward Southern slaveholders was similar to the attitude native Americans took toward the Irish and German Roman Catholic immigrants. As Americans expected the immigrant eventually to accept Protestantism, or at least the values of Protestantism, so did they expect the South to shift gradually from the plantation and slave system to the more republican New England system of small farms operated by free men, a pattern already largely accepted on the Western frontier. While Americanizers counted on the common schools to homogenize the next generation of Roman Catholics, a group that settled largely in the North and West, they had no equivalent instrument for dealing with the South. Schools were under local control, and the Southern leadership was loathe to emulate the common schools of New England, preferring the more aristocratic approach of private education for the elite. Given their lack of control over the South, Northerners depended entirely on the republican impulses abroad in the land to convince slaveholders to release their human property.
 Southern plantation owners, however, seemed in no rush to free their slaves. Conditions in the South changed after 1800 to increase the importance of slavery to that section. Introduction of the cotton gin made the South economically more dependent upon the slave system. The diminishing fertility of the soil persuaded some planters to work for the legalization of slavery in the virgin Southwestern territories. Entry of Missouri into the Union in 1821 as a slave state marked a victory for the planters and opened the way for some of them to move west with their Negroes. A Southern cultural nationalism rapidly developed based on human bondage. By 1829 Governor Stephen D. Miller of South Carolina proclaimed, "Slavery <u>is not a national evil; on the contrary, it is a natural benefit</u>".
 The apparent unwillingness of Southerners to let slavery die in their section prompted an educational campaign for abolition by a small group of Northerners who sought to bring the South into line with the national ideology. "... The subject of slavery," William Lloyd Garrison of New England wrote, "involves interest of a greater moment to our welfare as a republic ... than any other which has come before the American people since the Revo-

lutionary struggle...." While they differed with Garrison as to methods and timing, such transplanted New Englanders as Theodore Weld, Beriah Green, Joshua Giddings, Elizur Wright, and Henry Stanton joined with him to lead the fight to Americanize the South by expunging this institution that tarnished the U.S. example.

Overcoming original indifference and later persecution, the abolitionists slowly won over many people in the North and West to the view that the South was attempting to maintain and extend slavery. A key factor in the growing success of the antislavery movement was the militant counterattack on it by Southerners. When Garrison sent copies of his little-read publication, <u>Liberator</u>, to Southern editors, they responded to his passionate and harshly critical columns by enraged editorials of their own against proponents of abolition. The popular Northern press reprinted these controversial exchanges and created reader interest in the issue of slavery. Attempting to protect their economic, political, and cultural interests, Southern politicians in Washington achieved annexation of Texas as a slave state in 1844, defeated efforts to prohibit slavery in territory acquired in the Mexican War, and gained enactment of a more stringent Fugitive Slave Act in 1850. Enforcement of this act dramatized to Northerners the growing infringement on freedom in the United States, as fellow townsmen were fined or jailed for their part in the "underground railroad" that assisted escaping slaves and as some blacks in the North were accused of being fugitive slaves and shipped back to bondage in the South with little chance for legal defense. More and more Americans came to believe abolitionist claims that their own freedom, as well as the reputation of their country, was in jeopardy from a militant antirepublicanism.

Earlier Americanizers had succeeded in creating a concern for the ideological purity of the republic, an interest to which the abolitionists now appealed with ever-increasing success. By 1840 more than 150,000 people in the U.S. were members of antislavery societies. These organizations produced hymnals, almanacs, and children's books that included abolitionist materials. One speller opened its alphabet lesson with:

> A is an Abolitionist
> A man who wants to free
> The wretched slave, and give to all
> An equal liberty.

Theodore Weld's <u>American Slavery As It Is</u> was one of many publications that attacked the un-American nature of the institution. Antislavery conventions, public speakers, periodicals, tracts, and petition campaigns depicted Southern slaveholders as immoral, opulent, and aristocratic enemies of the middle class republican ideal, whose souls needed redemption.

Respected Northern and Western leaders enlisted in the antislavery effort. As early as 1835 the leading American Unitarian minister, William Ellery Channing of Boston, spoke out against slavery. Henry Ward Beecher, an important figure in the Congregational Church, took an unequivocal stand in 1850. Many people of New England and Presbyterian background who had worked to Americanize the nation's children by initiating or improving public schooling in the North and West joined in the effort to Americanize the South. Horace Mann left his post with the Massachusetts State Board of Education to become a congressman in 1848 as an antislavery Whig. Ohio public school founders Samuel Galloway and Samuel Lewis were active in the political struggle against slavery. Harriet Beecher Stowe, Henry Ward Beecher's schoolteacher sister and the wife of Ohio public school advocate Calvin Stowe, published her influential antislavery novel, <u>Uncle Tom's Cabin</u>, in 1851. Mainstream opposition coalesced in the new Republican Party, founded in 1854 to oppose the extension of slavery.

While they wished to cleanse the national soul, few opponents of slavery disagreed with the racist arguments of the defenders of the institution. With the exception of Garrison and a relatively few humanitarians like him, including those Quakers who maintained the tradition of John Woolman, Northerners generally accepted the Southern belief that blacks were inferior to Causasians. They viewed the United States as a white nation and saw little place in it for the emancipated Negro. Some backed the efforts of the American Colonization Society, organized in 1816, which assisted more than a thousand free Negroes to emigrate to Africa by 1828 and helped to send another seven thousand to Haiti. Large-scale emancipation, however, would make colonization extremely expensive. Whether they favored deportation or the education of blacks to make them more like whites, most Northerners were prepared to deal with that problem after abolishing slavery and restoring their republic's integrity. Southern agitation after 1850 for renewal of the slave trade, the violent controversy in Kansas and Nebraska over the extension of slavery, and the Supreme Court's proslavery Dred Scott decision in 1858 convinced Northerners that the survival of the republic was at stake. Abraham Lincoln, a moderate Illinois politician who favored gradual emancipation and deportation of blacks, mirrored growing public opinion in 1854: "I hate it [slavery] because it deprives our republican example of its just influence in the world ... and especially because it forces so many really good men amongst ourselves into an open war with the very fundamental principles of civil liberty...." After the Supreme Court found in the Dred Scott decision that the U.S. constitution forbade prohibitions against the extension of slavery, Lincoln marshalled evidence of a conspiracy operating to spread slavery throughout the nation. Declaring "this government cannot endure, permanently half **slave** and half **free**," Lincoln urged vigorous educational and political action to overcome the alleged plot and bring the South into line with the North and West.

The fear of a conspiracy, long fostered by abolitionist Joshua Giddings, soon grew into an hysteria that pictured the South in league with the pope and European monarchs to destroy the American way of life. Robert Breckinridge, the Kentucky advocate of common schooling, crusaded vigorously, as he had for years, against slavery, monarchy, and the papacy - institutions he believed threatened American freedom. Americanizers could point to the antirepublican pronouncements of such popes as Gregory XVI and Pius IX, to the U.S. Roman Catholic hierarchy's opposition to the abolitionists, and to the attitudes of many Irish immigrants toward blacks that culminated in burnings, mutilations, and lynchings of black people in New York City in 1863. The friendly relations between the aristocratic South and such European monarchies as France and England, both with an economic interest in the South's cotton exports, also gave the illusion of reality to this extreme conspiracy concept. Historian George Bancroft would soon describe the North-South struggle as a moral drama between the free Protestant republic and the slave confederacy supported by the "worn out aristocracies of Europe" and the "Pope of Rome." The aggressiveness of the South in promoting an institution Americans considered unrepublican evoked as frenzied a public reaction as the militancy of the Roman Catholic leadership had brought down earlier upon the Irish and German Catholic immigrants.

The election to the Presidency of Abraham Lincoln as a Republican pledged to halt the spread of slavery led to the South's secession in 1861. Lincoln vowed to preserve the republic but acted with restraint until Southerners attacked Union-held Fort Sumter, South Carolina, and unleashed the bloody Civil War. Northerners now began to assume the attitude taken toward slaveholding Southerners two decades earlier by William Lloyd Garrison: "We do not acknowledge them to be within the pale of Christianity, of republicanism, of humanity."

While a number of economic, political, and other factors combined to cause the Civil War, the threat of slavery to the Protestant, republican, and middle class civic religion of the United States was a crucial precipitant. People of the North and West were brought up on school books, sermons, and a popular press that pictured America as a land of liberty. This education created an environment in which abolitionists were able to convince Americans that slavery made a mockery of the national ideal. After the Civil War, the United States amended its constitution to outlaw slavery and thereby preserved its national identity as a free republic.

The people of the South thought their defeat simply meant the continuation of the Union and the end of slavery, as the assassinated Lincoln had pledged. Southerners did not expect that they would have to accept blacks on equal terms. Indeed, in 1865 and 1866 the conquered South imposed "Black Codes" of conduct on freed Negroes, similar to the old slave codes, to keep this "inferior" race under control. The Southerners, however, did not reckon with Congressman Thaddeus Stevens and the small but influential group of Radical Republicans who demanded that the South emulate their idealized view of the New England republican.

Reconstruction, a Radical Republican policy passed by Congress over President Andrew Johnson's veto, was instituted to Americanize black and white Southerner alike and create, as well, a Republican

Redefining the Ideology

Party in the South based on the franchise of the blacks. "Is it not time that these men [white Southerners] were transplanted at least into the nineteenth century," asked New Englander James Russell Lowell in the North American Review, "and, if they cannot be suddenly Americanized, made to understand something of the country...?" The morality of the newly freed slaves was the concern of missionaries from Northern churches who hastened South to upgrade the new black citizens. Under the fourteenth and fifteenth amendments to the constitution and the Civil Rights Act of 1875, and with the protection of the U.S. Army, a coalition of black and white legislators liberalized the South's election system, tried to achieve a social revolution on behalf of the poor, and established the first effective public school system in most of the Southern states. School teachers and philanthropic money from New England poured into the South in an effort to strengthen the developing schools. Encouraging attendance by the promise of literacy and the possibility of upward mobility in American society, schoolmen worked to improve the Southerners, a people they considered indolent, ignorant, and unrepublican. Through a common school education enriched by the increasingly popular manual arts, educators sought to homogenize the thinking of white and black Southerners, indoctrinate the Protestant republican consensus, build individual industry, and open the way to economic independence and moral maturity New England style. Americans believed that Reconstruction's attempted transplantation of the New England school to the South extended the same opportunity to Southerners as these schools had earlier afforded Roman Catholic immigrants - the chance to learn the national ideology, to achieve entry into the middle class, and to become good, conforming citizens.

While the freed Negro welcomed the opportunity to become Americanized, white Southerners were less appreciative of the North's efforts. By playing on Northerners' guilt feelings and on the deep desire in the North for national reconciliation, they were able to defeat the campaign to gain political and social equality for Southern blacks. Northerners, who never disagreed on the relative inferiority of non-Caucasian peoples, began to sense that Radical Republican policy was asking more of the South than of the rest of the country after achieving the Civil War goals of ending slavery and preserving the Union. They listened gravely and with growing concern to white Southerners' complaints of corruption in Reconstruction governments and of unethical actions by some of the freed slaves. Although such immorality was widespread in American society at the time, white Americans were especially alarmed when blacks engaged in improper practices. At the same time, white Southern writers surfeited the nation with romantic tales of the prewar South, packed with dashing colonels, magnolia trees, gentle ladies, and lovable but child-like "darky" servants. Thomas Nelson Page took the mythical South to its extreme in his novel, Red Rock, an allegory of national unity in which a heroine from the North married the gallant and noble Ku Klux Klansman whom she rescued from an unjust imprisonment. When President Rutherford B. Hayes fulfilled a political deal by withdrawing the remaining federal troops from the South in 1877, public opinion in the North was ready to accept his decision.

Northerners were prepared to give up the attempt at Reconstruction and Americanization of the South. They did not wish to alienate white Southerners any further, and they had no desire to see blacks and white radicals in control of the South. Changes such as the abolition of slavery, the breakup of the large plantations, and the growth of public schools gave people in the North the feeling that the South was conforming more closely to middle class and republican values that they defined as the American way. The development of public education in the South seemed to reassure Northerners that schooling's unfair exchange of knowledge and access to the middle class in return for the disavowal of peculiar values and patterns of life would at last be nationwide. Twenty years after his 1865 report on the South's recalcitrance that helped to trigger Reconstruction, influential Republican political figure Carl Schurz wrote that Southerners were "as loyal to the Union as the people of any part of the country."

Abandonment of Reconstruction meant that Northerners were willing to compromise the interests of black people in order to gain the good will of white Southerners. By 1886 the Supreme Court virtually nullified the Civil Rights Act of 1875 and the fourteenth amendment to the constitution, thus enabling the South to disenfranchise blacks, to prohibit interracial marriages and racial mixing in

Redefining the Ideology

church congregations, and to require separate educational and other facilities for blacks and whites. In the interest of national unity, Northerners sacrificed the political and social equality of the blacks they emancipated and left the future of Southern blacks in the hands of white Southerners. The attempt to Americanize the South to an idealistic model fell apart, as white Northerners and Southerners increasingly cemented their own reunion with a spirit of nationalism based on Anglo-Saxon racism.

The cohesive force of Anglo-Saxonism was strong. There was no question but what most Southern whites belonged to that race. Popular thinking also accorded membership to most white Northerners, including immigrants and their children of Germanic, Scandinavian, and sometimes even Irish background. The racist togetherness could paper over the continuing religious differences, especially since the schools were working to overcome that problem throughout the country.

Despite the nation's return to a white racist ideology, the influential black leader Booker T. Washington believed he could gain entry for his people into the mainstream of U.S. life by Americanizing them. He believed that the emancipated Negroes had to bring themselves up to the white man's level before they could realistically ask for equality. Vocational or industrial education, Washington thought, would make it possible for the new citizens to gain financial self-sufficiency and the equality offered by membership in the middle class. He was confident, too, that it could indoctrinate patterns of industriousness, punctuality, cleanliness, and a whole litany of personal habits becoming identified with the American way of life in a nation with a closing frontier. He proposed that blacks accept political and social inferiority for the time-being. Once black people upgraded themselves economically and in the social graces through this special kind of education, Washington assumed that white Americans would accept them as equals.

W.E.B. DuBois, a black sociologist and educator, questioned whether the South would ever accord equality to blacks without the application of intense pressures. DuBois favored liberal arts college education for the development of a black leadership elite that could help to apply these pressures. The skepticism of DuBois toward the

South proved correct, for a new populist leadership replaced the aristocrats who were prepared for eventual accommodation with blacks. DuBois warned, "... The ignorant Southerner hates the Negro, the workingmen fear his competition, the money-makers wish to use him as a laborer, some of the educated see a menace in his upward development...." These were the men who by the turn of the century gained control of the South and who, with the acquiescence of the North, were about to return the United States to its traditional racist patterns and to erase the aberrations introduced during the Civil War and Reconstruction.

Americanization education would be viewed as an insufficient means of dealing with non-Caucasian peoples in the U.S., as the Chinese in the American West were discovering. Westerners, like Southerners, preferred harsher methods for dealing with these outsiders. Protestant missionary work, much of it supported and staffed from the Eastern U.S., was ridiculed as ineffective. It was the rougher elements among the Irish and native American workers who conducted the West's major effort to Americanize the Chinese. These self-appointed "educators" attempted to terrorize the Chinese into conformity with American life by burning their separate Chinatowns and cutting off their distinctive queues, the long braid of hair that was meaningful in Chinese culture. Westerners, however, expected little success from any educational efforts directed at the Chinese. "During their entire settlement in California," the legislature reported to Congress, "they have never adapted themselves to our habits, modes of dress, or our educational system, ... never ceased the worship of their idol gods, or advanced a step beyond the musty traditions of their native hive." While the South was banishing blacks to a life of segregation, Westerners pressed for Congressional restriction of further immigration from China.

A joint investigating committee of Congress in 1876, headed by the fair-minded Senator Oliver P. Morton of Indiana, temporarily blunted the efforts of restrictionists. Morton dismissed the claims of white union leaders that Chinese willingness to work for low wages was proving disastrous to white workers and their families. "Difference in color, dress, manners, and religion," he wrote, "have ... more to do with this hostility than ... any actual injury to the white people of California." But

Redefining the Ideology

with the national Republican and Democratic parties courting votes in the West, New Englanders and others interested in the China trade and in church missions to the Chinese both in the United States and China had difficulty maintaining immigration laws for the Chinese equal to those for other nationalities. Arguing that big business was sacrificing poor white people for narrow self-interest and that Protestant missionaries were deluding themselves in believing they could successfully Americanize the Chinese, the restrictionists overcame the opposition and achieved a national immigration law in 1882 that excluded Chinese workers.

Restriction of immigration on racial grounds by the United States three months before it got around to excluding lunatics, idiots, convicts, and those likely to become a public charge brought strong protests from the government of China. But the Chinese were politically and militarily weak. American leaders thus felt no serious international pressure to mitigate the anti-Chinese policy the West had imposed on the rest of the country.

When Californians turned their discriminatory efforts against Japanese and Americans of Japanese descent after 1904, however, it became a dangerous international matter. Japan, recent victor in its war with the Russians, forcefully objected to the San Francisco school board's 1906 order requiring all ninety-three Japanese children in the city's white schools to attend the segregated Chinese school. The school board persisted in its policy while public opinion in Japan escalated into a war fever over this stigmatizing of the Japanese as inferior. Only by inviting the board, the superintendent of schools, and the mayor to Washington and promising action to check Japanese immigration did President Theodore Roosevelt convince San Francisco to reverse its policy. Although racist actions by Westerners did not lead immediately to war, they did create enmities in China and Japan that were to plague Americans after 1940.

Persecution of another non-Caucasian group, the American Indian, had gone so far by the 1870s that Americans were discussing what they could do with the surviving remnants. Some would have executed all Indians summarily on the frontier dictum that the only good Indian was a dead Indian. Others wished to Christianize and Americanize young Indians on the reservations. One of the most well-meaning white advocates of Indian education at the time was a young army officer, Richard Henry Pratt, who saw no future for reservation Indians in the United States. He wanted to integrate Indians into the life of the Caucasian victors by educating Indian children to adopt the English language, American dress, and American customs. With the backing of Secretary of the Interior Carl Schurz, Pratt established the Carlisle Indian School in 1879 where he attempted to eradicate the Indian culture of more than four thousand children during his twenty-four years of service. Gaining the assent of Western Indians to teach their children the white man's ways so they could better defend Indian rights, Pratt proceeded to take the children to his boarding school, shear their hair, clothe them in military uniforms, equip them with a trade, and train them up as white men.

Like Booker T. Washington, Pratt failed to realize that Americans rejected non-Caucasians, however Americanized, as a part of the national community. Instead of integrating the children into white society, the Indian Bureau regularly returned the children to their reservations after they had completed their few years of schooling. Back with their tribes, they either shed the white man's culture or became displaced persons, unacceptable in either Indian or white society. Pratt's well-intentioned Americanization program proved disastrous to those he was dedicated to helping. Even when they accepted Americanization, the fate of Indians and other non-Caucasians in the promised land was to be some form of banishment.

The rising influence of Anglo-Saxon racism also twisted an equally presumptuous yet well-meaning demand for uniformity in the U.S. into an American quest for empire. Josiah Strong, a Congregational minister who traced his lineage to Puritan New England, argued in 1885 that if the United States could overcome the perils of Roman Catholicism, Mormonism, immigration, intemperance, socialism, extreme wealth, and the growth of the carnal city, it could look forward to the voluntary adoption of the American way of life throughout South America, Africa, and the rest of the world. In his Our Country, a book that sold 176,000 copies by 1916, Strong urged Americans to cleanse their nation so that it would possess "the largest liberty, the purest Christianity, the highest civilization." Convinced that the American was "divinely commissioned to be, in a peculiar sense, his brother's

Redefining the Ideology

keeper," Dr. Strong hoped that the purified U.S. example would help to civilize, Protestantize, and Anglo-Saxonize the non-Caucasian, backward, and non-Christian peoples of the world. When the non-Caucasian targets for improvement overseas seemed too backward to learn from the American example, others used Strong's rhetoric to justify the use of force to impose U.S. institutions upon territories in the Caribbean and the Pacific.

From the notion of serving as an example, a policy that began in the days of the Puritans, there developed in the 1890s a powerful sentiment for overseas expansion cloaked in the rhetoric of Anglo-Saxonism and Christian duty. Senator Albert Beveridge, Republican from Indiana, reflected the attitude when he told Congress, "God ... has made us the master organizers of the world to establish system where chaos reigns.... He has made us adept in government that we may administer government among savage and senile peoples.... And of all our race He has marked the American people as His chosen nation to finally lead in the regeneration of the world." Beveridge and many of his fellow Republican congressmen found themselves justifying international expansion into the Philippine Islands, Hawaii, and Puerto Rico on the same grounds of Anglo-Saxon superiority used by racist Southern Democrats to justify white domination of the U.S. South.

Racism played an important part in the debate over expansion. Antiimperialists warned that the admission of non-Caucasians to citizenship would pollute Anglo-Saxon blood and institutions while the governing of peoples without their consent and representation would destroy at home the very ideology of republicanism that the expansionists ostensibly sought to export. Those who favored expansion, however, won public opinion to their side. Americans rejected allegations that such aggrandizement might threaten their own freedom. Having acted contrary to the U.S. charter of government in compromising the domestic freedom and equality of Indians, of blacks, and of Chinese on pragmatic grounds, Americans simply extended their racist double standard to the international scene for equally practical reasons.

The expansionist philosophy was compelling. The North and South together had won a war with Spain that proved the Union strong and dropped into American hands a number of former Spanish island

57

possessions. It was difficult to reject the spoils of what to Americans was so glorious a war, especially when such possessions could prove strategic for hemispheric defense and for trade with China and when both Germany and Japan seemed interested in the Philippines if the Americans withdrew. President William McKinley, considered at one time an antiexpansionist, finally rose from prayer one day with divine assurance that "there was nothing left for us to do but to take them all, and to educate the Filipinos, and uplift and civilize and Christianize them, and by God's grace do the very best we could by them as our fellow-men for whom Christ also died." The United States, therefore, took possession of Puerto Rico in the Caribbean and, until 1946, the Philippines in the Pacific, seeking to transform them with American government, law, and education while at the same time using them economically and militarily.

While attempting to export America's free institutions to "uncivilized" people abroad, back home the United States was closing doors on blacks North and South. By 1910 most Southern states had instituted full-scale segregation. Between 1884 and 1900 Americans lynched 1,678 black people, mostly in the South. Reasons given for lynchings ranged from murder and rape to talking with white girls and insulting a white man. In 1898 a former U.S. congressman led a mob into Wilmington, North Carolina, to ravage the black district. In South Carolina that year whites burned a newly appointed black postmaster to death in his house for his insolence in accepting the post, then shot down his escaping family. White mobs celebrated a racist victory that disenfranchised blacks in Louisiana by taking over New Orleans and assaulting black people for three days. In 1906 whites attacked and murdered blacks in a four-day binge in Atlanta, Georgia, honoring another white supremacy victory. Seeking refuge, many black people emigrated to Northern cities. Chicago's black population swelled more than six hundred per cent, from less than sixty-five hundred in 1880 to forty-five thousand in 1908. New York, Philadelphia, and other cities experienced similar population changes. The influx frightened white workers who feared for their jobs, and it worried middle class citizens who doubted that such an "inferior race" would prove an asset to their cities. Instead of a promised land in the North, blacks found that they could gain employment usually in menial jobs only and that they faced de facto segregation. North and South, black people discovered they were marked as "inferior" and were now more effectively banished from American society than during slavery.

Americanizers, seeking a uniform and harmonious society, had struggled to gain the South's conformity to republican and middle class values. Contrary to their intentions, they contributed to the outbreak of the Civil War and then to a reconciliation based on a harsh Anglo-Saxon racism. The racist reaction aroused by the activities of some of the Americanizers negated later attempts by others to Americanize blacks, Chinese, and Indians for entry into the society as equals. Even if non-Caucasians submitted to cultural genocide at the hands of the Americanizers, they simply could not conform with the color that white Americans associated with ideological purity in the U.S. While whites were prepared to end slavery, they had no intention of sharing their nation equally with non-Caucasians. Ironically, these racists sought to export American notions of freedom, equality, law, and order to nonwhites throughout the world by military force. The outward thrust beyond continental limits was blunted, however, when Americans discovered another situation within the United States that seemed to menace the purity of the American example. After learning that the source of European immigration had shifted from the Northwest to the Southeast of Europe, Americans realigned their national priorities and made an all-out effort back home to preserve the Anglo-Saxon and Protestant republic from this internal threat. It was the educational aspect of this drive that would eventually become widely known as the Americanization movement.

5 HELPING IMMIGRANTS BECOME AMERICAN: THE HUMANITARIAN AMERICANIZERS

With the attention of most Americans focussed on the attempts to spread the U.S. ideology overseas, the increasing numbers of Eastern and Southern European immigrants reaching the United States late in the nineteenth century experienced a relatively gentle and open-minded Americanizer. The social settlement workers, concerned coreligionists, and some schoolmen who greeted the "new immigration" in the 1890s worked to meet the needs of the newcomers and to interpret those needs to the wider community. Many sought to learn from the immigrants and to preserve, at least temporarily, portions of their native cultures. Yet, like Americanizers before and after, they too were advocates of the unfair exchange. In return for an education that offered a way into the middle class, they expected the immigrant to repudiate cultural "peculiarities" eventually and to adopt the American civic religion.

Young college graduates like Jane Addams, Ellen Gates Starr, and Robert Woods found that American society was not the happy, cooperative place their grammar school books had pictured. They were dismayed at the growing disparity between rich and poor. Like Horace Mann before them, these young Americans feared that the national community was in danger of collapse. Prompted by their commitment to the American rhetoric of freedom and justice, they moved into immigrant neighborhoods to help the people there and to try to understand their problems.

These middle class idealists gave rise to the settlement house movement in the United States. Jane Addams and her Rockford College classmate, Ellen Gates Starr, took up residence in a poor

Helping Immigrants Become American

immigrant area of Chicago in 1889. The ladies obtained the free use of an old mansion that they named Hull-House in honor of the family that owned it. At the same time, other such settlements were springing up independently in New York City, Boston, and other large cities around the country. By 1900 the United States had a hundred settlement houses. This figure doubled by 1905 and doubled again by 1910. Young men and women flocked from the colleges and from courses like those of Francis Peabody at Harvard University and Richard T. Ely at Johns Hopkins University, dedicated to doing good for the immigrants and other poor people. "I think it is hard for us to realize," Jane Addams wrote in 1892, "how seriously many of them are taking to the notion of human brotherhood, how eagerly they long to give tangible expression to the democratic ideal." It was this new generation of Americanizers that met the influx of Eastern and Southern Europeans in the large metropolitan centers starting in the 1890s.

The settlement workers and the new immigrants could hardly have been more disparate. The Eastern and Southern Europeans were mostly of peasant farmer background, possessed little formal education, and were usually Roman Catholic, Jewish, or Greek Orthodox in religion. From 1890 to 1910 about two-thirds of the thirteen million immigrants to the U.S. came from such backgrounds in Russia, Italy, Austria-Hungary, Poland, and other areas in the South and East of Europe.

The settlement workers, on the other hand, were largely middle class college graduates of Protestant background. More than half were of Congregational or Presbyterian faith, and many could trace their lineage back to colonial New England. Committed to the American civic religion, they set out to share their faith with the newcomers in classes and talks about republican government, the nation's Protestant heritage, Anglo-Saxon law, and middle class views of the rights and responsibilities of U.S. citizenship.

While some of the settlement workers were interested only in teaching the immigrant how to be more like the image they had of themselves, the more sensitive among them quickly learned that the immigrant had values and commitments that were the equal of their own. Jane Addams told of her Thanksgiving Day program in which she extolled the Pilgrim Fathers to an audience of Greek immigrants.

"...I was uneasily conscious of the somewhat feeble attempt to boast of Anglo-Saxon achievement in hardihood and privation to men whose powers of admiration were absorbed in their Greek background of philosophy and beauty." An eleven-year-old Irish boy translated the comments of one of the Greeks in the audience to Miss Addams. "He says if that is what your ancestors are like, that his could beat them out." Jane Addams learned from the experience the inclination of Americans "for ignoring the past" and for taking no heed of what the immigrant thought of them. William English Walling, a resident of University Settlement on New York's East Side, told new settlement workers, "[The immigrants have] a lot to teach us boys, so for the love of Jesus Christ don't let's be uplifters here."

Still, attempts to demonstrate the "gracious living" that the middle class associated with the "higher" Anglo-Saxon civilization were common in the settlements and often led to incongruous situations. Settlement house lessons in the proper handling of the silver tea service gave immigrant women an excuse for time away from the tenements but were hardly the most helpful use of that time. Miss Starr achieved the absurd in her ceremony of the salad bowl and in her concern that the color of the soups served at Hull-House not clash with the mauve dresses she always wore. Although Hull-House art exhibitions and college level course work did help some of the immigrants, the settlement residents soon came to recognize that they could not build the community they desired by trying to mold the newcomers immediately into perfect likenesses of themselves.

Out of their experience, settlement workers began to adapt their educational programs to the individual needs and interests of the immigrants. They provided manual arts programs, kindergartens, and classes in English, homemaking, and child care. There were club activities for people of all ages, receptions for different ethnic groups, summer excursions, athletics, and a wide range of other activities. Jane Addams and Ellen Gates Starr established the Hull-House Labor Museum in 1900 to preserve the art of spinning and weaving in which Italian immigrant women excelled. Through programs like this the settlements attempted to help the children of the newcomers to understand and appreciate the Old Country languages, customs, and traditions of their parents. Such native American concern for the immediate needs of the immigrants, the social workers thought, would elicit sympathetic feelings for the United States and ultimately lead to that harmonious community that Americanizers continually sought.

Settlement residents found that immigrants often did not respond to traditional educational methods, so they improvised new ones. Miss Addams discovered, for example, that dramatic presentation was often more effective with immigrants than the lecture or the printed word. When they experienced difficulty in classroom teaching about housekeeping American-style, many settlements established a model apartment in a tenement where staff members could teach cooking, cleaning, and child care by practical example. Jane Addams in 1899 told how Hull-House residents persuaded Italian mothers to feed their children breakfasts that were more substantial than pieces of bread soaked in tea or wine. The staff invited a small group of the mothers to Hull-House for enjoyable Sunday morning meals at which oatmeal and cod liver oil were served. Gradually, others in the Italian neighborhood began to serve these "American breakfasts." With their acceptance of cod liver oil, mothers in the Italian community found they no longer needed to tie salt bags around the children's necks to fight the evil eye they believed weakened their children's bones. Thus the Hull-House workers overcame the calcium and vitamin D deficiencies that induced rickets without the need to convince the mothers of the validity of nutritional science. "Teaching in a Settlement requires distinct methods," Miss Addams wrote. "It has to be diffused in a social atmosphere, information must be held in solution, in a medium of fellowship and good will."

The settlement house workers could learn to improve their methods, but they found it more difficult to surmount the middle class assumptions that were so much a part of them. They were intruders in the immigrant neighborhoods, attempting to bring American middle class culture and customs into the tenements. While they were prepared to attend to the needs expressed by the immigrants and to nurture for a time some of the Old Country traditions, the social workers also had as their ultimate goal the conversion of the immigrant to a middle class life style and to the prevailing American ideology. Anglo-Saxon, Protestant, and middle class republicanism was to the humanitarian Americanizers, as to other Americans, the highest form of civilization they could imagine. They found it difficult to accord equality to immigrants who seemed out of step with the American consensus and who failed to practice American fashions of dress and grooming. Even Jane Addams, perhaps the most humanitarian and open-minded of all the social settlement workers, showed condescension in asking Americans not to expect "the same human development of an Italian peasant and a New England scholar."

This was the attitude that enabled these Americanizers to be so humanitarian and kindly. They attributed the alleged inferiority of Eastern and Southern Europeans, not to inherent racial differences, but to cultural background. They were confident that education could achieve cultural upgrading. Unlike later Americanizers whose greater haste would change the kindly tone taken toward the "new immigration," these settlement workers were patient. They held strong commitments to the American civic religion and were optimistic enough to believe that eventually experience and education would bring the immigrants to accept the most vital aspects of the U.S. ideology.

Dedicated to American political institutions and the private enterprise economic system, the humanitarian Americanizers taught the immigrant to accept the status quo in the U.S. until they began to recognize the harsh effect of the American system on the immigrants, blacks, and other poverty stricken people. When they saw the unequal justice of the system and industry's use of poor people as just another of its raw materials, the settlement workers' point of view changed somewhat. They now saw a need to work to overhaul the system, to humanize it, and to show Americans that their way of life needed improvement.

In speeches, books, and in magazine and newspaper articles the settlement residents tried to educate the American public to understand the immigrants and to support laws that would remove the grievances immigrants felt toward American society. The social workers attempted to show that the failure of cities to provide equal sanitation facilities and police protection to immigrant neighborhoods led to infestations of rats, disease, and crime. They claimed that native prejudice against the immigrants caused much of the social friction.

Helping Immigrants Become American

Slum landlords, they reported, charged exorbitant rents for substandard housing. It was only natural, the settlement workers wrote, that the more perceptive among the immigrants might seize on ideas such as unions, strikes, and socialism - ideas considered wildly radical at the time. The social workers thought Americans should calmly and rationally redress grievances in "the American way" and thereby overcome radicalism.

Jane Addams realized that her classes in citizenship could not win foreigners to "the American way" if Americans failed to live up to their own standards in dealing with protesting immigrants. Writing in 1908, she indicated that the Russian Jewish community in Chicago saw little difference between the Czarist secret police and the Chicago police who raided Jewish homes and halls after arresting a recent Russian Jewish immigrant and charging him with plotting to assassinate the city police chief. The accusers claimed that he was disgruntled because the police prevented a parade of the unemployed and threatened to break up a meeting if an "agitator" was allowed to speak. The Chicago police cited their own repression as the cause of the potential violent act, Miss Addams pointed out. "With the curious logic of the policeman, [the authorities] insist that unless further repressive measures are used such acts will constantly occur," she wrote. Focussing on the radical methods of strikes, bombings, and marches that immigrants and others were forced to use to obtain public notice of their grievances, Americans overlooked what the protests were all about, then proceeded to try to crush the protestors by police-state methods, all the while piously demanding that immigrants practice Americanism.

Jane Addams and Mary McDowell of the University of Chicago settlement plunged into political action to get the American reality more into line with their ideals. They pressured the city council for improved garbage collection and eventually got it. They supported the Chicago stockyards strike in 1904 and intervened personally with businessman J. Ogden Armour to gain management recognition of the Amalgamated Meat Cutters and Butcher Workmen. Miss Addams ran against the local ward boss at election time. Defeated in that effort, she succeeded in gaining a seat on the school board. In this new role, she brought the concerns of the settlements to bear on the public schools.

As in politics and economics, social workers challenged the narrow patterns of thought and action in control of public education. Miss Addams believed the schools discriminated against the children of immigrants by rewarding intellectual achievements and denigrating the dignity of labor. She charged that classes were abstract, repetitive, and geared to indoctrinating the businessman's interest that children be punctual and obey orders without question. Miss Addams advocated a more practical education that she thought would prove inspiring to children whose "parents have had to do only with tangible things."

Jane Addams and the social workers supported the American educational philosopher, John Dewey, in urging the schools to deal with the everyday lives of the children. Indeed, the educational activities at Hull-House and several other social settlements served as practical models for Dewey in developing his philosophy of education. "What we want," Dewey told the National Education Association in 1902, "is to see ... every public school ... doing something of the same sort of work that is now done by a settlement or two scattered at wide distances through the city."

Dewey and the settlement workers wanted the schools to be, in the words of Jane Addams, "a socializing and harmonizing factor" in American society. Dewey described the settlements, like the schools he desired, as "bringing people together, of doing away with barriers of caste, or class, or race, or type of experience that keep people from real communion with each other." They were echoing the cry of the Americanizers throughout the nation's history and calling for the reform of the public school so that it would accomplish in an urban and industrial setting the goals set for it by Horace Mann a half century earlier in an agrarian society.

The "new education," as it was popularly termed, caught on slowly during the first decade of the twentieth century. Encouraged by the settlement workers, most major U.S. cities introduced vocational education to provide for immigrants and others who desired it a practical training similar to that which Booker T. Washington had advocated for blacks. The more advanced schools borrowed from a Boston settlement house the idea of vocational guidance and counselling. New York City public schools, pressured by Lillian Wald of Henry

Helping Immigrants Become American

Street Settlement, introduced a nursing service and hot lunches to help solve community problems of health and nutrition. Rochester, New York, operated sixteen schools as neighborhood recreation and education centers that were open mornings, afternoons, and well into the evenings. The people of Rochester studied together in the school libraries and classrooms, attended the school theaters together, and segregated by sex, bathed together in the school baths. The schools of company towns like Eveleth and Ely, Minnesota, and Gary, Indiana, also became deeply involved in practical, community education.

Newcomers from Eastern and Southern Europe had long expressed interest in the free schooling offered to them and their children in the U.S. Even before the introduction of the "new education," immigrants were participating in the few public school extension programs like that in New York City established by English immigrant Henry Leipziger in 1890. Many of the newcomers encouraged their children to attend the public schools as long as it was economically feasible. They petitioned for adult English and civics classes for themselves in some of the large cities like Chicago, Detroit, and Philadelphia. These immigrants wanted the schools to teach them and their children to read and write English and to understand their rights and duties in their adopted country. To this extent, at least, they wanted to become Americanized.

While settlement workers hoped the "new education" would be a more flexible means of helping immigrants become Americanized, in the long run it merely instituted a new rigidity. Schoolmen would eventually categorize virtually all Eastern and Southern European children as assimilable only through a differentiated type of education that would prepare them for a job in industry. The "new education" would prove to be no panacea for the individual immigrant.

The churches, too, could be harsh in dealing with the "new immigration." American religious groups had little sympathy for the distinctive European habits and views the immigrants displayed. Protestants, Catholics, and Jews alike expected that Americanization education would rapidly erode most of the Old Country cultural patterns of the newcomers and replace them with American ways.

Although their attitude toward the immigrants

was often unfriendly and alienating, Protestant church members expected the newcomers to convert to Protestantism. They took great pride in immigrants like Edward A. Steiner and Constantine Panunzio. Steiner, a Jewish immigrant from Austria-Hungary, became a Congregational minister. Panunzio, a Roman Catholic from Southern Italy, joined the Methodist clergy. Steiner, Panunzio, and others like them were to Protestant Americans early in the twentieth century what Wussausmon had been to New England Puritans, living symbols of acculturation and the hope of the future.

Protestants were happy to have Steiner tell them of their responsibility to explain their values to the immigrant who had "fallen heir to Protestant traditions, without fully realizing ... [the] spiritual inheritance and ... moral obligations" involved. They were less pleased with these disciples when both Steiner and Panunzio raged at Protestant missions to the immigrants for being more concerned with numbers converted than with serving the needs and interests of the newcomers. These Americanized immigrants showed that the Protestant American's fear of the newcomer and disgust toward his manners and poverty alienated many potential converts from the church. "Nothing can be more repellent," Steiner wrote in 1906, "than the attitude of the average Protestant Christian toward the immigrant of to-day. As a rule he is prejudiced, is grossly ignorant of the historic and religious background of the strangers and meets every one of them with suspicion."

It was not only Protestants who viewed with dismay the influx of Eastern and Southern Europeans. American Roman Catholics, led by the dominant Irish immigrant faction of the clergy, and American Jews who came into the country in large numbers with the nineteenth century wave of German immigration, accepted many elements of the U.S ideology, rejecting for the most part only the extreme concept that one had to belong to a Protestant church to be a true American. These coreligionists of the newcomers were just as offended as Protestants by the "un-American" ways they saw in the appearances, personal habits, and backgrounds of the "new immigration." As these Roman Catholics and Jews had only recently established themselves in the United States, sometimes in the face of strong prejudice, they feared that the newcomers would arouse American Protestant hostility against themselves and threaten their improving position in the society. American Roman Catholics and Jews, therefore, busied themselves with Americanizing the immigrants. The Roman Catholic Church used its clergy, schools, press, charity institutions, and fraternal organizations to persuade immigrants to give up their foreign cultural patterns and conform to American customs. Archbishop John Ireland of St. Paul, Minnesota, an Irish immigrant, was a leader among the Americanizing bishops. Not only did he fear an American reaction against Roman Catholics if the church did not quickly Americanize the immigrant; he also feared that the Roman Catholic Church itself might split apart in the United States on the basis of cultural nationalism. He struggled against the efforts of immigrant Catholics to preserve their languages and traditions as staunchly as Benjamin Franklin had fought the inroads of "foreign culture" more than a hundred years earlier. In the interests of Catholic Church unity and public relations in the United States, many parochial schools became as dedicated as the public schools to Americanization education. Instead of equating the "true American" with Protestantism, as in the public schools, the parochial schools associated the concept with Roman Catholic practice.

Jewish settlement houses developed in many cities to encourage Jewish immigrant children to learn American ways, to attend public school, and to preserve their identity within American parameters. Mrs. Simon Kander of Milwaukee was one of the Jewish leaders who helped to overcome the suspicion of Russian parents to the Americanization of their children, in whom, she said, "our great hope lies." "It is a selfish motive that spurs us on," Mrs. Kander wrote. "It is to protect ourselves, our own reputation in the community that we must work ... to better the home conditions of our people."

Americanization meant changes for the immigrants and their children, some of them related to meaningful American traditions but most simply destructive of immigrant cultures. Mary Antin, a Jewish immigrant from Russia who attended Barnard College, exemplified the exchange Americans offered the newcomers through schooling. She discarded most of the "peculiar" aspects of her religion for allegiance to American nationalism. "Never had I

69

prayed, never had I chanted the songs of David, never had I called upon the Most Holy, in such utter reverence and worship," she wrote in describing how she felt when reading in school about George Washington, "the noble boy who would not tell a lie to save himself from punishment." Old stock Boston adopted her as a kind of mascot when she was a school girl declaiming the Protestant republican values they cherished while retaining her loose cultural ties to Judaism. In adopting the American civic religion like Mary Antin, immigrants of Jewish, Roman Catholic, and Eastern Orthodox backgrounds relinquished many of their unique cultural traditions while maintaining their own religious organizational structures.

Mary Antin was one of a large number of immigrant and second generation Eastern and Southern Europeans who entered teaching or social work and other community-building efforts after 1900. Their entry was the final blow that effectively ended the more than two hundred and fifty year reign of New Englanders and Presbyterians in dispensing Americanization education. Americans of virtually all backgrounds would soon provide leadership in the effort to Americanize the nation.

Gino Speranza, a second generation Italian American who was a Yale graduate and a lawyer, was one of the first lay Roman Catholics to join with Protestant Anglo-Saxons in an effort to Americanize largely Roman Catholic immigrants. The Society for the Protection of Italian Immigrants, which he served as the lone Italian and one of two Roman Catholic board members, existed to find shelter for new arrivals, to furnish them with background on the language and customs of the land, to provide them with legal aid, and to help find them jobs so that they would not "through want of work become a charge to the State or an enemy of society."

Speranza found he had to walk a tightrope between the various elements with which he dealt. From the Roman Catholic Italian community in the U.S. he found suspicion and obstruction resulting from fears that his nonsectarian organization was a Protestant missionary attempt or at least a likely competitor for funds with existing Roman Catholic organizations. Some potential patrons of the society who lived in Italy did not want the immigrants to become Americanized and feared that Speranza's organization contained too many "Anglo-saxons who were corrupting Latin Morals." He, too, chafed over the activities of some of the Anglo-Saxon staff members of the Society. "Our naive cocksureness that what is American is necessarily the best and most desirable, rises almost to the dignity of a national sin," he wrote in 1904. Speranza resigned from the board of the Society in June of 1905, charging that staff members failed to practice an "intelligent Americanization" that honored the heritage of Italians while assimilating them into American life. "... I feel that I would fail in my duty as an American," he wrote, "if I participated in a work which tended to make an Italian ashamed of or indifferent to his Italian antecedents."

Speranza urged the native American to help Italian immigrants to love the country by being kind to them and by showing them the good side of life in the United States. "Too many of them ... know of America only what they learn from the corrupt politician, the boss, the banker and the rough handed policeman," he wrote. "It is friendliness that is the leaven of assimilation...," he argued, noting that immigrants needed to feel "that the American people are their friends, true friends upon whom they can rely." Speranza blamed American apathy for allowing Italian work gang leaders to victimize their fellow countrymen by enforcing a kind of peonage on them, taking most of their wages in payment for poor food and miserable lodgings. He wanted Americans to take a positive interest in the immigrants and to associate directly with them. He believed in the original melting pot concept, at least as far as Americans and Italian immigrants were concerned, anticipating a finer human type resulting from the combination.

Like Gino Speranza, most of the Americanizers who ministered to the Southern and Eastern Europeans at the turn of the century were humanitarian and patient. They were prepared to work for gradual rather than immediate assimilation of immigrants and wanted to help the newcomers in whatever ways they could. Unlike Speranza, however, most of the humanitarian Americanizers, even the kindly Jane Addams, expected that their patience would pay off in the eventual disappearance of the cultures of the immigrants. Speranza, on the other hand, seemed committed to the assimilation concept of Hector St. John de Crèvecoeur that immigrant contributions would change the American type into something better and more desirable. Even though

Speranza opposed the assumption that the immigrants should eventually exchange their cultures for uniform American patterns, he could join with the humanitarian Americanizers in trying to educate native Americans to be tolerant and understanding of immigrants and to involve themselves with the newcomers. "It is my firm belief," he wrote, "that the basis of assimilation is a <u>spirit of true friendliness</u>." He would find, however, that most Americans paid little heed to his advice.

6 REDUCING THE INTAKE OF IMPURITIES: THE IMMIGRATION RESTRICTIONISTS

While vaguely aware of the burgeoning cities with their foreign populations, the average middle class American in a farmhouse or small town home contemplated the opening of the twentieth century with a smug satisfaction. The United States had just defeated the country Americans considered the archetype of backward Europe - monarchical, aristocratic, Roman Catholic Spain. The victory had vastly increased American self-esteem by bringing the beginnings of empire and considerable world prestige to the U.S. Convinced of the innate superiority of their Anglo-Saxon race and institutions, the generally prosperous Americans confidently awaited the assimilation of the inferior "new immigration" from Europe. They believed they could afford to be patient and depend upon the U.S. environment, the schools, and perhaps the settlement workers in the cities to Americanize the newcomers. The social workers sought to overcome this complacency in order to gain active middle class involvement in their programs, a change they hoped would lead to increased financial support and to an understanding of the problems immigrants were facing. Success in obtaining such participation, however, proved less than a blessing to the immigrants or to the humanitarian Americanizers.

In the attempt to stir the middle class from its apathy toward immigrants and their social condition, humanitarian Americanizers received the aid of a number of "muckraking" journalists after the turn of the century. Lincoln Steffens in his series of magazine articles on "The Shame of the Cities" showed how Irish American political "bosses" were sewing up the vote of the various immigrant groups and ruling the cities as feudal

73

princes were imagined to rule their fiefs. Americans concluded from articles by Steffens and other writers that the political backgrounds and "peculiar" religions and nationalities of these newcomers presented a challenge to their Anglo-Saxon and Protestant republic. They also feared a threat to their middle class ideal as a result of the stratification that was becoming increasingly apparent in American society. The poverty and industrial exploitation of the immigrants was creating an underclass and enabling a small group of parvenu capitalists to amass inordinate wealth and power. The writings of the settlement workers and the muckrakers had impact. Many Americans became concerned that the traditional Protestant and middle class republic might be in jeopardy unless they involved themselves in controlling the growth of business, in improving government and the schools, and in helping the immigrants understand the American way of life.

At an accelerating pace, the settlement workers found themselves in the company of other middle class Americans as they attempted to reform traditional U.S. institutions. Academicians, churchmen, those in the professions, and many others worked with the settlement residents to improve schooling, to make the existing structure of government more effective, and to control the activities of big business through the so-called Progressive movement. Together they sought to make the government more responsive to the people and to gain enactment of social justice legislation that would benefit immigrant and native alike.

A growing interest in the immigrants delighted the humanitarian Americanizers. They assumed that increased concern and involvement would lead to greater support of services for the newcomers. To their chagrin the developing interest led, instead, to a questioning of education as the method for dealing with the yearly influx of immigrants that between 1905 and 1914 never dropped below 750,000 and was composed largely of Southern and Eastern Europeans.

As these newly aroused Americans came into contact with the immigrant to help him and to enlist him in the effort to get the United States to return to what they felt were its traditional ideals of government, they increasingly sensed that his values were not their values. "The American has learned not only that this is a free government," wrote Professor John Commons of the University of Wisconsin in 1907, "but that its freedom is based on constitutional principles of an abstract nature." He reflected the middle class view that the native American thought and voted in accord with the Anglo-Saxon and Protestant republicanism that "percolated through his subconscious self." Commons listed freedom of the press, trial by jury, separation of powers, independence of the judiciary, and equality of opportunity as principles motivating native Americans. "But the immigrant has none of these ...," he charged. "He votes as instructed by his employer or his political 'boss,' because it will help his employer's business or because his boss will get him a job, or ... favor him and others of his nationality."

John Commons and the other latecomer reformers began to blame the immigrant for the evils they saw about them in America and to question the effectiveness of Americanization education. They realized that the immigrants were supporting the opponents of reform who were more adept than the Progressives in winning over the newcomers. Soon many middle class Americans were ready to back a quick solution to what they viewed as a growing "immigrant problem."

Increasingly, these anxious Americans were attracted to the arguments of social scientists who favored restricting European immigration. Relying heavily on British, French, and German work in racial heredity, these scholars reported that the influx of Eastern and Southern Europeans was threatening American homogeneity. Economist Richmond Mayo-Smith was one of the early advocates of a scientific approach to the building of the American nation. "We must set up our standard of what we desire this nation to be," he wrote in 1890, "and then consider whether the policy we have hitherto pursued in regard to immigration is calculated to maintain that standard or to endanger it."

With the American ideology having narrowed more explicitly along racist lines at the demise of Reconstruction, Mayo-Smith and other social scientists were now recommending racial criteria for the admission of immigrants. These scholars wished to maintain a Protestant, middle class, and republican society. To achieve their goal, they were convinced that America would have to remain Anglo-Saxon. In presenting his view of the U.S. standard to be preserved Mayo-Smith, who traced his lineage to colonial New England, emphasized "the social morality of the Puritan settlers of New England," America's "free political constitution," and "the ability to govern ourselves in the ordinary affairs of life, which we have inherited from England." Mayo-Smith questioned whether such cherished American patterns could survive if immigration went unchecked.

From a questioning attitude, American academics moved rapidly to the advocacy of immigration restriction despite warnings from some respected colleagues that their science was not advanced enough to warrant the generalizations that they made regarding race. Acknowledging that there was "provocation" for concern with race, American sociologist William Z. Ripley in 1900 nevertheless worried over the "decided inclination to sink the racial explanation up to the handle in every possible phase of social life...." A number of U.S. anthropologists, led by Franz Boas, argued that national achievements and physical appearances of different nationality groups had little relationship to the quality of citizenship of individual immigrants. Their arguments, however, failed to deter or to weaken the influence on public opinion of such of their social science colleagues as Richard Ely, Edward Bemis, Franklin Giddings, Thomas N. Carver, Francis A. Walker, and Thomas Bailey Aldrich. Utilizing a series of theoretical models borrowed from European anthropologists, from the scientific breeders of cattle, and from eugenics, American social scientists proceeded to classify nationality groups according to their physical characteristics, rating them from superior to inferior.

While helping middle class Progressives to justify consideration of immigration restriction, social science also legitimized restrictionist efforts by organized labor and by lineage-minded descendants of old-line Eastern families. The workers wanted to lessen competition for the available jobs and push wage rates up. Unrestricted immigration blocked these goals. The Easterners had been left in the backwash of post-Civil War industrial development, surpassed in wealth and prestige by the rising industrialists, deprived of their one-time political power by Irish American politicians, mauled financially by the economic crisis of 1893, and disturbed by the vision of non-Anglo-Saxon immigrants clawing toward economic parity. With only their racial heritage and longer

Reducing the Intake of Impurities

connection with U.S. history to distinguish them as "superior" to the newcomers, it was no wonder that people of this background founded the Immigration Restriction League in 1894. The support of social science gave respectability to such influential groups that were ready to reject the U.S. tradition of serving as an asylum for the oppressed of Europe. The restrictionists won some important victories after 1900 that reflected a waning faith in Americanization education. The United States doubled the immigrant head tax from one to two dollars and outlawed the entry or naturalization of anarchists in 1903. Four years later the appointment of a federal Immigration Commission to restudy the entire question of immigration advanced the cause of restriction. The Commission presented its report in 1911, surrounding its preconceived notions with a massive forty-two volumes of immigration statistics, policy studies, and a Dictionary of Races that translated Anglo-Saxonism into a scientific classification system. The commissioners, who included such restrictionists as Senator Henry Cabot Lodge and economist Jeremiah Jenks, suggested that materialism alone drove the Southern and Eastern European to the United States and implied that the earlier immigrant from Northern and Western Europe came for more idealistic reasons. Even though America was becoming urbanized, they faulted the newcomers for settling in the cities unlike many of the earlier immigrants who were able to homestead on cheap land. Insinuating that Southern and Eastern Europeans were an ignorant and morally debased people incapable of being Americanized, the Immigration Commission's study purported to show that the "new immigration" endangered American society.

While American prejudice toward immigrants was not limited to those from Southern and Eastern Europe, for political reasons the Immigration Commission carefully avoided attacks on the Irish, the Germans, or the Scandinavians. These people were now termed the "old immigration" even though the Scandinavians had come to the U.S. largely in the post-Civil War years up to about 1890. The Commission's Dictionary of Races even suggested that the Irish were closer in blood to the revered Anglo-Saxon than to the Celt. Inclusion of the Irish within the pale was politically essential. Lodge, for instance, depended for his Senate seat on continued Irish support. The Immigration Commission's report set the boundaries for the assault on the immigration laws. Restrictionists would concentrate their attack on the most vulnerable target, the "new immigration," and avoid encounter with the Germans, Irish, and Scandinavians who had by then gained a grudging acceptance within the American consensus and whose economic and political power in America was rapidly increasing.

The most successful popularizer of the Immigration Commission's findings was Professor Edward A. Ross who in 1911 took an unequivocal position in favor of immigration restriction. This University of Wisconsin sociologist was a hard-hitting and effective proponent of liberal reforms. A middle class Progressive, he supported legislation that would help the workers and control big business. Ross, who was of Scots-Irish Presbyterian background, resembled the Americanizers in longing for the homogeneous America of his grammar school textbooks. He had little faith, however, in the capacity of existing patterns of education to indoctrinate the "new immigration" in the civic religion. Ross viewed Americanization education, he wrote, "with that half amused contempt which is felt by sociologists generally."

Dismissing Americanization education as sentimentalism, Ross claimed that restriction was the scientific solution for the social ills he and many other social scientists believed immigrants were causing in American society. Basing his analysis of the current immigration on physical stature and the size and shape of heads, lacing both models with his native prejudice that associated character weakness with variations from Anglo-Saxon physical norms, Ross in 1911 hied off to street corners, churches, and other gathering places of the immigrants to study the newcomers. He had already developed in 1904 a "Value Rank of the American People" in which he suggested that the "cheap stucco manikins from Southeastern Europe" seemed out of place among the stronger, healthier, more energetic, more pure and honest Anglo-Saxons. From his 1911 study Ross concluded, "The blood now being injected into the veins of our people is subcommon." "To the practiced eye," he wrote, "the physiognomy of certain groups unmistakably proclaims inferiority of type. I have seen gatherings of the foreign-born in which narrow and sloping foreheads were the rule. The shortness and smallness of the crania were very noticeable." In order to save Americans from "race suicide," as well as from a low standard of living, yellow journalism, illiteracy, pauperism, urban slums, and municipal crime and corruption, Ross advocated the limiting of further Eastern and Southern European immigration to the U.S.

Ross's ably written series of articles in The Century Magazine in 1913 and 1914, expanded into a book in 1914 titled Old World in the New, brought the restrictionist argument to the general public in a way the arid Immigration Commission report could never do. He carefully avoided specific recommendations of restrictive legislation, heeding the advice of the Immigration Commission's expert on economics, Jeremiah Jenks. Ross jotted Jenks's admonition in his notebook: "Better use ... [the] series to create a public opinion favorable to restriction but not champion any particular method of restriction."

The "new immigration" did not lack defenders, however. The popular social settlement pioneer, Jane Addams, wrote in The Ladies Home Journal that much of the agitation against immigrants was a scapegoating that blamed a helpless group for the ills of the entire community. Author Mary Antin, an immigrant from Russia, questioned the competency of social science to infringe "on the right of free men to choose their place of residence." "By all means," she wrote, "register the cephalic index of the alien, - the anthropologist will make something of it at his leisure, - but do not let it determine his [the immigrant's] right to life, liberty, and the pursuit of happiness." Clergyman-author Edward A. Steiner, another immigrant from Eastern Europe, also questioned the race classifications of the social scientists, arguing that "underneath all the differences in races and classes, humanity is essentially one."

The North American Civic League was another friend of the "new immigration" although its motives mixed humanitarianism with the self-interest of U.S. industrialists. The League was founded in 1907 to engage in social welfare work on behalf of the newcomers. It also encouraged employers to support English and civics classes for their workers in an effort to offset claims by the radical Industrial Workers of the World that management cared little for the welfare of its employees. The League was a staunch defender of the existing immigration policy that encouraged a flow of cheap labor into the United States.

Although the policy of unrestricted immigration had the support of big business and a strong humanitarian tradition behind it, restrictionists persisted in their struggle to win public opinion away from the proimmigration forces. They were able to show rather easily that self-interest, not concern for the welfare of the immigrants, motivated the business advocates of the existing policy. It was a more difficult task to overcome the pride Americans took in the tradition of the U.S. as an asylum for Europe's oppressed. "This sentimental humanitarian attitude," restrictionist Robert De C. Ward believed, was "the chief obstacle" the restrictionists faced in gaining the support of public opinion for their solution to the "immigration problem."

By 1913, however, the restrictionists were waxing strong. The Immigration Restriction League had enlisted Professors Ross and Commons, Boston settlement worker Robert Woods, and a wide range of college presidents around the country into its national committee that also included business and professional people and former holders of federal political office. Some current and former settlement workers voiced their support for the position of the League. Paul Kellogg, the editor of Survey and a former resident of Greenwich House settlement in New York, came out for immigration restriction in 1911. And in 1912 Walter Weyl, a resident for several years at University Settlement in New York, published The New Democracy in which he argued for restriction. "America," he wrote, "was to be the eternal land of liberty, the refuge of the world's oppressed, the mentor of Europe." Directly attacking the cherished tradition of unrestricted European immigration, Weyl contended that it was, paradoxically, destroying the purity of the American example and would have to cease if the U.S. was to remain a free land and a model to the world.

By tarring the humanitarian Americanizers as "sentimentalists," Edward A. Ross and the other immigration restrictionists were undermining American confidence in existing modes of education. It was a dangerous approach to take. In the past, a shaken faith in education provided an important impulse for Americans to resort to harsh and sometimes violent means of achieving conformity. In his efforts to limit diversity by restricting immigration, Ross walked in the path of the Puritans, Samuel F.B. Morse, and the anti-Chinese workers of California. It would be more than twenty years before he would write, "I blush to confess that nearly two-thirds of my life had passed before I awoke to the fallacy of rating peoples according to the grade of their culture." Guilt feelings in the 1930s, however, could not undo his earlier success in furthering racist sentiment in America. Ross and the restrictionists were also responsible, in large measure, for forcing a change in the philosophy of Americanization education. Since the humanitarian approach to Americanization could no longer maintain public support against the advocates of restriction, a shift in emphasis was not long in coming.

7 THE IMPERIOUS DEMAND FOR CONFORMITY: THE SCIENTIFIC AMERICANIZERS

The man on horseback who rode to the rescue of Americanization education and of continued free immigration from Europe was no man at all. She was a crisp, orderly-minded young social researcher, Miss Frances Kellor, who sought to overcome the efforts of immigration restrictionists to portray Americanization as sentimental and ineffective. In her propaganda, the field took on the appearance of a hard-headed and precise science with potential for "final indestructible definitions and principles ... and ... finally approved methods." Americanization education, she argued, could become a cool and dispassionate profession capable of forging the harmonious and homogeneous nation Americans desired. Society, rather than the immigrant, was her primary concern. She worked zealously to involve industry, the schools, and virtually all the institutions of the United States in a scientific approach to what was now formally termed the Americanization movement.

Frances Kellor was convinced that Americanizers could engineer a one-minded nation and achieve full public support if they borrowed concepts being introduced into U.S. industry at the time by a celebrated group of "efficiency experts." Organization analysis, cost accounting, time and motion studies, and output measurements could be adapted to her field, she believed, and would result in the assimilation of immigrants and their children by the society in a less costly and more effective manner than ever before. Her goal was to supplement "scientific management with citizenship management." "Some of us believe," she wrote, "that in this new spirit lies the hope of the nation."

Miss Kellor became the leading researcher and

propagandist for this scientific Americanization movement. A social researcher and former settlement worker active in Progressive politics and liberal causes, from 1909 to 1914 she headed the New York branch of the proimmigration North American Civic League. The national organization's commitment to the interests of business, however, involved its personnel increasingly in crossing picket lines and reporting on unionists, actions that alienated it from the immigrants and caused Miss Kellor to break with the parent group. She took her New York branch out of the League in 1914, renamed it the Committee for Immigrants in America, and led it onto the national level as a clearinghouse to involve, assist, and coordinate public and private agencies in Americanization education. She used her monthly journal, <u>Immigrants in America Review</u>, to gain support for her ideas. She also capitalized on the many important contacts she had made in her reform activities and in her work with the North American Civic League. Her associations ranged from the business community, government, and social work to such reform groups as the women's suffrage movement. Taking advantage of the interest of U.S. Secretary of the Interior Franklin K. Lane in her approach to Americanization, she raised funds from some of her wealthy friends to provide the U.S. Bureau of Education with a Division of Immigrant Education complete with staff. Miss Kellor and her entire New York operation would become a part of this U.S. governmental agency during World War I, thus gaining official endorsement for her efforts in behalf of scientific Americanization.

Miss Kellor represented a new breed of social worker, the social researcher-lobbyist. Settlement pioneer Jane Addams had noted the changing interests among settlement house recruits after the turn of the century. She observed that new staff members were often motivated less by a desire to engage in philanthropy than by an interest in conducting scientific research into existing conditions in the society. They assumed that Americans would act to improve those conditions if the facts indicated change was needed. These new professionals charged that social work often suffered from an amateurish and sentimental concern for individual needs that ignored the interests of the broader community. The old humanitarian approach to Americanization had little place in this "pro-

83

fessional" and "scientific" view of social work.
   Attempts to achieve legislation that would protect the immigrants received Miss Kellor's support, but in return she demanded a high price from the newcomers. She urged, for example, the passage of laws to control the padrone system that subjected foreign workers to virtual peonage. In exchange, she expected the immigrants to eat American food, wear acceptable garb, and discard rapidly the cultural and class qualities that differentiated them from Protestant, middle class, and republican Americans. Through her entire career, she viewed outward expressions of nonconformity by the immigrants as symptomatic of their failure to adhere to the American civic religion. In applying the concept of reciprocity not only to the schools where it had been traditional but to adults in the broad context of U.S. society, Frances Kellor became the Americanization movement's leading advocate of the unfair exchange.
   Miss Kellor urged the mobilization of all the institutions of the society in her ostensibly objective and scientific approach to Americanization education. She was convinced that a systematically planned educational campaign by school, factory, and community could gain the Eastern and Southern European's acceptance of the prevailing norms in America. She believed that scientific assimilation required, at the very least, the full and efficient application of the schools and factories, including the introduction of effective Americanization classes in both and careful measurement of results obtained. Miss Kellor promoted her cause extensively within the Americanization movement, in the educational establishment, in the business community, and among the general public. In achieving widespread discussion of Americanization in her philosophical terms, she returned the rapidly developing profession to its traditional pattern, the imperious demand for conformity of the outsider to national norms.
   For several years, this propaganda on behalf of scientific Americanization would prove sufficient in itself to maintain public confidence in education and in continued unrestricted immigration. Americans trusted the propaganda although it offered no substantial proof of the widespread adoption, or even the applicability, of scientific management techniques for Americanization. It would not be necessary, at least for a time, for

efficiency concepts to be widely implemented and successful. As long as Americans were satisfied that scientific methodology would eventually be utilized effectively to homogenize the outsiders, they would continue to support Americanization education over harsher alternatives for achieving uniformity.

Miss Kellor and others who advocated scientific Americanization worked very hard indeed to enlist U.S. industry in the campaign to nationalize the immigrants. She told employers that English and civics classes in the factory would not only improve the safety record and lead to a more stable work force but make America a more united and more vigorous nation. "We are passing out of the phase of welfare work into the field of national citizenship efficiency...," she wrote. "... The primary needs of workmen, namely order and Americanization, must fall primarily upon the local industry, and if American traditions and standards of living are to be preserved, the burden must be placed there." In the winter of 1915-1916, Miss Kellor achieved the establishment of an Immigration Committee within that important national organization of American business, the Chamber of Commerce, with her wealthy New York friend, Frank Trumbull, as chairman and herself as assistant to the chairman.

Employee welfare and safety education programs were already under way in industry, designed to develop worker loyalty to the company and enmity to labor unions. Many factory managers no doubt agreed with Miss Kellor when the wrote, "Strikes and plots that have been fostered and developed by un-American agitators and foreign propaganda are not easily carried on among men who have acquired, with the English language and citizenship, an understanding of American industrial standards and an American point of view." But most companies were not yet ready to enlist their in-plant education programs in her cause of national "citizenship management."

Employers were inclined to rely on less dogmatic adult education consultants like Peter Roberts, head of the national industrial department of the Young Men's Christian Association. In the early stages of his work this immigrant from Wales seemed committed to the humanitarian concepts then in vogue in Americanization, operating on that "spirit of true friendliness" between native American and immigrant advocated by Gino Speranza of the Society

85

for the Protection of Italian Immigrants. Roberts recruited volunteer language instructors to teach immigrants in the factories and elsewhere and prepared instructional materials that focussed on practical language used in the home and in industry. His early emphasis was on education of the workers for safety and communication in the factory.

Gradually, however, Roberts and the YMCA came to accept Miss Kellor's concept of education for citizenship management. The Association articulated its changing philosophy in these words: "Years ago ... immigration was largely English, Irish, German and Scandinavian - wholesome, earnest, faithful citizens and nation builders. Of late years, however, ... masses of suspicious, clannish people from southern and southeastern Europe have swarmed to our already congested cities.... It is not a question of whether we want them or not. They are here and their numbers are increasing.... Unless we can assimilate, develop, train and make good citizens out of them, they are certain to make ignorant, suspicious, and un-Americanized citizens out of us." Paraphrasing Benjamin Franklin, the YMCA warned, "Unless we Americanize them they will foreignize us."

Roberts joined actively in Miss Kellor's efficiency crusade by responding to the call for assistance by the public school leadership and industrialists of Detroit, Michigan. Detroit was one of the few American cities where businessmen put their factories to work in the interest of militant nationalism prior to U.S. involvement in World War I. With Frances Kellor's Committee for Immigrants in America providing them with encouragement and advice, the Bureau of Commerce, leading Detroit industries, and the Board of Education cooperated in 1915 in an English-first program, or as it was soon termed, an Americans-first program. Motivated by fears of mixed loyalties and by a brief period of unemployment, both occasioned by the outbreak of the war in Europe, the Detroit Americanizers put pressure on foreigners to learn English, to study American government, and to become naturalized citizens.

"From August 17 to September 13, 1915, the whole city embarked on a gigantic campaign of publicity for the benefit of its adopted children from Europe...," wrote Gregory Mason in The Outlook. To get attendance at the Americanization classes that

The Imperious Demand for Conformity

Peter Roberts had helped the Board of Education to organize, the Board of Commerce advertised intensively. It arranged for posters on factory bulletin boards and at area gathering places of immigrants. Promotional pieces were placed in pay envelopes, foreign language books borrowed from the library, and in packages brought home from the stores by anyone "who looked like a foreigner." Immigrants were bombarded with the message that attendance at Americanization classes would get them better jobs and make them better citizens.

To encourage its "adopted children" to learn English some factories established systematically discriminatory hiring and promotion policies. The Saxon Motor Company made attendance at night school compulsory for its non-English-speaking workers. The Northway Motor and Manufacturing Company required such employees to attend either the public evening school or its own factory school, or face discharge. The Cadillac Company and most other firms merely gave strong encouragement to their employees to attend the public evening schools. Miss Kellor particularly applauded the decision of Packard Motor Company and Paige-Detroit Company to pressure immigrants to become citizens by a policy of non-promotion for noncitizens.

Frances Kellor praised the Detroit campaign and also spoke well of less ambitious programs conducted in cities like Syracuse, Rochester, Pittsburgh, Wilmington, Youngstown, Minneapolis, and St. Louis. At Detroit's Ford Motor Company, however, Americanization education went too far even for her. Ford ran its own school where the pupils were told to "walk to the American blackboard, take a piece of American chalk, and explain how the American workman walks to his American home and sits down with his American family to their good American dinner." Most Americanizers in 1916 viewed the Ford approach as "grotesquely exaggerated patriotism." While such fanaticism proved embarrassing to the movement, it was simply further evidence that Miss Kellor's propaganda was capable of stirring public interest and a considerable degree of business support.

Miss Kellor and her colleagues encouraged the schools to join with the factories in scientifically fashioning good citizens out of immigrants and their children. She expressed disappointment in the general lack of interest on the part of the schools in dealing with the adult and in the practice of overloading tired daytime teachers of children with night school responsibilities. In these criticisms, she received the backing of the U.S. Bureau of Education, which reported in 1916 that only eleven states gave grants to support evening schools. The Bureau also attacked the weak administration of the night schools and criticized their failure to train their staffs in techniques of teaching adult foreigners. Miss Kellor's *Immigrants in America Review* complained in 1915, "The content of English instruction is in a chaotic condition," with texts and teachers alike unadapted to adults. "The night school student...," she argued, "is a grown man ... sharply conscious of his need in very particular directions. This is why he can not be given a child's primer and set to declaiming - 'I see a cat' or 'What does little birdie say.'" One of the goals Miss Kellor set for the Americanization movement was the improvement and "ultimate standardization of immigrant education in each state thruout the country."

To encourage the schools in improving their Americanization of children and adults, Miss Kellor supported the activities of innovative schoolmen like William A. Wirt of Gary, Indiana. Wirt, who was superintendent of that city's schools from 1907 to 1938, introduced the "platoon school" for the efficient transformation of the many immigrants and their children in Gary into "true Americans." Wirt's system moved students on a tight schedule through classroom, auditorium, playground, gymnasium, and swimming pool. "The first principle in turning waste into profit in school management," Wirt wrote in 1916, "is to use every facility all the time for all the people." The resources of the schools would be used "all day long by all children alternately, and out of school hours, they should be used by adults...." To do otherwise, Wirt added, would be to engage in a "Great Lockout in America's Citizenship Plants."

William Wirt and the small band of "new breed" educational administrators like him were in no way challenging the basic goals of education in the United States. From the time of Horace Mann schoolmen had worked to gain the conformity of children to a model of homogeneity. It was no different with Wirt and such kindred souls as S.C. Hartwell, superintendent of schools in Kalamazoo and later in St. Paul; Joseph S. Taylor, district superintendent of schools in New York City, and

The Imperious Demand for Conformity

David Snedden, commissioner of education in Massachusetts. These efficiency-minded educators of the twentieth century simply added adults to their responsibilities and applied new techniques for achieving a uniform America. Through the years a "peculiar" religion, unusual clothing, or some other deviation from the norm had marked a child for harassment and terrorization in school, as Americanizers strove to stamp him into conformity. Speaking about the school teachers of nineteenth century Lowell, Massachusetts, William Cardinal O'Connell remembered how, as a child, he "sensed the bitter antipathy, scarcely concealed, which nearly all these good women ... felt toward those of us who had Catholic faith and Irish names. For any slight pretext we were severely punished. We were made to feel the slur against our faith and race, which hurt us to our very hearts' core." Such social pressure and a curriculum geared to inculcate the prevailing ideology had a lifetime of influence upon immigrant children, almost all of whom wanted very deeply to be considered Americans.

Scientific Americanizers like Frances Kellor and William Wirt did not want to terminate the pressure for conformity exerted by the schools. They wanted to make this citizenship education more efficient. Their methods and rhetoric provided twentieth century packaging for the continuing interest in what Charles Dole of the Patriotic League in 1897 had called "The Religion of Citizenship." All Americans, he thought, believed in this religion of "working together to make a righteous city and nation." Now, however, many Americanizers were keeping pace with society by invoking "the science of citizenship." In articulating their goals, twentieth century advocates of scientific Americanization through schooling spoke less of the righteous society than of the efficient society.

In the name of efficiency, scientific Americanizers influenced many schools with high enrollments of Eastern and Southern European children to differentiate their classes according to the ethnic origins of their pupils. "The question of how to handle a Scotch immigrant child is very different from that of how to teach an Italian," wrote Leonard P. Ayres of the Russell Sage Foundation. "The educating of an English boy is not at all the same task as the educating of a Russian." M. Catherine Mahy, supervisor of English in the Hope

Street School of Providence, Rhode Island, reflected the scientific approach in 1916. "Think of it!" she wrote. "Think of asking the Jew from Russia to read The Courtship of Miles Standish with the same zest and appreciation as is felt by the little girl in IA in whose veins runs the blood of Miles Standish...." Although Supervisor Mahy added that a differentiated course should be urged only upon "the alien not capable of taking the classical course," teachers and guidance counsellors often disregarded this portion of her advice. Many of the more forward-looking schools began to treat Southern and Eastern European children as they already treated blacks, as a special group requiring a special, nonacademic education.

In developing this differentiated education, schoolmen allowed their racism to distort the philosophy of education that Jane Addams and John Dewey had promoted at least partly on humanitarian grounds. Dewey and Miss Addams had urged the schools to appeal to the needs and interests of immigrant children. After catching their interest, the schools were to lead them to an understanding and appreciation of American culture and to eventual assimilation by it. Schoolmen turned this philosophy into a racial stereotyping and placed many Eastern and Southern European children who could have excelled academically on a treadmill to a factory job.

Progressive, innovative schoolmen tended to look upon the children of the "new immigration" as requiring a practical curriculum that emphasized American government, home economics, and the vocations. They assumed that such courses would interest the pupils in staying in school long enough to undergo a thorough indoctrination in the civic religion and to learn a trade. Mastery of a vocation, it was expected, would provide the opportunity for their entry into the middle class. Those who wished to enroll in the college preparatory course soon found this stereotyping a major obstacle in their path. That the intellectual potential of a number of Eastern and Southern European children was thwarted by the vocational curriculum was generally not recognized by the scientific Americanizers.

Vocational education for all the children of the "new immigration" fit well into Frances Kellor's approach to the assimilation of outsiders. The racial stereotyping and disregard of individuality that schoolmen practiced under her banner of scientific Americanization caused her little concern. She agreed with School Superintendent Addison B. Poland of Newark, New Jersey, who argued that the efficient and harmonious community desired by progressive educators was "rarely, or never, attained except by and thru uniformity of some kind." She complimented vocational education in 1914 for seeking to provide "the sort of training that will enable them [immigrant children] to fit into the social and industrial scheme at the point for which their endowment and capacity best suit them."

Despite all the rhetoric scientific Americanization failed to attain widespread adoption. Most factory educational programs continued to deal with safety more than with patriotism; most settlements with the individual needs of immigrants and their children. Only those schools with large enrollments of Eastern and Southern Europeans that were administered by innovative schoolmen introduced vocational education and scientific Americanization techniques. None the less, Miss Kellor was able to convince Americans of the potential of scientific Americanization. Her success had two outcomes. She undermined the work of the humanitarian Americanizers, if only by implication, as inefficient sentimentalism. But she also maintained the political viability of the Americanization option against the advocates of immigration restriction. Miss Kellor believed that her approach had to achieve wider implementation to sustain Americanization education as national policy. She therefore prepared to turn the growing war fever in the United States to the benefit of scientific Americanization.

8 LET THE PROFESSIONALS DO IT

U.S. preparation for war and eventual entry into World War I marked the flaring forth of a powerful campaign to Americanize immigrants. The drive continued into the post-war period, fed by the fear of an international conspiracy by the new Communist regime in Russia. While scientific Americanizers worked to systematize these activities, the education that thrived in this climate of fear and suspicion was more hysterical than scientific. The campaigners devoted themselves to promoting "democracy," an expression that had replaced "republic" as the popular term for describing the traditional American civic religion. Widespread commitment to the preservation of this ideology swelled the ranks of the Americanizers between 1917 and the early 1920s.

Frances Kellor, the Americanization movement's leading propagandist, had seemed to welcome the outbreak of World War I in Europe. She believed the interest immigrants from the belligerent countries expressed in the fate of their native lands, even after U.S. President Woodrow Wilson asked everyone in America to maintain neutrality, demonstrated a need for a more effective Americanization of the newcomers. "Thanks to the war," she wrote, "we have been freed from the delusion that we are a united nation marching steadily along an American highway of peace, prosperity, common ideals, beliefs, language, and purpose." Brewing a mixture of fear and guilt, she urged Americans to dedicate themselves to what she termed their forgotten responsibility, that "of making Americans of the people that have come to ... [the nation's] shores."

Responding to Frances Kellor's propaganda, new

Let the Professionals Do It

enthusiasts tumbled over each other to join the Americanization bandwagon. The National Americanization Day Committee she helped to organize in 1915 had already seeded the nation with educational materials and encouragement for local Fourth of July ceremonies to foster patriotism among the immigrants. Now the Committee on Public Information and other federal agencies aided Miss Kellor in encouraging and organizing this increasingly popular movement. Such mushrooming patriotic organizations as the National Security League, the Council of National Defense, and the American Protective League were enlisted in the campaign. When the United States entered the war in 1917, Miss Kellor's previously uphill Americanization drive received strong impetus.

Miss Kellor's persistent pleas for the involvement of industry paid off at last, as the wartime situation led many businessmen to intensify their pressures on employees to speak English and become citizens. They believed that the growth in plant harmony, which she had led them to expect, would increase war production and profits. Employees who failed to adhere to these norms of language and citizenship received harsh lectures on their lack of "100 per cent Americanism." Industry's professional and trade magazines abounded with advice to managers and efficiency engineers to Americanize employees in the name of business efficiency and profit. Such educational programs, management consultant Winthrop Talbot contended, were necessary "for maintaining the proper functioning of the human mechanisms employed for production purposes." Although harmony for profit was not Miss Kellor's interest, she was happy for industry's involvement, whatever the motive, in programs that furthered her own conception of a uniform and harmonious national community.

In the schools, too, more administrators hoisted the banner of scientific Americanization. In the name of the war effort, schoolmen in many parts of the nation implemented programs they claimed were scientifically designed to produce loyal and efficient finished products. They eliminated German from the curriculum as a disloyal subject and began to give report card grades not only on class work but on the citizenship of their charges. Just as the workers' use of English on the job had become a gauge of their level of Americanization, so now did children's behavior in the classroom become an index of their level of citizenship, a measure of their dedication to the creation of a happy, harmonious America.

As with the factory, the school also seemed to be an excellent institution in which to impose and enforce regulations designed to produce "better citizens." Utah went to the extreme of passing a law in 1919 requiring boys and girls up to the age of eighteen to attend school or to have a job. The Utah statute led to the registration by the State Department of Education of all young people in the state and the compilation of records on each that showed their levels of civic righteousness. These dossiers followed them whenever they moved from one location in the state to another. The war hysteria also helped to bring the hold-out states to enact compulsory school attendance laws and those with such laws to improve their enforcement.

The wartime drive for the ideological purity of the immigrants and the unity of the United States sometimes took a serpentine course. While the Postmaster General sought to crush the foreign-language press in the name of Americanism, Frances Kellor and others were using it to spread Americanization propaganda. While some tried to use the ethnic associations in the United States in a similar manner and pressed them to buy Liberty Bonds, the Attorney General illegally raided their meetings and the Office of Alien Property attempted to seize their assets. The same Americans who claimed they were fighting for democracy and the freedom of people in Europe supported an American government that infiltrated the organizations of the European ethnic groups in the U.S. with government agents and with volunteer citizen snoopers.

While Miss Kellor was delighted with the involvement of legions of Americans in her campaign, she found that wartime emotionalism was more conducive to the rhetoric than to the methodology of scientific Americanization. Most of the new recruits to the movement failed to grasp the scientific approaches she advocated. Panic, not scientific method, dominated the Americanization movement during this period, and for a time Miss Kellor seemed to tolerate the overzealousness.

In the early stages of the war, the hysteria focussed on immigrants from Germany and its allied nations. They were watched carefully by their neighbors and dunned for Liberty Bond contributions. Their children were prime targets for the

Let the Professionals Do It

Americanization education of the schools. Parents and children alike experienced community pressure and intimidation. If an immigrant somehow rankled a native, he might be punished by the furtive painting of yellow stripes on his home to symbolize his "disloyalty." As in the days of the witchcraft trials of Puritan New England, the animal world was not exempt from attack by the fanatics. Dachshunds, identified with Germany by the public, sometimes found it unsafe to scamper alone on the streets of America during World War I.

Schooled to reject diversity as unpatriotic and convinced of the inferiority of Eastern and Southern Europeans, Americans soon extended the application of their severe wartime demands for loyalty to all the "new immigration." It made little difference that the governments or popular resistance movements in the native lands of many of these people supported the U.S. war effort against the Central Powers. Jane Addams, the social worker, told of a man who rushed into Hull-House one day to report that the Rumanians north of Madison Street were "hatching a plot against the government." Miss Addams exasperated him by pointing out that these people were allies of the United States. "'I never can get those Balkan countries straightened out' was his apology," she wrote, "and I was in no position to remind him that it was not his geography that was at fault but his state of mind." In another incident that reflected the hysteria, a group of natives stoned some Czech Americans who wore their national garb when seeing off their sons and husbands to fight in the U.S. Army. When revolution put a Communist government into power in Russia, which then signed an early and separate peace treaty with Germany, Americans felt more justified in harassing the immigrants from Eastern Europe. All the foreign-born in the U.S., not just those from nations then hostile to the country, were expected to submit to Americanization education programs, to speak only English in public, and to accept the other norms that prevailed in the Unites States.

Before long Americanizers sought to extend their influence a step further by advocating what became known as the Americanizing of Americans. Native citizens who spoke the wrong language or who "thought wrongly" became targets for purification. Royal Dixon, a colleague of Miss Kellor, wanted to expunge the United States of pacifism, political

95

machines, and materialistic selfishness. He thought that such manifestations, although long a part of American life, threatened the survival of traditional Protestant values and of democracy in the U.S. Such "un-American" thinking, he argued, required the application of Americanization education. In 1919 the National Education Association recommended that Congress require a year of "compulsory civic, physical, and vocational training" for all young people in the U.S. For anyone, young or old, who could not read and write English, the NEA requested "legal provision for compulsory classes in Americanization...."

By this time Americanizers were lock-stepping to the beat of anti-Communism. They attempted to overcome what they believed was an increasingly popular concept that only a class struggle could achieve justice for the workers of the nation. Businessmen, who had seen how Attorney General Mitchell Palmer's post-war crusade against Bolshevism had blunted union strikes for higher wages and better working conditions, seemed ready to provide increased funding for programs in this type of "patriotism." Frances Kellor quickly associated herself with what appeared to be the new Americanization bandwagon. She now conducted virtually all her educational activities from the newly formed Inter-Racial Council, a business-supported and business-oriented private organization.

It proved impossible, however, for Miss Kellor and other Americanizers to maintain the national frenzy indefinitely. The same disillusionment with crusading that elected Warren G. Harding President on a "back to normalcy" platform began to work against the Americanization campaign. People in the United States were becoming ready to rethink these activities.

Critics suddenly surfaced on the left and blasted Americanization education as "cultural tyranny" by middle class natives over "the imported plebs." In an important inquiry by thirty Americans on the state of civilization in the U.S., the journalist and former university teacher Robert Morss Lovett termed the Americanization campaign a crude "attempt to put something over" on the immigrants. "Education," he wrote, "is the propaganda department of the State, and the existing social system." Writing in <u>The New Republic</u>, Edward Hale Bierstadt urged a reassessment of the philosophy behind Americanization education. "To Americanize

Let the Professionals Do It

is an active, transitive verb...," he wrote. "It implies something done to somebody by someone else.... What it should mean, what we must make it mean, is a mutuality of action."

These critics received support from advocates of the increasingly publicized philosophy of cultural pluralism. One of its most articulate proponents, many of whom were descended from recent immigrants, was Horace M. Kallen. "The ideal of liberty is no longer rooted in the like-mindedness of a group...," Kallen wrote, taking dead aim on the assumptions of the Americanizers. "In essence, democracy involves, not the elimination of differences, but the perfection and conservation of differences. It aims, through union, not at uniformity, but at variety."

Salvos from the right also ripped into Americanization education for failing to keep its promise of maintaining ideological purity in the American example. Influential critics like Lothrop Stoddard and Henry Pratt Fairchild, decrying the "mongrelization" of the Anglo-Saxon nation, argued that Americanizers had encouraged immigrants to become citizens without expunging them of such "un-American" ideas as trade unionism and Bolshevism. The Saturday Evening Post helped to popularize this point of view. "In spite of the evidence on every side," the Post editorialized in 1921, "sentimentalists still picture Uncle Sam as a clever chef who can take a handful of foreign scraps, a sprig of Americanism and a clove of democracy, and skillfully blend the mess into something fine and desirable." According to the Post, race character was a fixed and unchanging fact that made Americanization of most of the more recent immigrants a hopeless task. "They will always be Americanski - near-Americans with un-American ideas and ideals."

Sensing that the campaign was losing its momentum, leaders among the Americanizers increased their emphasis on professionalizing the field, an effort that became known as the Americanizing of Americanization. Miss Kellor, ascribing the problems of Americanization education to a surfeit of zeal and an "absence of definition, of principles, and of methods," called for the creation of an institute of immigration research to provide basic data and professional guidance. John J. Mahoney, a professor at Boston University who studied Americanization for the U.S. Bureau of Education, agreed with her analysis of the difficulties. "Probably no word in the English language to-day," he wrote, "is quite as meaningless as Americanization." They encouraged the organization of university programs to develop trained professionals and supported the recommendation of a study, financed by the Carnegie Corporation, which in 1920 called for institutionalizing the movement within the educational establishment.

The National Education Association in 1921 organized a Department of Immigrant Education, signifying that public schoolmen were now ready to take over responsibility for the full range of twentieth century Americanization education. Many school administrators had come to recognize advantages in expanding their domain to include adults and in providing the scientific citizenship education the public was demanding for outsiders. Institutionalization, however, came too late to keep the reputation of the movement intact.

With Americanization education widely questioned, it was no longer able to serve as a viable bulwark against the arguments of the immigration restrictionists. For nearly a decade "scientific Americanization" had been the panacea relied upon to maintain both the prevailing civic religion and America's image as the asylum for the oppressed of Europe. Americans now were beginning to believe they had to choose between the two. The restrictionists, who for years had articulated this choice as a major problem facing the United States, sensed that victory could finally be theirs.

Accepting a more professional Americanization education for indoctrinating immigrants already in the land, restrictionists thrust home their arguments for curtailing further immigration. They claimed that it was no longer necessary for the United States to serve as an asylum since World War I had democratized Europe by splitting up the old dynasties into republics of free people organized along linguistic and ethnic lines. It was now more important than ever, according to the restrictionists, to maintain America as the purest example of democracy for these new nations to emulate. Under these conditions, they argued, the immigration of alien races with divisive ideals and customs needed close regulation. They argued further that America no longer possessed an open frontier and required fewer immigrants than in earlier years. The strongest case against the immigrants, however, was biological. Restrictionists trotted out the old social science models that ranked nationality groups from superior to inferior. They pointed to the results of World War I U.S. Army intelligence tests that, because of built-in bias, seemed to corroborate the models. Using these scientific arguments, the restrictionists gained increasing public acceptance of their view that America was becoming polluted by Southern and Eastern European blood.

Restrictionists effectively used the statements of a convert to Anglo-Saxonism, Italian American Gino Speranza, in support of their efforts to limit immigration. Prior to World War I Speranza had favored a humanitarian form of Americanization education, claiming then that assimilation of immigrants should be based on "a spirit of true friendliness." A series of events in his life led him to change this position. His marriage by a Methodist minister to Florence Colgate, an Anglo-Saxon Protestant, signified his break with Catholicism. The wartime hysteria over the possibility of divided loyalties among the different nationality groups in the U.S. also had a lasting influence upon him. Speranza came to believe, as well, that a continuing influx of immigrants nullified the efforts of Americanizers. In the early 1920s Gino Speranza became an able exponent of the racist views of American social science, advocating Anglo-Saxonism in the name of science and national solidarity.

In an influential series of articles in The World's Work in 1923, soon revised and published as a book, Speranza lamented the heterogeneity in the land. He claimed that, instead of accepting American ways, foreigners were imposing their customs on the United States. He expressed dismay at the flouting of prohibition and Sabbath laws. He raged at the opposition of aliens to ordinances requiring the use of English. He opposed the use of foreign languages in some churches and parochial schools. He attacked "Israelitic Americans and Romanist Americans" for attempting to weaken the influence of the public school by eliminating its use of the Protestant Bible, "as much the symbol of self-government and of the national conscience as the American Flag." He had no time for "New Stock special pleaders" who promoted cultural pluralism with "finely phrased nonsense and spurious scholarship." The "basis of the democracy which George Washington fathered," wrote Speranza, "was ... distinctly Anglo-Saxon ... and specifically Protestant." Americans listened attentively when an Italian American, an "unbiased observer," propounded Protestantism and Anglo-Saxonism as the proper U.S. way of life. The propaganda of the Anglo-Saxonists succeeded in gaining political support for severe limitations on immigration from Eastern and Southern Europe. It had helped to achieve a literacy test for immigrants in 1917 and an emergency quota on immigration in 1921. Speranza and the other advocates now gained the public backing of U.S. President Calvin Coolidge who told Congress in 1923, "America must be kept American." The lawmakers responded by passing a stringent National Origins Act in 1924 that limited immigration to the U.S. from outside North and South America to 164,000 persons a year until 1929 and then cut it to 150,000 per year after that. The provisions for selection of the yearly quotas discriminated harshly against the "new immigration." The failure of Americanization education to make Anglo-Saxons out of the newcomers played a vital role in the decision to adopt a policy of immigration restriction. But Americans were not prepared to give up completely on Americanization education, as long as it could be professionalized and applied more efficiently to those Eastern and Southern Europeans who had already achieved entry into the United States.

9 BROADENING THE CONSENSUS

After judging their fanatical attempts to assimilate Eastern and Southern Europeans a failure, Americans sought to professionalize the practice of Americanization education and, through the public schools, to generalize its implementation across the country. Such an Americanizing of all Americans together was thought to be a more democratic approach then the recently discredited effort to Americanize a specific group. Accordingly, the U.S. turned Americanization education over to the virtually exclusive jurisdiction of the public school, the same institution to which it had earlier entrusted the homogenization of Roman Catholics. Once again the teaching profession would be the primary group relied upon to expunge distinguishing peculiarities of all Americans, including Eastern and Southern European immigrants and their children. During the 1930s and 1940s these most recent newcomers did, in fact, come to look more and more like the prevailing American ideal. Their adjustment was rewarded by acceptance into the American mainstream and by a modification of the civic religion to include them. Once established, these newly Americanized Jewish, Eastern Orthodox, and Roman Catholic citizens became stalwart defenders of the new consensus against demands for entry by the nation's black people and other minorities Americans branded as non-Caucasians.

The notion of schooling as a community-building science gained wide currency by the late 1920s, as professional schoolmen institutionalized the effort to obtain conformity of all Americans to the national consensus. Community after community, whether it had a large immigrant population or not, committed its schools to citizenship education.

101

Sociologists Robert and Helen Lynd described in 1929 how the community of "Middletown" sought to homogenize its children through the curriculum and the daily school rituals. They noted that this attempt to build a harmonious community included the indoctrination of respect for God, private property, and private enterprise. William Heard Kilpatrick of Columbia University observed in 1932 that the public schools generally promulgated Protestant, Anglo-Saxon, democratic-republican, and middle class values through opening exercises, songs, holidays, textbooks, and teaching emphasis. In keeping with the public's expectations, the schools spared no effort in seeking to purge all real differences in the name of national unity.

It was probably the public's expectations for Americanization education more than the efforts of the schools that actually benefited the immigrants. For many newcomers school was a grueling apprenticeship in Americanism in which their unique backgrounds and capacities were devalued and ridiculed. But public belief in the educational alternative bought time for the U.S. social, economic, and political environment to exert its effect, time during which many immigrants found a niche in the economy and gradually became acculturated to existing American ways and values. Public confidence that the schools were solving the "immigrant problem" blocked or blunted resort to more drastic measures against the outsiders. The illusion that the professionalized and institutionalized Americanization program was effective gave the U.S. milieu time to function as the operative force for assimilation of the immigrants.

As the environment influenced the Eastern and Southern Europeans and their children to look, act, and believe more and more like the rest of the population, the United States gradually expanded its consensus to include these Americanized outsiders. Roman Catholics and the Eastern Orthodox were included first in a white Christian civic religion. Later, in the aftermath of the holocaust of World War II, the Jews were also accepted. The consensus became a white Judeo-Christian consensus. The adoption by these newcomers of most existing American patterns and values reduced the threat they presented to the native American. As in the past, most Americans were willing to believe that assimilation was under way if white outsiders conformed to existing patterns in most areas of life, even if they maintained separate organizational commitments in religion. These organizational shells of old world culture achieved a larger degree of toleration, as did other non-threatening European manifestations. Few native Americans worried inordinately if immigrants and their descendants indulged their taste for foreign cuisine in their American kitchens or dining rooms. Nor did they balk at letting immigrants, and later their grandchildren who wanted to recapture a sense of their European heritage, wear outdated European clothing at ethnic gatherings and folk festivals and play at being Europeans.

When the Ku Klux Klan and other extremist groups occasionally resorted to violence against such manifestations of "foreignism," Americans experienced a sense of guilt. This self-reproach, often part of the Americanization syndrome, contributed to the demise of the Anglo-Saxon, Protestant nature of the civic religion, as did American wartime propaganda against the Aryan superiority doctrine of Nazi Germany. After World War II, the ethos to be preserved became the broader ideal of a white, Judeo-Christian, middle class democracy.

Almost immediately the question arose whether Americans could expand this recently articulated doctrine quickly enough to satisfy increasingly militant black people and meet a new world situation in which West vied with East for influence in the newly independent and largely non-Caucasian Third World. Those seeking to alter the racist patterns of life in the United States would discover that the newly modified consensus was an impediment. Protestant, Catholic, and Jew thought of America as a white society. Authorities would find it difficult to convince people in the U.S. that racism was no longer in the national interest.

Beginning in the 1940s, events were set in motion that would lead eventually to a panic reaction. They included a series of federal judicial decisions in behalf of civil rights for non-Caucasians and executive actions that put the Office of the President on record against segregation. Having helped to exact the new establishment support, the black community's long-standing agitation for justice now strengthened with these gains and developed into the national civil rights movement, directed largely by highly visible and articulate leaders like A. Philip Randolph, James Farmer, and the Reverend Dr. Martin

103

Luther King, Jr. The black churches of the South, along with the Highlander adult education center in Tennessee, headed by Myles Horton, provided indigenous religious, intellectual, and educational sustenance for the movement in the South. In reaction, white Southern segregationists mounted massive resistance. National and world news media in the 1950s and 1960s presented a picture of armed white Southern law officers bullying peaceful black demonstrators with clubs, pistols, high pressure water hoses, and tear gas.

Northerners and Westerners could empathize with blacks, as long as the civil rights movement confined itself to a legal assault on Jim Crow laws in the South. When the challenge extended to more subtle forms of racial discrimination throughout the country, U.S. public opinion became more equivocal. In 1966 in Chicago, King found himself pelted with stones by lower middle class whites, including those of Eastern and Southern European origin, as he demonstrated with supporters in behalf of racial desegregation. Riots by poor blacks in Detroit, Los Angeles, and other cities around the country diminished white support for civil rights. Panic among whites mounted in the cities of America, North and South.

While American leaders recognized that the U.S. would have to broaden its consensus to include blacks in order to avoid violence and world censure, they were becoming aware that many Caucasians in the United States would reject such a move unless blacks acted more middle class, more "American." It was difficult for blacks to appear white despite the hair pomades and skin lighteners long on the market. They might, however, as many already did, learn to think, act, dress, talk, and in most ways look and behave more like the average middle class Caucasian. If Americans could be convinced that blacks were willing and able to behave more like whites, the authorities could see that the democratic imperative might prompt public acceptance of a widening of the consensus to encompass this visible minority.

An important step in this direction was public school desegregation, a policy mandated by decisions of the Supreme Court in 1954 and 1955. Enforcement of the court action would bring disadvantaged black children into closer proximity to white children and white teachers from whom they would gratefully learn and accept white middle class standards. Progress, however, was slow. When for various reasons court-ordered desegregation of the public schools failed to provide a quick panacea, additional reforms were recommended. As early as 1961, former Harvard University President James Conant advocated a plan to speed up the process of making poor blacks more like whites. He recommended the injection of vast sums of money to improve the nation's slum elementary schools with their predominantly black student bodies and to bus high school pupils from their inner-city ghettoes to comprehensive schools in white sections of the community. Later, he called for the states to require a "radical redistricting" of schools to create racially mixed administrative units by combining city slum districts with white suburban districts. His goal was to overcome what he called "the adverse influences of the home and the street" on black children.

The assumptions underlying Conant's proposal linked him to the tradition of the nation's Americanizers. He wanted to improve the schools so that they could bring blacks, the outsiders, into closer association with whites, prepare them more effectively for earning their way into the middle class, and motivate them to discard their black, lower class culture for more "American" ways. He was operating on Horace Mann's philosophy of the public school as the balance wheel of the social order and the homogenizer of the nation. Demands to allow blacks into the mainstream had the best chance of being met, Conant seemed to believe, if Americans knew the schools were seriously engaged in the indoctrination of these outsiders in the civic religion.

The desegregated public school continued to be viewed as the basic institution for Americanizing the poor black population, but authorities judged the task too great for immediate accomplishment by the public school system alone. As some one hundred riots by blacks hit the cities of the North and the West from 1965 through 1967, programs to reach, upgrade, and homogenize out-of-school blacks, i.e., pre-school children, teen-age school dropouts, and adults, were seen as urgently needed. In 1968 Stewart Alsop, an influential national columnist, supported the call of the Brookings Institution for a bold new initiative. "An enormous educational effort, starting as early as the second year of life," he wrote, "will have to be made if the children of the Negro ... are to become Americans first, and Afro-Americans only second." The president of the University of South Carolina, Thomas F. Jones, urged a conference of adult educators in 1969 to "bring order and light" into lives of ignorance by "upgrading the value system" of blacks and other poor people. Government officials and adult educators talked of providing blacks with an "educational ladder" to the middle class.

At the same time as it helped to fund the schools to offer compensatory programs for disadvantaged children, the U.S. government also established supplementary programs of its own to benefit blacks who were beyond the influence of the school system. The violent racial conflict in the country encouraged the direct involvement by the federal government in Americanization education. Federal agencies attached particular urgency to reaching unemployed black youths and adults, especially the teen-aged school dropouts identified by the public and by the authorities with crime, disorder in the streets, black disaffection generally, and even with black separatism. An antipoverty program, ostensibly designed to help these people, soon began to take on the traditional pattern of the unfair exchange. Job Corps camps demanded that black participants groom and conduct themselves according to white middle class standards. Efforts were made to require welfare recipients to accept training along with the "handouts," as many members of the middle class termed such entitlements. The ultimate in Americanization was the U.S. military's "Project 100,000." This program drafted "tens of thousands" of "substandard" blacks and others with "poverty-encrusted" backgrounds into a special military educational project designed to "upgrade" and "salvage" these people.

Just as the Americanization of immigrants was described as "cultural tyranny" and an effort to maintain the status quo, so too was the attempt to Americanize black Americans. Critics pointed out that education to adapt blacks to the mainstream society disregarded the need to overhaul and humanize the existing political, economic, and social system. Saul Alinsky, one of the leading community organizers in the U.S., termed elements of the antipoverty program "welfare colonialism."

It was difficult for supporters of Americanization to accept the charges. They saw so clearly that America was the finest example of freedom and good government in the world. They assumed that a willingness on their part to open the way to economic and political opportunity should be reciprocated by the outsider giving up his "idiosyncracies." They were so committed to the U.S. civic religion that they viewed a recipient of welfare as morally weak; a Black Muslim as either subversive or crazy. Advocates of Americanization were, as always, good-hearted and appallingly presumptuous seekers of conformity to their own conceptions of what constituted the good American.

While civil rights organizations agreed on their major goal, racial equality, they exhibited different reactions to the conformity demanded as the nation's price tag for that equality. Some black leaders accepted the concept of total integration with whites, even if that were to mean the disappearance of the black minority culture, even the disappearance of the evidence of a black presence in America. Integration was what Benjamin Franklin was talking about when he argued for "early friendships" and "intermarriages" to "create that sameness of interests, and conformity of manners, which is absolutely necessary to the forming them into one people, and bringing them to love, and peaceably submit to the same laws and government." Franklin was talking of integrating Germans into the society, of course, not blacks, but the concept of integration was the same. However, such ultimate and final Americanization of the black minority, a group that formed only ten to twelve per cent of the U.S. population, was anathema to people like the Black Muslims who argued for Afro American identity, pride, and separatism.

Assimilation was not the only issue dividing civil rights activists. They also argued over strategy and tactics. While Martin Luther King and many of his supporters advocated nonviolent means for achieving equality, some of the other black leaders took a more militant stance. Stokely Carmichael, Rap Brown, and the Black Panthers emulated the bravado of nineteenth century Roman Catholic Bishop John Hughes and evoked as violent a reaction from whites as Hughes had stirred among Protestants.

There were other splits within the civil rights movement. While black militants doubted the good will of whites, other racial groups were uncertain about cooperation with blacks. They knew that many black people, like the European immigrants

107

before them, were interested primarily in improving their own situation. Once that was accomplished, the black minority might prove the most dedicated enemy of any further widening of the U.S. consensus. These other outsiders feared that blacks might prove as negative to them in success as many of the descendants of recent Southern and Eastern European immigrants were proving toward the aspirations of black people.

In the midst of all this turmoil in the society, the Americanization syndrome was once again discernible. A perceived threat to the existing consensus had created panic. The outside force of international conditions had strengthened the hand of a minority that exerted continuing pressure to change the status quo. The awakened consciences, as well as the guilt feelings, of many white Americans became evident in the numbers of these people attracted to the civil rights cause and in the national grief occasioned by the assassination of Martin Luther King by a white man. As in the past, Americans again became convinced they could use the schools and, at least for awhile, other public agencies like the Job Corps and the military to conduct an Americanization program to achieve the necessary level of conformity demanded of the outsiders. In time, it seemed that the consensus to which conformity was required had entered the beginning stages of a modification consistent with the operation of the Americanization syndrome.

The public had become convinced that under the shells of separate religious organizations and behind the facade of Eastern and Southern European ethnicity lay standardized, conforming Americans who had assimilated majority manners and values. It had thus become possible to expand the consensus to include these former outsiders. The same process was now at work with a native minority. A crucial part of the process was public confidence that education would cleanse black people, especially poor ghetto dwellers, of their alleged impurities. Americans believed that education would transform poor blacks from being what whites imagined them to be: indolent, violence-prone burdens upon the public purse addicted to speaking a substandard dialect of English called "jive." As with the earlier Americanization of immigrants, it was not the education itself that was of much significance. What was important was the breathing

Broadening the Consensus

space provided by the trust Americans put in the educational option. Americanization education allowed time for an increasingly integrated society to furnish more economic opportunity, to condition blacks to be more like whites, and to bring whites into contact with blacks to see that they did indeed seem to be more like whites. If the vestigial religious and ethnic peculiarities of Eastern and Southern Europeans could be accepted as mere facades, it seemed that blackness would eventually be perceived as only skin deep. With its imperious demand for conformity satisfied by the application of new programs of Americanization education to the nation's black underclass, the United States slowly began to move toward expanding its consensus. Despite setbacks to the civil rights movement, disagreement among civil right leaders and groups, and a lack of enthusiasm by the Ronald Reagan administration in the 1980s for the change that was taking place, the U.S. had begun to expand its consensus toward a nonracial, middle class, Judeo-Christian democracy. The results of the black-led struggle for racial equality in America would have ramifications for the nation that transcended black people. Other minority groups, too, would begin to come closer to gaining the economic and social opportunities they had sought for years.

10 HISPANICS AND THE LANGUAGE QUESTION

The beginning stages of an expansion of the national ethos from a Judeo-Christian, middle class democracy for whites only to one increasingly non-racial brought not only blacks closer to access to the mainstream of American life. Another less nationally visible minority which had struggled to improve its lot in the United States for more than a century also made gains. Action by the Hispanics would have to accelerate, though, if they wanted to preserve a crucial part of their cultures. They generally fit the Judeo-Christian criterion of the national consensus. They seemed prepared to honor most middle class and democratic norms. The widening of the consensus to accept what most Americans considered to be their racial distinctiveness, however, might not be enough to gain them acceptance unless they gave up, in exchange, the right of some in their group to speak only Spanish and any intention of pressing for equality of that language with the English language. The next manifestation of the Americanization syndrome seemed to be shaping up over language rights.

Language was an issue that had been repeatedly resolved in America. Obviously, Wussausmon, the Indian, had to learn English. The Puritans, not the Indians, were the bearers of God's word. Of course, the Germans had to be taught English rather than become a force for divisiveness. Benjamin Franklin thought so. Archbishop John Ireland thought so. The American people thought so, as evidenced by their attitudes toward anyone speaking German during the two world wars. The work of Frances Kellor, Peter Roberts, and the cooperating Americanizers of Detroit's "Americans-first program" of 1915 exemplified the commitment of most

Americans to English as the sole language of general usage in the United States. But English had never been formally designated the nation's official language. In the last quarter of the twentieth century, the language issue was coming to the fore again, as an increasing presence of Hispanics in the land caught the attention of Americans. The high birth rate among the some seventeen million Hispanics in the U.S. and the high rate of Spanish-speaking immigration, much of it undocumented and therefore illegal, caused concern. For some Americans, the proximity of the United States to a porous southern border beyond which lay what appeared to be increasingly unstable countries containing an endless sea of potential immigrants to the U.S., people who spoke only Spanish, raised the concern to a level of fear.

The fear seemed justified to those holding it when neighborhoods in some areas of the country rapidly became Spanish-speaking. Long-time residents in lower middle class neighborhoods could hardly go shopping for food in their corner grocery stores unless they spoke Spanish or were prepared to point to what they wanted, thus being forced to act like foreigners in their own country. By 1980 high visibility areas of the United States like parts of Miami, New York, Philadelphia, Chicago, and Los Angeles had become virtual English-free zones where Hispanics could get by quite well by speaking only Spanish. The likelihood of some sort of reaction was considerable.

The response, in the American tradition, was varied. A number of individuals and groups, including religiously motivated organizations like the American Friends Service Committee, worked to help the Hispanics and to maintain the tradition of openness to diversity embodied earlier by John Woolman. Others worried over reported estimates by the U.S. Border Patrol that it would apprehend 1.8 million aliens entering the U.S. from Mexico in 1986 alone and that up to ten times that number might successfully be entering the country every year without documentation. These people advocated equally traditional American responses to diversity in calling for more effective immigration restriction and for a new Americanization campaign aimed at keeping the U.S. monolingual.

The catalyst for a renewed drive for Americanization education was a conservative former U.S.

senator from California, Samuel Ichiye Hayakawa. He was an immigrant from Canada who had achieved recognition as a professor of English, a semantics scholar, and a tough-minded university administrator. As president of San Francisco State University from 1968 to 1973, Hayakawa had taken a hard line toward student activists. As a U.S. senator, he began to worry that the work of Hispanic social, cultural, and political organizations might be creating a climate favorable to a bilingual U.S. society. His concern led him to propose a constitutional amendment to declare English the official language of the U.S.

After his retirement from the Senate, Hayakawa helped to create in 1983 a "national public interest oganization" to lobby for this constitutional change. "We're calling it U.S.ENGLISH," Hayakawa wrote. "Its purpose is to restore the English-only ballot, and to limit bilingual education to a transitional role." The purpose was considerably wider than that. U.S.ENGLISH wanted to stop government agencies and discourage private businesses from providing public services in languages other than English. It also sought to nip in the bud "current Puerto Rican assumptions ... that it can become the 51st state without adopting English as the official language."

While the organization had its own mandate, it also had a link with the immigration restrictionists. The connection was in the person of its chairman, John Tanton. He was also the founder and chairman of the board of the Federation for American Immigration Reform (FAIR), an active lobby group seeking to limit Hispanic and other immigration. For their part, Hayakawa and U.S.ENGLISH had embarked on a program in support of the Americanization of Hispanics and others in the United States. These new Americanizers sought to serve the interests of the United States, as they understood them. They wanted to prevent the divisiveness they foresaw in a growing commitment within the United States to an alternative language and, therefore, to an alternative culture.

For its executive director U.S.ENGLISH hired a professional social worker who had been employed previously by FAIR. She was Gerda Bikales, whose interests in social policy were reminiscent of those of the earlier Americanizer, Frances Kellor. Ms. Bikales was an immigrant herself. She had experienced a form of Americanization education in

New York City schools after she and her parents emigrated from Europe at the end of World War II. She could empathize with those undergoing Americanization by recalling the pain she said she felt as a French-speaking Polish immigrant experiencing acculturation in New York. But she accepted the unfair exchange of Americanization - the giving up of ethnically unique qualities in exchange for the privileges of citizenship and the opportunity for entry into the middle class - as an inevitable process for anyone settling in the country who wished to rise socially and economically. She viewed her work in behalf of the use of English as in the interest of the minority group person as well as in the interest of a cohesive nation.

Whatever their own interests and reasons, by June of 1986 a reported 180,000 Americans of varied backgrounds had become members of U.S.ENGLISH. Its board of advisers included such authors and media pundits as Walter Cronkite, Alistair Cooke, Gore Vidal, Norman Cousins, and Norman Podhoretz. From the arts and academe the board drew the likes of Jacques Barzun, an immigrant from France; Saul Bellow, who was born in Canada, and Bruno Bettelheim, who originated in Austria. Publisher Walter Annenberg, whose father had come to America as a child in 1885, represented the nouveau riche. Former diplomat Angier Biddle Duke represented old wealth and old-line American stock. There were other advisers and a board of directors that included former Senator Hayakawa as honorary chairman. Hayakawa saw himself as opening an opportunity for all concerned and dedicated Americans to rally in support of the English language as a bulwark of national unity. Others, including some Hispanics, charged that what he had opened was a Pandora's box of U.S. nativism and racism.

Hayakawa did not see himself as an advocate of nativism and racism. What he wanted, he said, was to avoid in the United States "a situation like the province of Quebec." He worried over the politicization of language differences. "... It shocks me that French Canadians, reasonably far away from the Negro civil rights movement, would imitate the same methods, the same rhetoric, to defend French Canadian rights." Through U.S.ENGLISH Hayakawa worked to prevent what appeared to him to be a rising tide of Hispanic immigration and consciousness from threatening the dominance of the English language. To him the use of English was the basis of the American consensus, the cement that held an increasingly diverse nation together. He sought, by force of law, to make that unity more secure.

Ironically, Hayakawa's proposed constitutional amendment and support organization could have the opposite effect of creating an open struggle in the body politic, the usual pattern associated with the Americanization syndrome. Benjamin Franklin's much earlier program to Anglify the "too thick settled" Germans of Pennsylvania solidified resistance within the German community. Hayakawa's effort was generating a similar response. Among the many Hispanics united in attacking the proposed amendment were Baltasar Corrada, resident commissioner of Puerto Rico and vice-chairman of the Congressional Hispanic Caucus; Arnoldo Torres, executive director of the League of United Latin American Citizens, and Raul Yzaguirre, president of the National Council of La Raza. The proposal to make English the official language, the work of U.S.ENGLISH, and efforts to restrict Hispanic immigration could result in increasingly effective cooperative action by Hispanics, a group historically divided into factions because of differing traditions and varied experiences with life in the United States.

The Hispanic experience in the U.S. was diverse. Some Hispanics in the country were recent immigrants or refugees from the Caribbean and Central and South America. Others were part of a long-term and continuing flow of people from Mexico. Still others moved to the U.S. mainland from the nation's island possession of Puerto Rico where the population had become American citizens early in the twentieth century. Many Hispanics in the American Southwest had a much longer family tradition as American citizens and a history and background quite different from the more recent arrivals, a history that seemed to be forgotten by many Americans. Indeed, Hispanics held sway in Texas until the 1830s and in California, New Mexico, and other parts of the Southwest until the 1840s. The heritage of some Mexican Americans, particularly in New Mexico, could be traced to the Spanish conquistadors who had settled parts of the American Southwest prior to the permanent establishment by the English immigrants of their colonies along the east coast.

The native Mexican population in Mexico's northern provinces was always small, however. Immigration from the Unites States in the 1820s - some of it legal and much of it illegal - resulted in an imbalance which worried authorities in Mexico City. By 1830 some 25,000 Americans resided in Texas alongside a mere 4,000 to 5,000 native Mexicans. Efforts by the newly independent Mexican government to strengthen control from the capital only exacerbated the situation. Native Mexicans, immigrant Americans who had acculturated to Mexican values, and Americans with a vision of their race's Manifest Destiny to control the area who were resident in Texas for economic or political reasons could unite to resist interference from the Mexican central government and to declare independence in 1836. It was the Anglo Americans, however, who for the most part made the economic and political gains from the new situation.

The United States finally moved into the power vacuum in 1845 by accepting the request of Texans for annexation and by maneuvering the Mexican government into a war resulting in the Treaty of Guadalupe Hidalgo. The treaty required Mexico to cede half of its territory with less than one per cent of its population to the United States. For legal consideration of fifteen million U.S. dollars the United States received what became the states of Arizona, California, Nevada, New Mexico, Utah, and half of Colorado. It also received clear title to Texas. To retain their Mexican citizenship some 2,000 residents of the conquered territory moved across the new border. But the vast majority of the fewer than 75,000 Mexicans living in the newly acquired U.S. territory became U.S. citizens. These new Mexican Americans expected the United States government to protect their political and civil rights and their property rights, all of which were guaranteed by the treaty and its later protocol.

These new citizens would be disappointed. The flood of Anglo-Saxon Protestants into the former Mexican territory pitted two cultures against each other. The settlers were committed to "Anglo-Saxon Republican America," as New England author Richard Henry Dana, Jr., put it. They viewed the white or light skinned aristocrats of the old Spanish social order as part of a decadent, feudal society. The darker skinned Mexican Americans were dismissed as Indians. Like the earlier Scots-Irish frontiersmen of Pennsylvania, these new bearers of truth and righteousness felt justified in homesteading or otherwise appropriating any apparently "vacant" land, even land being used for the grazing of cattle, treaties and land grants notwithstanding. They took the land and suppressed as "banditos" those Mexican Americans who resisted. In Texas the violence against the conquered was institutionalized in the form of the Texas Rangers. An institution of suppression in California was the Board of Land Commissioners, an organization that made it difficult, expensive, and often impossible for Spanish-speaking landholders to validate their land grants. These attitudes in the Southwest were legitimized nationally by the 1877 compromise between North and South that ended Reconstruction in the South and formalized the U.S. consensus as distinctly Anglo-Saxon.

The Mexican American, Spanish-speaking culture reeled before the numbers, the unfamiliar legal system, and the self-righteous acquisitiveness of the newcomers. Some lighter skinned of the Mexican Americans disappeared into the new dominant society or, particularly in New Mexico, became an elite upper class with ties to the Anglo leadership community. Most, especially the darker skinned, gradually became a dispossessed and segregated working class, utilized in jobs deemed appropriate for blacks and other allegedly inferior people. But the history and tradition of the Mexican American could not be erased. The banishment to segregation, in some places by custom or regulation and in others by poverty and low wages, encouraged the maintenance of a separate culture with its wellspring, the Spanish language, which was learned in the segregated barrio and reinforced by continuing contacts across the nearby border.

Although schooling of the Mexican American was not always enforced, it was often segregated, even in California, and designed for Americanization. Teachers sought to educate the children to forget their history, to feel shame over their racial and cultural heritage, and to stop speaking Spanish. "The subtle prejudice and the not so subtle arrogance of Anglos came at me at a very early age," Mexican American Antonio Gomez recalled in 1968, "although it took many years to realize and comprehend what took place. The SPEAK ENGLISH signs in every hall and doorway and the unmitigated efforts of the Anglo teachers to eradicate the Spanish language, coupled with their demands for behavioral changes, clearly pointed out to me that I was not acceptable." In 1974 the U.S. Commission on Civil Rights reported, "The language which most Chicano children have learned - Spanish - is not the language of the school and is either ignored or actively suppressed." Speaking Spanish on some school grounds could result in Spanish detention, suspension from school, or even corporal punishment.

Despite the extensive violations of their rights, Mexican Americans achieved some cultural and political victories which set important precedents. A small coterie of Spanish-speaking delegates to California's constitutional convention of 1849 was able to prevent the limiting of the vote to whites only and to get unanimous agreement that the legislature would print all laws in Spanish as well as English. New Mexico, with the largest number of Mexican Americans of all the former Mexican holdings, achieved entry into the Union with a constitution that recognized Spanish language rights. The accomplishments, however, were insufficient to prevent the rapid descent of the Mexican American into an economically impoverished underclass, a pool of cheap labor.

There were times when these resident Mexican American citizens of the U.S. proved an insufficient labor source for the farms and mines of the Southwest and later the railroads and factories of the nation. Additional workers were then imported from Mexico, some legally and many illegally, to do the needed work, especially after the severe restriction of European immigration following World War I. The two world wars worsened the situation by draining the labor pool of Americans, including Mexican Americans, to serve in the U.S. military. Through the years, those charged with enforcing administratively-determined rules of entry at the Mexican border were pressed to look the other way when workers were needed. The pressure to turn a blind eye continued even after 1968 when a law became effective limiting immigration from the Western Hemisphere to no more that 120,000 persons per year. The known desire for cheap labor contributed to expectations of easy movement across the border with Mexico.

There were other times when the worker from Mexico was unwelcome in the land. When the Depression forced Anglo workers into the fields, the U.S. engaged in a major deportation program aimed at undocumented Mexican nationals in the country but

117

which swept away some native Mexican Americans as well. In the 1950s Operation Wetback expelled some 3.8 million Hispanics, including a number of Mexican American citizens. Mexican Americans came to recognize that campaigns aimed at Mexican nationals threatened them, too, since at all times Anglos tended to make little or no distinction between the documented and the undocumented, between Mexicans and Mexican Americans. An American of brownish hue and Spanish surname tended to be thought of by most Americans as just another one of those Mexicans.

Despite the deportations and restrictions, the flow of population during and after World War II was clearly northward, gaining momentum after 1965, and by 1986 including a new group, the Mexican professional and business class. High interest rates and a worldwide recession in the 1970s were followed in the 1980s by a collapse in the price of oil, an export upon which the Mexican economy had become dependent and which served as shrinking collateral for massive foreign debts owed mostly to U.S. banks. The economic fallout involved devaluation of the peso and galloping inflation. One way or another, wealthy and entrepreneurial Mexicans converted their pesos to U.S. dollars and deposited the money in U.S. banks, invested it in U.S. property, or purchased small businesses in the American Southwest. Soon these doctors, lawyers, engineers, and small businessmen began to follow their money north. Alex Dey, a Mexican American adviser to some of the new arrivals, quipped: "People from Mexico are saying that they are going to take over Texas and California again."

It was an ironic jest that other Hispanics could relate to since Mexicans were not the only Spanish-speaking people in territory taken over by the United States. Puerto Rico was another American conquest. The Puerto Ricans were obtained in 1898 when Spain ceded the small Caribbean island to the U.S. as part of the price of its defeat in the Spanish-American War.

The Puerto Rican people experienced Americanization efforts from the beginning of their relationship with the United States. The Americanizers went to the island to teach the new Americans "the spirit of American institutions and the ideals of the American people," as U.S. Commissioner Martin S. Brumbaugh put it. They insisted that Puerto Ricans exercise their "inalienable right to learn the English language." By the

1930s, however, the enforced use of English in the public schools to Americanize the people was seen as a failed policy. It was the Roman Catholic Church that became the major institution for the Americanization of the Puerto Rican. Eventually, in Puerto Rico itself, the United States let a "free market" operate in education. Economic self-interest was relied upon to motivate the competitive-minded among the Puerto Ricans to send their children to private schools established by English-speaking Roman Catholic teaching orders from the U.S. Here the children were taught in English to accept mainland values, thus helping to develop and perpetuate an elite class of "Americanized" Puerto Ricans. The economic situation also encouraged many poor Puerto Ricans to emigrate to the mainland. There the Irish American-dominated higher clergy met the Hispanic Roman Catholic from the island as the Protestant had earlier met the European Roman Catholic immigrant - as a potential convert to the truth. In this case the truth was an ascetic, Irish American loyalism to the organization, a "truth" with little fascination for most Latin American Catholics. Their faith was based more on a community of personal relationships than on loyalty to an institution and its structures. Their attitude, including sometimes an anticlerical stance, antagonized American Roman Catholics. Furthermore, the tradition of Archbishop John Ireland and his commitment to the English language had become an inheritance of the institution. Given these factors, it was understandable that Archbishop Francis Spellman allowed practical administrative considerations to convince him in 1939 to absorb Puerto Rican Roman Catholics in New York into existing parishes. Little was done to adapt to the newcomers, and Spanish language services were relegated to chapels or to school halls. Despite the sensitive ministry of some clergy, like that of adult educator Ivan Illich in the 1950s, Roman Catholic Puerto Ricans on the mainland tended to experience an Americanizing church.

In Puerto Rico, meanwhile, Americanization, both planned and "free market" variety, had helped foment a reaction, the development of a distinct Puerto Rican identity based largely on the Spanish language as spoken on the island. Puerto Ricans, who were accorded U.S. citizenship in 1917, gained control of their own public educational system after 1947 and restored Spanish as the language of instruction, with English as a second language. Americanizers had believed that a true understanding of American principles and ideals required their communication in the English language. But Luis Ferré, an advocate of statehood for Puerto Rico, could say in 1963: "We Puerto Ricans may speak Spanish, but we are American and we think American."

It would not be until after World War II that the full impact of the Puerto Rican factor in American society would begin to be felt by English-speaking Americans. Cheap air fares between the island and New York after the war gave Puerto Ricans easy access to the American mainland. They were U.S. citizens, and they needed jobs since American business interests had destroyed the island's subsistence economy. American investors had turned Puerto Rico into a sugar producer-exporter and locked it into the American economic orbit. As a result, 2.5 million uprooted Puerto Ricans had found their way to the mainland by 1985.

The Puerto Ricans in the U.S. were joined by another exodus from the Caribbean after 1959, this one by Cubans in the wake of the revolution led by Fidel Castro. The first arrivals from Cuba were upper and middle class refugees, including many small businessmen. They settled mostly in Florida where they established an effective Cuban American network of self-help. By 1985 a Cuban American, Xavier Suarez, was elected mayor of Miami. These lighter skinned Hispanics initially welcomed a later influx that included a large number of black and lower class Cubans. In time, though, the Cuban American network turned its back on most of these so-called Mariel immigrants who arrived in 1980. These newcomers included many single persons, a group not as well looked after by revolutionary Cuba as families. Because of their lower class status, their lesser stature in the community as single people, and their blackness, a number of the Mariel group became rejects among the Cubans in the U.S. Sponsorship, housing, and jobs which the Cuban American community had initially made available became closed to them. Some became desperate, with no family, no home, no job, no hope. Negotiations with Cuba for their repatriation proved difficult, and some became, at least for a time, wards of the Immigration and Naturalization Service in the Krome Detention Center near Miami.

Still other Spanish-speaking people looked northward in the 1970s and 1980s. These were refugees from South America and, increasingly, from Central America. Arrivals from Central America included Nicaraguans opposed to a revolutionary regime that had overthrown a right-wing dictatorship in their country. Other Central American refugees were from nations caught up in U.S. efforts to depose the Nicaraguan government and to contain further leftist inroads in the area. They fled a political and military crossfire between the left and the right to seek asylum in the United States. The U.S. government's politically motivated reticence to accord this latter group refugee status under the law spawned the sanctuary movement. The government proved less reticent to uphold the law against conscientious acts by this group, indicting participating U.S. citizens for helping to establish a twentieth century version of the "underground railroad" of slavery days, this one to transport and shelter undocumented Central American refugees.

Despite all their different backgrounds and their varying experiences with U.S. culture and society, by the 1980s the Hispanics had achieved major gains in the United States. An Hispanic of Cuban background was mayor of Miami. He succeeded a Puerto Rican. A Mexican American had become mayor of San Antonio. A strong Hispanic caucus of national politicians existed in Congress. A political consciousness was developing which furthered a cultural consciousness based on the Spanish language.

The growing political clout of Mexican Americans had been recognized in 1968 by U.S. President Lyndon Johnson, a Texan, when he signed the Bilingual Education Act. This law promoted provision of educational services in the native languages of minority group children, where numbers warranted it, on the basis that such instruction was essential to ensuring them an adequate education. Bilingual education took varying forms across the country. In some places, classroom instruction was given in both English and Spanish (or other minority language) for just a few years, usually at the primary level, until the minority children became proficient in English. This so-called transitional model of bilingual education, which former Senator Hayakawa favored, contrasted with the maintenance model, utilized elsewhere in the nation, in which

121

sustained provision of bilingual, bicultural education for the minority group became the goal. In school districts that had a mixture of non-English-speaking pupils from a number of different countries, the definition of bilingual education was often stretched to allow the teaching of remedial English or "English as a Second Language." During the Reagan administration, it even became possible for a limited number of schools to provide unilingual English instruction to pupils with "limited English proficiency" funded under the Bilingual Education Act. By 1985 more than twenty states had legislation encouraging some form of bilingual education, usually involving Spanish.

Government support for what some Americans saw as a competing language and culture resulted in a backlash. Even though its diverse patterns of implementation were hardly conducive to turning the U.S. into a Spanish-speaking country, bilingual education bore the brunt of the reaction. Harold Evans, editorial director of U.S. News and World Report, complained in March of 1986 that "bilingualism has come to mean not a year or two's transition to English, but a means of retaining Spanish language and culture.... Bilingualism has become a badge of separateness, not a route to assimilation." For U.S.ENGLISH bilingual education symbolized "the breakdown of institutional support for assimilation," a regrettable outcome of the encouragement by the civil rights movement of minority group pride. Former Senator Hayakawa attacked bilingual education as retarding the learning of English and, reminiscent of those who spoke of remedial education for blacks as a ladder to the middle class, declared that "the most rapid way of getting out of the ghetto is to speak good English."

Many Hispanics did not quarrel with this restatement of Americanization's unfair exchange. Spokespersons for the Mexican American Legal Defense and Education Fund denied any Hispanic desire to prevent their children from learning English. Instead, they pointed to those studies in the controversial research on bilingualism that proved to their satisfaction that children in bilingual programs achieved better results in English than children in standard programs.

U.S.ENGLISH, however, worried that Hispanics might also see merit in attempting to preserve and create a viable Hispanic culture in the U.S., a culture competitive with the dominant Anglo culture based on the English language. The Puerto Rican example was not one that set well with Americanizers. They fretted over the availability of all-Spanish radio and TV stations in parts of the country and a National Spanish Television Network to service many of the Hispanic TV stations. They were concerned that businessmen in those areas of the country were issuing Spanish-language credit application forms, providing bilingual directories in their stores, publishing catalogues in Spanish, and establishing personal-shopper services and toll-free telephone lines for Spanish-speaking customers. Efforts by Hispanics to establish a federally endowed national Hispanic university system exasperated them.

In its newsletter and its other publications U.S.ENGLISH quoted what it believed were the more frightening and extreme statements of Spanish cultural pride to stir its membership in behalf of English hegemony. It republished from the May, 1983, edition of *Esquire Magazine* a quotation attributed to Puerto Rican Maurice Ferre, then mayor of Miami: "You can be born here [in the United States] in a Cuban hospital, be baptized by a Cuban priest, buy all your food from a Cuban grocer, take your insurance from a Cuban bank. You can get all the news in Spanish - read the Spanish daily paper, watch Spanish TV, listen to Spanish radio. You can go through life without having to speak English at all.... Nowhere does the Constitution say that English is our language." U.S.ENGLISH also cited the view of Mario Obledo, national president of the League of United Latin American Citizens, that "every American child ought to be taught both English and Spanish." In addition, it reprinted the statement of Aurora Helton of the Governor of Oklahoma's Hispanic Advisory Committee: "Let's face it, we are not going to be a totally English speaking country any more." And it quoted Robert Cordova, a professor of Spanish: "To prepare American youth for the America and world of the not-too-distant future, the present monolingual, monocultural Anglocentric public education system must be replaced by a multilingual, multicultural, pluralistic one.... The Hispanic population is becoming larger and Hispanic culture is becoming stronger.... American society and ideas of old no longer exist."

These statements in behalf of toleration

disturbed Americanizers by implicitly encouraging a further broadening of the U.S. consensus. The ideology had so recently and so tentatively adjusted toward acceptance of a nonracial orientation. Was it sensible policy to try to expand again so soon and so significantly? Could the society become, if not immediately multilingual and multicultural, at least bilingual and bicultural? Not if the Americanizers of U.S.ENGLISH were to have their way.

CONCLUSION: Civil Strife or Expansion of the Consensus?

The Hispanics of the United States were facing a resurgence of the Americanization syndrome. Minority encounters with fearful efforts to indoctrinate the currently dominant pattern, this study has shown, were nothing new in American history. From Puritan times to the present members of one minority group after another have had to decide how to contend with the imperious demand for conformity. Those who have resisted have played a crucial role in changing the American consensus. America developed from a society based on freedom to impose its own narrow, dissenting conformity to one predicated upon a relatively broad Judeo-Christian, middle class, democratic consensus with a new opening toward nonracialism. Was this to be the ultimate and final formulation of the American way, or would the consensus be open to further refinement, further change, further expansion? This was the question facing Americans toward the end of the twentieth century.

The country's new Americanizers saw a serious threat to the nation's identity in the "encroachment of Spanish," as U.S.ENGLISH put it, upon the long-time dominance of the English language and Anglo culture in the United States. They also worried about a growing Asian influence in the country. Ironically, Anglo-Saxon expansionism had justified the incorporation into the U.S. of the Spanish-speaking people of the Southwest and Puerto Rico, as well as the population of Hawaii which included a considerable number of Asians. Racist, segregationist attitudes and policies had obstructed the assimilation of these Asians and Hispanics, and now the Americanizer arrogantly took alarm at their interest in maintaining their own identities.

125

Conclusion

Intensifying the fright was the fact that the numbers of Hispanics and Asians in the U.S. were increasing. Natural population growth was augmented by immigration. The same law by which Congress attempted but failed to restrict immigration from the Americas in the 1960s succeeded in slightly liberalizing the numbers allowed into the country from Asia. What followed was an increase in arrivals from both areas. In 1985, Asians accounted for nearly fifty per cent of the documented newcomers, Hispanics roughly forty per cent. Undocumented immigration bolstered the Hispanic numbers. In its July 8, 1985, issue titled "The Changing Face of America," Time Magazine reported to the nation that by the year 2000 Hispanics could constitute the largest minority in the U.S., outnumbering blacks. Also in 1985, the Population Reference Bureau, a private research organization based in Washington, D.C., announced its estimate that early in the twenty-first century Hispanics and Asians together could assume majority status in the state of California, placing Anglos in the minority. The organization projected Hispanics to compose 38.1 per cent of the California population by the year 2030 and Asians to make up 15.6 per cent. With its Mexican border as an entry point for Hispanics and its Los Angeles International Airport as a gateway for Asians, California had become a major focus of the new immigration.

California was also the home state of S.I. Hayakawa and others who were deeply concerned about the impact of these developments. A California-based organization, the Institute for Contemporary Studies, commissioned a book published in 1985 on the issue of current immigration to the United States. Titled Clamor at the Gates: The New American Immigration, the book had as its purpose the communication of the "critical immediacy" of the subject of immigration. The problem was not limited to the West Coast, according to the organization's president. Glenn Dumke worried that the "economy, mores, and politics" in various parts of the nation were "being rapidly changed by incursions of peoples whose backgrounds are far different from those of citizens of the nineteenth-century U.S." His concerns of 1985 were reminiscent of those expressed earlier in the century by the YMCA regarding the changing source of immigration at that time. Dumke was particularly upset by his perception that "some of the arriving

Conclusion

groups ... want top priority to be given to preservation of their own culture, and, in some cases, even language." Reflecting the thinking of Hayakawa, Dumke noted that southern Californians were becoming concerned about "Quebecization."

A more popularized and more inflammatory discussion of the new immigration appeared early in 1986. The Immigration Time Bomb: The Fragmenting of America was written with a free-lance co-author by then governor of Colorado Richard D. Lamm. Their book promoted the twin messages of John Tanton and his Washington, D.C.-based organizations, U.S.ENGLISH and the Federation for American Immigration Reform (FAIR): the English language should be recognized as "the tie that binds" the U.S. together and more effective immigration restriction laws should be put into place and rigorously enforced.

Lamm painted a bleak picture, emphasizing extreme situations. He pointed to some criminals, including drug dealers, among Hispanic immigrants. He noted that even some Hispanics felt disillusioned about the Mariel immigration from Cuba. He recounted stories of Asians and Hispanics, especially the undocumented among the latter, taking work from Americans and then permitting themselves to be treated virtually as slaves in the land of liberty. He spoke of Hispanic work gang recruiters and bosses preying on fellow Hispanics, as earlier padrones had done to their fellow Italians in the U.S. He showed how the immigrants were forced to live and work in substandard conditions for little or no wages. He wrung his hands over the vulnerability of Hispanics to banditry and other criminal acts along the U.S.-Mexican border, as they sought to enter the United States in desolate, less controlled areas. His solutions were to make it unlawful for employers to hire those he disparaged more than 365 times in his book with the term illegal, decrease the numbers permitted to enter the country, and patrol the Mexican border more tightly to apprehend and deport those "yearning to breathe free," now equated with criminals and competitors for the jobs of American workers.

In a later article, Lamm summarized his position on language. "We should be color-blind but linguistically cohesive," he wrote. "We should be a rainbow but not a cacophony. We should welcome different peoples but not different languages. We can teach English through bilingual education, but

Conclusion

we should take great care not to become a bilingual society." Lamm accepted the new nonracial consensus but drew the line at the English language and the Anglo American culture.

In his book, Lamm railed at Hispanic leaders in the U.S. He claimed that Congressmen Edward Roybal of California, Robert Garcia of New York, Henry B. Gonzales of Texas, and Kika de la Garza of Texas misunderstood or misrepresented legislation he favored. He quoted a syndicated newspaper columnist's dismissal of such organizations as the Mexican American Legal Defense and Education Fund (founded in 1968), the National Council of La Raza (also founded in 1968), and even the venerable League of United Latin American Citizens (founded in 1929) as artificially created by philanthropic foundations and out of touch with the interests of Hispanic Americans. At the grass roots, Lamm wrote, "there is no conflict among the interests of working people, middle-class people, blacks, and Hispanic Americans on the immigration issue - all of these groups feel that immigration must be controlled."

The immigration restrictionists certainly hoped that such was the case as the issue reached panic proportions in some parts of the country. In April of 1986 the Brownsville, Texas, City Commission requested U.S. President Ronald Reagan to increase the number of federal immigration service officers to help overcome "an alarming and ever-increasing number of robberies, rapes, physical assaults and thefts." Some Anglo political candidates in Arizona and Texas sought office on the border question. They aroused passions by pointing to potential increases in the crime rate and the unemployment rate and to an alleged "massive infiltration of drugs and terrorists" if the border were not more adequately policed. In January of 1986 the Los Angeles County Board of Supervisors requested that federal troops be sent to seal the border with Mexico. "I believe the military ought to be used now, because we are in a period of war," the sponsor of the motion argued. He was Mike Antonovich, a county supervisor and candidate for the Republican nomination for U.S. senator. "We have a crisis with drugs on the border," he said, "and then you add [Libyan leader Muammar] Qadhafi saying he's going to disrupt the United States through terror." Mexican sociologist Jorge Bustamante reported from Tijuana, Mexico, in May of 1986:

Conclusion

"I've been doing research on immigration for 18 years, and I've never seen the paranoia so high in the U.S."

The panic rose, at least in parts of the United States, even as Americans in July of 1986 celebrated the one hundredth anniversary of the dedication of their Statue of Liberty and reveled in their vision of America as a City on a Hill, a haven of freedom open to immigrants from around the world. U.S. President Reagan, who some time earlier had invoked the myth of Americans as "the chosen people of God," expatiated on the theme to those gathered for opening ceremonies in New York Harbor on the evening of July 3. "Call it mysticism if you will," he said. "I have always believed there was some divine providence that placed this great land here ... to be found by a special kind of people from every corner of the world ... [who would] build a new world of peace and freedom and hope.... We are the keepers of the flame of liberty. We hold it high ... for the world to see, a beacon of hope, a light unto the nations." About the same time, a New York Times/CBS News poll indicated that forty-nine per cent of adult Americans, as compared with thirty-three per cent the previous year, favored tighter restriction of immigration. The poll also found that in most parts of the country the majority did not believe the U.S. should welcome immigrants who came to the country with minimal resources in an effort "to make a success of their lives." One immigrant in New York City was unable to contain his frustration with the hypocrisy. On July 7, as the ferry boat on which he was a passenger glided past the Statue of Liberty, a homeless Mariel Cuban immigrant slashed eleven fellow passengers at random, killing two, with a sword he had smuggled aboard in some newspapers. Having heard the rhetoric but having experienced a different reality in the promised land, he finally gave vent to his despair. The havoc thus being wreaked on the lives of the nation's immigrants and others by the often hostile and hypocritical response of some Americans to the newcomers seemed to demand reflection upon this reemergence of the Americanization syndrome.

The United States could consider five of its six traditional options for dealing with diversity in meeting the immigration of the late twentieth century. Public opinion was unfavorable toward the final alternative, genocide. Three of the options

Conclusion

- immigration restriction, banishment (deportation), and Americanization education - were arrayed against the other two options, a dependence upon the environment alone and a commitment to cultural pluralism. Despite the promoters of restriction, deportation, and Americanization and despite the growing panic in parts of the United States, the ideal of cultural pluralism maintained considerable public support, encouraging efforts by Hispanics and Asians to assert their identities and to demand greater respect. It is true that some individual Hispanics and Asians supported the policies of organizations like FAIR and U.S.ENGLISH. But many had the political savvy to realize that the long-term interests of their communities seldom coincided with the policies of immigration restriction, deportation, or Americanization. Hispanic Americans had repeatedly found themselves vulnerable to these policies and disadvantaged by them. With the assistance of able organizers, community educators, and politicians such as César Chávez and Dolores Huerta of the United Farm Workers of America, Roberto Vargas of the leadership development organization, Razagente Associates, and Representative Edward Roybal of the Congressional Hispanic Caucus, Hispanics sought to clarify their values and interests and to work in behalf of them. The farm workers' movement fought an uphill battle for better living and working conditions against powerful U.S. business interests. The need to deal with health and mental health problems led Mexican Americans associated with Vargas to struggle communally to develop culturally-grounded Chicano approaches to building healthier, less exploitative communities. Congressman Roybal and other Hispanics both in and out of Congress worked long and hard to obtain increased funding for bilingual education, a program they saw as necessary to ensure equal educational opportunity for Hispanic children.

Asians, too, had begun to assert their right to a pluralistic America. When Asian Americans sensed in 1980 that a revival of a popular American motion picture stereotype of the Asian, Detective Charlie Chan, could revive old prejudices, they organized a resistance group, the Coalition of Asians to Nix Charlie Chan or CAN Charlie Chan. Their acronym contained more humor and perhaps more candor than John Tanton's FAIR, an organization dedicated to

Conclusion

what some considered extremely UNfair policies of immigration restriction. The rising consciousness and increasing organization of the country's Asian and Hispanic minorities made all the more urgent the need for Americans to weigh thoughtfully the arguments for immigration restriction, deportation, and Americanization against those for cultural pluralism and reliance on the U.S. milieu.

The basis for a policy of cultural pluralism was particularly compelling in the case of the Hispanics. To begin with, they could identify their cultures with the Spanish and Mexican American traditions in the land, a history that predated the arrival of the Anglos. Furthermore, proximity to various manifestations of Spanish culture south of the Mexican border and in Puerto Rico provided access to Hispanic roots, sometimes including friends and relatives, and to total immersion in the Spanish language. And visitors from Puerto Rico and from south of the border, as well as Hispanic immigrants, could come north and reinforce the use of Spanish throughout the U.S. The bilingual education movement in the United States, to the extent that it encouraged appreciation and use of languages other than English, was becoming another force in support of Hispanic culture.

Hispanics could draw encouragement from continuing traces of the pluralist philosophy of John Woolman in the U.S. This humanitarian impulse found expression in the 1980s in the work of religiously motivated individuals and organizations who sought to learn from and help undocumented Hispanics, the group in most jeopardy from the new outbreak of the Americanization syndrome. The American Friends Service Committee, for example, provided assistance programs in Florida, south Texas, southern California, and Mexico. These programs aided Hispanics to resist "overzealous enforcement by the Immigration and Naturalization Service (INS)." Toward that end the AFSC assisted in the organization and development of a self-help network that included a bail fund and a corps of volunteer paralegal representatives. It also provided legal aid to Kanjobal Indians to resist an INS deportation order to return to Guatemala where some 30,000 civilians had died in the early 1980s in a reign of terror and repression. The Service Committee also helped farm workers to complete Labor Standard Complaint forms against employers who would take advantage of them. It maintained

Conclusion

contacts with the Border Patrol and encouraged the monitoring and protesting of harassment of Hispanics by law enforcement agencies. And it sought "to promote genuine public understanding and awareness of the nature and causes of the migration of Mexican undocumented persons to the United States, the problems they face here, and the contributions they make to the U.S. economy and culture."

Spokesmen for the AFSC challenged the immigration figures underlying the growing panic. Noting the Border Patrol's rough estimates of four to ten successful illegal entries into the United States for every one apprehension, as reported by the New York Times, they observed wryly that the maximum estimate would mean the complete emptying of Mexico and Central America in less than a decade. They could point to an analysis in that same newspaper in June of 1986 that cited figures from Charles B. Keely of the Population Council. Only seven per cent of the U.S. population was foreign born, based on the 1980 census, compared with eleven per cent for France, sixteen per cent for Canada, and twenty per cent for Australia. Even including the undocumented, Keely said, yearly immigration to the U.S. totaled only 0.3 per cent of the population compared to 1.5 per cent at the historic peak of immigration to the U.S. "... Though the public rhetoric talks of a 'tidal wave' of migrants, and while their impact has been enormous on certain areas of the Mexican border," the paper reported, "in fact, immigration remains a comparative trickle when taken as a percentage of population." The figures of fear fostered by the self-serving Border Patrol bureaucracy were clearly overblown.

AFSC workers provided a further dose of hard-to-swallow truth when they said that much of the immigration from Mexico and Central America, which the restrictionists claimed threatened America, was in fact promoted by U.S. foreign policies. These ill-conceived strategies and tactics included the maintenance in power of Latin American dictators, support of right-wing guerrillas to destabilize and unseat left-wing governments like that of Nicaragua, and encouragement of the International Monetary Fund to pressure Latin American governments to repay loans to U.S. banks by cutting back on public expenditures for economic development and for social programs. Some of the more indomitable victims of these policies, they said, tended to be

Conclusion

those seeking to enter the United States in search of asylum and economic opportunity. The United States, by its policies, was thus very much involved in unleashing the alleged flood of immigrants that the restrictionists so desperately wished to restrain and in draining Latin American countries of some of their most capable leadership. A change in U.S. foreign policy could result in improvements in their native lands that would draw many Hispanics back home.

The compassion, understanding of the realities, and commitment to cultural pluralism demonstrated by AFSC personnel could offer hope to the Hispanics and counter the policy demands of the Americanizers and immigration restrictionists. It was a matter of record that virtually every new wave of immigration to the U.S. at some point triggered a needless panic reaction and policies that punished the immigrants and, in some cases, even long-time citizens of the same heritage as the immigrants. It also seemed that humanitarian alternatives, far from being mere sentimentalism, could serve U.S. interests equally well or better than the harsh policies engendered by fear. When undocumented Hispanics eventually returned to their home countries, for example, the memories they would carry of the United States could have influence on the future of the colossus of the north. If some kind of intervention were seen as imperative to reduce the inflow from foreign countries, Americans could consider the relatively humanitarian recommendation drawn from recent U.S. history by Tony Bonilla, chairman of the National Hispanic Leadership Conference. He challenged the negative responses of the panic stricken that would undermine civil liberties and pour money into securing the Mexican border against those seeking asylum and economic opportunity. If the problem were as severe as the immigration restrictionists claimed, Bonilla had a positive suggestion for reducing the human necessity for immigration from Mexico: "If we can rebuild Europe after wiping them out during the second world war, if we can rebuild Japan and make them a top adversary economically, we ought to be able to help Mexico rebuild their economy."

The spirit of cultural pluralism touched Hispanics once again when the National Conference of Catholic Bishops in 1983 approved a pastoral letter calling for a more respectful and compassionate ministry to Roman Catholic Hispanics, a ministry

Conclusion

that would see an increase in the use of Spanish by the church. "Although ... [the Hispanics'] faith is deep and strong," the bishops stated, "it is being challenged and eroded by social pressures to assimilate." In the article in its newsletter describing the pastoral letter, U.S.ENGLISH juxtaposed information suggesting that the action of the bishops may have been motivated by "inroads made among Hispanics" by evangelical Protestant groups like the Pentecostals. In a later issue, it pointed to what it called New York Archbishop John O'Connor's skepticism and "misgivings" about serving Hispanics in Spanish. This cleric of Irish American heritage was well aware of the traditional role of the U.S. Roman Catholic Church as Americanizer. He acknowledged that "when the Poles, the Italians and the others came to the United States, they had to adapt to the language...." But in August of 1984 he was in Puerto Rico as part of an intensive course in Spanish and prepared to accept the advice of priests in Hispanic parishes that, at least for the next fifty years, the church should respond affirmatively to the Hispanic community with such measures as the provision of bilingual Masses. The fifty year limitation could suggest that O'Connor saw church policy deploying cultural pluralism in the short term to maintain Hispanic good will while relying in the long term on the U.S. milieu to bring Hispanics into conformity with the American or Anglo consensus. Still, support for a combination of openness to cultural pluralism and a patient wait upon the assimilative processes of the environment seemed a more humane position than endorsement of restriction, deportation, or Americanization.

A factor aiding the survival of pluralism in the 1980s was policy confusion in the conservative Reagan administration. Ideological commitment to freedom of market forces could be interpreted as applying to a free flow of trade and people across borders, allowing prices and wages to find their own market levels. Such a laissez-faire concept might favor relying on the environment alone in immigration and assimilation policies. On the other hand, it could be argued that a conservative government could properly intervene in "defense of the border" and involve itself actively in immigration restriction, deportation, and Americanization. Caught between these arguments, policy was inconsistent, especially when the President sought to

Conclusion

woo Hispanic voters to his party and to appeal to the forty-two per cent minority of Americans the 1986 New York Times/CBS News poll found were opposed to further limits on immigration. In light of the present situation and in the perspective of American history, what would be appropriate policy for dealing, in particular, with the current Hispanic and Asian immigration? It has been suggested in this study that recommendations of those favoring tighter restriction, deportation, and Americanization are unsound. They merely inflame the body politic and wreak further injustice upon those already so burdened. It would seem that, within the United States, policies consistent with cultural pluralism would be more in line with the country's highest ideals and more beneficial to the long-term interests of the United States.

In U.S. foreign policy, new initiatives may be essential. Unless oil and other commodity prices rebound quickly and dramatically from their early 1986 levels, bilateral and multilateral arrangements will be needed between the U.S. government and Latin American countries for the forgiveness of the debts of those countries to U.S. banks. Such arrangements may need to be made contingent upon acceptance by the Latin American governments of an aid program of the kind suggested by Tony Bonilla, a new Marshall Plan for the disadvantaged to be administered by indigenous church-related organizations and other such nongovernmental agencies. And U.S. foreign policy in the area must cease to rely on repressive surrogate military juntas. Support of an intelligently implemented plan for economic assistance and for the strengthening of the social fabric of Latin American nations seems a positive alternative to a buildup of men and materiel to seal the border against "the homeless, tempest-tossed."

Within the United States, attention needs to be given to bringing the national ideology more completely into accord with present realities. Eventually, in responding to the growing Asian population, it may be necessary to expand the Judeo-Christian aspect of the consensus. As well, the social and economic element of the consensus may very soon need to be re-examined and, perhaps, redefined in light of shifting international circumstances and the growing gap between rich and poor in the United States. Economic conditions are in a period of change world-wide. International

Conclusion

resistance to American economic influence is stiffening. Wealthy and middle class Americans may have to moderate their economic expectations and, at the same time, resolve to take steps to achieve greater redistribution of wealth within the country. The time-honored myth that the American middle class life style is available to anyone prepared to hold a full-time job and work hard is becoming increasingly difficult to reconcile with experience and with projections regarding international competition, automation, and long-term unemployment. These structural limitations in the nation's economy make the traditional argument of the Americanizer regarding the poor and the unemployed, that they are themselves primarily responsible for their situation and need only to become ambitious and submit to educational upgrading in order to obtain a middle class occupation, seem less and less convincing. Even the goal of middle class work, the middle class life style, is coming under scrutiny, as critics challenge its wastefulness of finite world resources, its toll on the environment, and its failure to provide the expected measure of health, happiness, and harmony. The country's middle class ideal of a competitive, consumption-oriented, efficient national work force may have to evolve toward the more humanitarian ethos of a cooperative, conserving, caring national family.

While the social and economic issue may eventually dwarf the religious, political, ethnic, racial, linguistic, and cultural issues, the most immediate conflict over the national ideology concerns the Hispanic reality in the country. This study recommends the renunciation of demands for English as the sole language of general usage and the continued provision of bilingual public services where numbers warrant them. This commitment toward an expansion of the consensus to include Spanish language and culture would not necessarily result in a totally bilingual and bicultural society. Paradoxically, openness to modification might better preserve the very culture and language U.S.ENGLISH so treasures by making them more worth preserving. In the process the dominant culture could be enriched by the humanism and innovation germinating in its midst in such groups as the United Farm Workers and the Chicano community health movement. In the long run, a culture open to others and willing to incorporate new realities

Conclusion

will prove more cohesive, resilient, and sustainable than one encumbered by an imperious demand for conformity.
 Already it appears that the relaxed, pluralistic policy on language so repugnant to the Americanizers has led to three quarters of second-generation Hispanics becoming monolingual in English or bilingual in Spanish and English. In a study published in 1983 Professor Calvin Veltman revealed a <u>Language Shift in the United States</u> among Hispanics similar to that of other ethnic groups. His work poured cold figures on what he called the "anglochauvinist" who peeked briefly at the situation from time to time and saw similar appearing people who "continued" to speak only Spanish. But they were replacements from south of the border who would be the next group to learn English and move into the American mainstream. They would be replaced, by the time the fearful next looked, by still another group of monolingual Hispanics in process of learning English. "When the facts of language shift are known," wrote Professor David F. Marshall in <u>English Today</u> in April of 1986, "The ELA [Hayakawa's English Language Amendment] appears unnecessary, a flagrant political 'slap in the face' to our most rapidly growing minority."
 But what of the so-called Quebecization of the United States of which Canadian immigrant Hayakawa warned? The former senator had his facts and interpretation wrong. What had happened in Quebec was that French-speaking natives of that province, even those who could make themselves understood in English, were refused economic and social opportunities, a situation not unlike that which had been faced by Hispanics and by blacks and other non-Caucasians in the U.S. <u>Québecois</u> could realistically identify with the black civil rights movement and seek to achieve equality in their province and nation.
 In response, a bilingualism-biculturalism policy was promoted across Canada, based on historical precedent, to ensure that language would not be used as a means of discrimination. Out of consideration for the traditions of more recent immigrants, a "heritage language" concept was also introduced which supported the teaching of languages other than French and English. Bilingualism and biculturalism, supplemented by multicultural initiatives, were not the cause of unrest in Canada. They were the basis of the

Conclusion

solution.
    Implementation of a similar policy in the United States might have considerable merit. Bilingualism in Spanish and English has historical and legal precedent in the U.S. Southwest. Hispanic culture in that area can be traced back about four hundred years. Such tradition might well be used to support a solution similar to that achieved in Canada. The Canadian policy of bilingualism and biculturalism offers both a precedent and a model for consideration by U.S. policy makers.
    In coming to grips with this language issue, the United States has an opportunity to design a policy consistent with cultural pluralism, a philosophy that may be the best antidote for the Americanization syndrome. Diagnosis of the syndrome in its most recent manifestation and such a sensible, sensitive remedy for it as an expansion of the consensus toward linguistic pluralism could mitigate or even avoid this time the suffering usually brought on by outbreaks of this disorder in the American body politic. Openness to diversity could prove a far more effective policy for social harmony than attempts to enforce loyalty to an outdated consensus.

IMPORTANT DATES IN THE HISTORY OF AMERICANIZATION

1697 Cotton Mather produces his Magnalia Christi Americana

1747 Benjamin Franklin publishes his "Plain Truth" pamphlet

1754 Franklin urges the Anglification of German immigrant children in Pennsylvania

1782 Hector St. John de Crèvecoeur's melting pot theory first publicized

1783 First printing of Noah Webster's American Spelling Book

1797 John Jay articulates the concept of Americanization

1831 William Lloyd Garrison founds the Liberator to agitate against slavery

1848 Treaty of Guadalupe Hidalgo promises to protect Hispanic political, civil, and property rights in territory taken from Mexico

1849 California's constitutional convention agrees to print all laws in Spanish and English

1850 Free public schooling established in many portions of the North and West by this time

1866 James Russell Lowell calls for Americanizing the South

Important Dates

1867	Congress enacts the Reconstruction Acts
1879	Richard Henry Pratt establishes the Carlisle Indian School
1885	Josiah Strong's <u>Our Country</u> restates the American interest in serving as an example to the world
1889	Jane Addams opens Hull-House
1890	Public school classes for adult immigrants begun in New York City by Henry Leipziger
1895	First campaign to Americanize U.S. blacks enunciated in Booker T. Washington's address to the Atlanta Exposition
1897	Patriotic League extols "The Religion of Citizenship"
1898	U.S. obtains Puerto Rico from Spain as part of the spoils of the Spanish-American War
1900	Senator Albert Beveridge advocates the Americanization of "backward" areas of the world
1902	John Dewey urges schoolmen to copy the methods of the social settlements
1906	Immigrant Edward A. Steiner attacks American attitudes toward Eastern and Southern European immigrants in his book, <u>On the Trail of the Immigrant</u>
1907	Walter F. Frear, the new governor of Hawaii, signs a charter of incorporation for a Buddhist mission, an action rejected the year before by his predecessor as incompatible "with the best future interests of this Territory"
1909	The report of Leonard P. Ayres, <u>Laggards in Our Schools</u>, raises questions regarding the effectiveness of Americanization education in the schools
1912	Mary Antin describes her Americanization in <u>The Promised Land</u>

Important Dates

1912 New Mexico enters the Union with a constitution recognizing Spanish language rights

1914 Frances Kellor establishes the Committee for Immigrants in America

1915 National Americanization Day Committee organized; Detroit launches its Americans-first program

1916 The Outlook magazine praises the public schools of Rochester, New York, as "An Americanization Factory"

1917 The Jones Act provides Puerto Ricans with U.S. citizenship

1918 Frances Kellor associates herself with the new business-oriented Inter-Racial Council

1919 Utah requires all its young people to have a job or to enroll in school; The National Education Association recommends Congress pass a compulsory citizenship education law

1920 Study supported by the Carnegie Corporation recommends institutionalizing Americanization education within the education establishment

1921 Edward Hale Bierstadt calls for reassessing the Americanization philosophy; The National Education Association organizes a Department of Immigrant Education

1922 Robert Morss Lovett, writing in Civilization in the United States, attacks Americanization education as nationalistic propaganda

1929 Robert and Helen Lynd report in Middletown: A Study in Contemporary American Culture that the public schools attempt to indoctrinate the American civic religion

1932 William Heard Kilpatrick of Teachers College, Columbia University, claims that the public schools try to inculcate commitment to Protestant, Anglo-Saxon, and middle class values

Important Dates

1954 Supreme Court decision, Brown vs. Board of Education, sets course toward a nonracial consensus

1961 James B. Conant publishes his Slums and Suburbs that urges the Americanization of blacks in the U.S.

1966 Secretary of Defense Robert McNamara announces "Project 100,000" - a program to "salvage poverty-encrusted" young blacks and other males by drafting them into military educational programs

1967 Canada publishes Volume 1 of the Report of the Royal Commission on Bilingualism and Biculturalism

1968 The Brookings Institution urges a $6.5-billion program to upgrade black Americans; Washington columnist Stewart Alsop calls for making black migrants from the South into standardized Americans;
President Lyndon B. Johnson signs the Bilingual Education Act

1969 Speakers at the Galaxy Conference on Adult Education in Washington, D.C., encourage the Americanization of blacks in the United States

1974 The U.S. Commission on Civil Rights publishes the last of the six volumes of its Mexican-American Education Study

1975 The American Legion adopts a resolution calling for English as the primary language to be taught in U.S. schools

1978 American Friends Service Committee organizes the U.S. Mexico Border Program after working in the area some forty years

1979 Federation for American Immigration Reform sets up shop in Washington, D.C., "to stop illegal immigration and to reform U.S. immigration policy to conform with the realities of the 1980's"

1981 Senator S.I. Hayakawa introduces an amend-

Important Dates

ment to the U.S. constitution to make English the official language of the country

1983 U.S.ENGLISH is organized to further the dominance of the English language in the United States;
Calvin Veltman publishes his seminal study on Language Shift in the United States, showing that Hispanics are shifting to the general use of English on the same pattern as other immigrants have done over the years;
Pastoral letter of the National Conference of Catholic Bishops urges policies consistent with cultural pluralism in dealing with Hispanic parishioners

1986 The Immigration Time Bomb by Richard D. Lamm, then governor of Colorado, appears in support of English language hegemony and tighter enforcement of more restrictive immigration laws;
Celebration of the Independence Day holiday as Liberty Weekend extols America's image as a refuge for immigrants;
Immigration Reform and Control Act of 1986 forbids employment of undocumented immigrants and provides amnesty for certain ones of those who can prove they arrived in the U.S. before January 1982

BIBLIOGRAPHICAL ESSAY

The major purpose of this essay is to enable the reader to determine the sources emphasized in the writing of this book. There has been an attempt to avoid a tedious listing of the basic studies and interpretations of U.S. history that it was necessary to consult in the absence of any serious longitudinal analysis of Americanization education. Such studies were used merely to corroborate facts; the interpretations were largely irrelevant to the story of Americanization. While attention will also be drawn to selected publications of value in the topic area, the thrust of this report will be upon materials that directly influenced this analysis.

The study relied largely upon primary sources, depending almost exclusively upon them in the period after 1900. Appreciation is due the Principal's Humanities and Social Science Research Fund at the University of Saskatchewan, Saskatoon, for underwriting archival research at the New York City Public Library, Columbia University, the American Arbitration Association, the Swarthmore College Library, the Free Library of Philadelphia, and at both the Social Welfare History Archives and Immigrant Archives at the University of Minnesota. Valuable assistance was provided by the libraries at the University of Wisconsin and the University of Minnesota, the Wisconsin State Historical Society, and the University of Saskatchewan Library System, especially its Reference Department. Appreciation is also due Domingo Gonzalez and Primitivo Rodriguez of the American Friends Service Committee and Gerda Bikales, executive director of U.S.ENGLISH, for consenting to be interviewed and for providing background information and materials

Bibliographical Essay

in support of their respective positions related to the most recent outbreak of the Americanization syndrome.
   The secondary sources listed in this essay covered a wide range of topics, but few of the authors expressed any recognition that they were dealing with some phase of Americanization education. Most treated an individual or a limited series of events that became interpreted in this book as part of Americanization. Even those studies that touched directly on Americanization while covering a broad sweep of history tended to interpret the phenomenon as an 1875 to 1925 occurrence and to deal with it only in the context of immigration and the struggle for immigration restriction. John W. Higham, Strangers in the Land, (New Brunswick, New Jersey: Rutgers University Press, 1955), provided the best of these studies concerned with the treatment of immigrants in America in the post-Civil War period. Maldwyn Allen Jones, American Immigration, (Chicago and London: The University of Chicago Press, 1960), John Bodnar, The Transplanted: A History of Immigrants in Urban America, (Bloomington, Indiana: Indiana University Press, 1985), and George M. Stephenson, A History of American Immigration 1820-1924, (Boston: Ginn & Co., 1926), dealt with a broader time span and also proved helpful to the study. Indeed, it was Stephenson who termed Americanization "benevolent nativism."
   With one exception the few writers who focussed on the Americanization movement confined their topic to the decade after 1914. The classic work on this period was Edward George Hartmann, The Movement to Americanize the Immigrant, (New York: Columbia University, 1948; reprinted in 1967 by AMS Press, Inc., of New York). More recent studies were John F. McClymer, "The Americanization Movement and the Education of the Foreign-Born Adult, 1914-1925," in Bernard J. Weiss, ed., American Education and the European Immigrant: 1840-1940, (Urbana, Illinois: University of Illinois Press, 1982), and Maxine Seller, "Success and Failure in Adult Education: The Immigrant Experience 1914-1924," Adult Education, XXVIII (Winter, 1978), pp.83-99. The exception to this time line was Mark Krug, The Melting of the Ethnics: Education of the Immigrants, 1880-1914, (Bloomington: PDK, 1976).
   The target populations, the immigrants, were the focus of Oscar Handlin, a respected author

Bibliographical Essay

whose works on newcomers throughout American history were consulted in the writing of this study but whose judgments were often rejected. Among Handlin's books that proved useful were Adventures in Freedom, (New York, Toronto, and London: McGraw-Hill Book Co., Inc., 1954); Boston's Immigrants, (Cambridge, Massachusetts: Harvard University Press, 1959); Immigration as a Factor in American History, (Englewood Cliffs, New Jersey: Prentice-Hall, Inc., 1959); The Newcomers, (Cambridge, Massachusetts: Harvard University Press, 1959); Race and Nationality in American Life, (Garden City, New York: Doubleday and Co., Inc., Anchor Book, 1957), and The Uprooted, (Boston: Little, Brown, and Co., 1951). A succinct report by Handlin showing most of the areas of disagreement with The Americanization Syndrome was ...Out of Many: A Study Guide to Cultural Pluralism in the United States, (New York: Anti-Defamation League of B'nai B'rith, 1964).

The differences with Handlin were not questions of fact but matters of interpretation and emphasis. Handlin, who wrote most of these materials during the 1950s, was himself caught up in the contemporary East-West "fight for men's minds." Reporting enthusiastically that "...this country is and always has been vitally concerned with the progressive diffusion of its democratic way of life throughout the world," Handlin suggested that the Americanization of immigrants had some positive lessons to offer U.S. leaders in their efforts to democratize the world.

Operating on such values and assumptions, it was only natural that Handlin would interpret nineteenth century nativism and twentieth century Anglo-Saxon racism as aberrations from a U.S. norm of individual freedom and justice for all. Nativist efforts to limit the political rights of immigrants during the 1800s, dismissed as short-term deviations, were dissociated from immigration restriction in Handlin's analysis. Yet Samual F.B. Morse and some of his followers clearly hoped that such limitations on political rights would discourage immigration. Handlin suggested that late nineteenth and early twentieth century Anglo-Saxonism, although quite harsh, was another passing phase. He assumed that the melting pot theory enunciated by Hector St. John de Crèvecoeur operated until the late nineteenth century, a view rejected in The Americanization Syndrome which sug-

Bibliographical Essay

gested that the melting pot philosophy was exchanged quite early for the concept of fitting outsiders into a standardized American mold. While Handlin viewed the urge for homogeneity as a series of discrete aberrations in U.S. history, this longitudinal study of Americanization has suggested a continuing pattern.

Handlin and The Americanization Syndrome differed in other ways, too. He took little note of the siege mentality of immigrants that was caused partly by native American demands for their conformity to the existing U.S. ideology. The conservatism that Handlin attributed to the Irish Roman Catholics, particularly, was clearly encouraged by such native demands, as well as by the social, cultural, philosophical, and religious outlook of the transplanted Irish peasant that Handlin emphasized.

Handlin also ascribed nativism less to ideological indoctrination than to socioeconomic factors. In Boston's Immigrants he tried to draw a dichotomy between native nonacceptance of Irish Catholics and native acceptance of German Catholics. The more bellicose Irish may have gained the headlines in the East, but there was considerable struggle between natives and German Roman Catholics around the country. Although there can be no doubting the importance of socioeconomic elements in outbursts of nativism, it was the Catholicism of the German and Irish immigrants that enabled the native Protestant to justify his harsh actions against them by labelling them as subversives.

The major difference in interpretation, however, is related to the meaning of cultural pluralism. While Handlin agreed that Protestant values infiltrated both Roman Catholicism and Judaism in America, he believed the toleration of religious forms organized separately from Protestantism somehow connoted a pluralistic point of view. In this study cultural pluralism has been interpreted as based on a philosophy that respects true diversity, not one that merely tolerates separate organizational shells.

The integrity of cultural pluralism proved to be wide open to subversion in a nation so dedicated to homogeneity. It was easy to blur the boundaries between pluralism, the melting pot, and the civic religion. The U.S. milieu in the early 1900s led even such an outstanding exponent of cultural pluralism as Horace Kallen to talk of this philo-

147

sophy as eventually blending all the cultures of the society into something approximating Crèvecoeur's melting pot. Using some of Kallen's writings, one could also describe cultural pluralism as a clever ruse for gaining the confidence of immigrants and then working on a long-term basis to achieve their conformity to existing norms. Such an interpretation, with which it appears that Handlin agrees, makes a mockery of the concept of pluralism.

This analysis has also rejected the interpretations of other respected historians regarding such issues as the civic religion, the melting pot, abolitionism, nativism, and the role of Booker T. Washington in the struggle for equality. Ernest Lee Tuveson, for example, in his Redeemer Nation, (Chicago: University of Chicago Press, 1968), interpreted the historical roots of the U.S. civic religion as being simply "Protestant." He failed to isolate the various elements of this complex religious group and to recognize the predominance of New England and Calvinist thought in the development of the national ethos. While Tuveson apparently did not recognize it, most of his proofs and quotations regarding the U.S. as a redeemer nation were drawn from persons of such Puritan, Presbyterian, Congregational, or Unitarian background.

During the 1970s considerable argument was made in behalf of the existence of "ethnics" in the United States, persons of largely Eastern and Southern European derivation who have refused to melt into the Americanizers' melting pot. Michael Novak, The Rise of the Unmeltable Ethnics, (New York: The Macmillan Co., 1971), emphasized their cultural backgrounds. Colin Greer, Cobweb Attitudes: Essays on Educational and Cultural Mythology, (New York: Teachers College Press, 1970), and The Great School Legend: A Revisionist Interpretation of American Public Education, (New York: Basic Books, Inc., 1972), focussed on their economic class background.

The first three chapters of the Novak book provide excellent complementary reading to that part of The Americanization Syndrome depicting efforts to Americanize the Eastern and Southern European immigrants and their descendants. Novak interpreted in some detail their reactions to the Americanizers and to the values such educators sought to disseminate.

Novak's "intelligent subjectivity," as he

Bibliographical Essay

termed his sensitive and valuable approach to research, proved seductive although not totally convincing. Perhaps there is an "ethnic" factor involved in how people react to pain. One wonders, though, if it is primarily "ethnic" to stress the individual's personal community, attachment to family and relatives, to stability, and to roots. Might it not be more a social and economic class trait than an "ethnic" trait? Even the Jew's kosher kitchen and the Italian American's love of Italian opera may be more social than cultural. In a time when "black is beautiful" and when nearly everybody believes that lower middle class neighborhoods are not, it may be necessary for dwellers therein to let their imaginations soar to any fancied roots of glory.

This study dealt cautiously with the alleged continued presence of these so-called European "ethnics" in the U.S. It was judged that they are likely no more European than black Americans today are African. It may be true that the "ethnics" have not spread quickly throughout the nation or across the social classes. It is quite probable, though, as Colin Greer suggested, that economic class is at the root of the situation. While "Italian" neighborhoods and "Slavic" neighborhoods may still remain, the values of these people are American - lower middle class American, perhaps, but not "ethnic."

Although their analysis of the situation in New York City in the 1960s showed that in many ways third and fourth generation descendants of immigrants conformed to the American civic religion, Nathan Glazer and Daniel Moynihan provided in Beyond the Melting Pot, (Cambridge, Massachusetts: The M.I.T. Press and Harvard University Press, 1963; 2nd edition, 1970), an interpretation of the situation in support of the existence of "ethnics." Glazer and Moynihan chose to emphasize the loyalties of New Yorkers to different sets of American religious and political institutions and to use these loyalties to suggest the existence of unassimilated ethnic groups. They pointed out, too, that New York City elections require a racially, ethnically, and religiously "balanced" ticket. They were much too quick, however, to reject the notion that these commitments may be based on economic and political interests improperly labelled with anachronistic terms related to ethnicity. The interpretation in The Americanization Syndrome

149

Bibliographical Essay

is that the environment has led descendants of the immigrants to conform so closely to a somewhat revised American civic religion that ethnic designations of these people today are more reflective of romanticism than of reality.

It might well be a further revision of the civic religion that has led historians to rehabilitate the abolitionists in U.S. history. Once rejected as fanatics and "redeemers," abolitionists have more recently been pictured as humanitarians seeking equality for black people. It is possible that the trend toward civil rights for blacks that accelerated in the 1960s enabled historians to empathize better with the antislavery crusaders. The genesis of a widening consensus may also have made it easier for historians to view the abolitionists as patriots wishing to expand the national ethos rather than as purveyors of divisiveness in a nation united on grounds of Anglo-Saxonism.

Martin Duberman's The Antislavery Vanguard: New Essays on the Abolitionists, (Princeton, New Jersey: Princeton University Press, 1965), was a collection of writings that went far in returning the abolitionists to favor. But even in this compilation, Leon Litwack's "The Emancipation of the Negro Abolitionist" showed how white abolitionists tried the souls of their black coworkers. It was quite clear that many of these nineteenth century white emancipators emphasized their commitment to the nation's republican purity over concern for the individual black person.

Historians have also attempted to refurbish the image of Booker T. Washington as a fighter for equality behind the scenes. See August Meier, Negro Thought in America, 1880-1915, (Ann Arbor: University of Michigan Press, 1963), and Francis L. Broderick and August Meier, Negro Protest Thought in the Twentieth Century, (Indianapolis and New York: The Bobbs-Merrill Co., Inc., 1965). It seems reasonable to assume, however, that Washington's major influence was his public one where he legitimized the national policy of withholding equal rights until blacks "upgraded" themselves through education.

A number of other publications are relevant to the topics of race, ethnicity, and assimilation in American life. They include Jack Aqueros, et al., The Immigrant Experience: The Anguish of Becoming American, (New York: Dial Press, 1971); Thomas J. Archdeacon, Becoming American: An Ethnic History,

Bibliographical Essay

(New York: The Free Press, Macmillan, 1983); Milton L. Barron, ed., Minorities in a Changing World, (New York: Alfred A. Knopf, 1967); Leonard Dinnerstein, Ethnic Americans: A History of Immigration and Assimilation, (New York: Dodd, Mead, 1975); Reginald Horsman, Race and Manifest Destiny: The Origins of American Racial Anglo-Saxonism, (Cambridge, Massachusetts: Harvard University Press, 1981); Institute for Research in History, Ethnic and Immigration Groups: The United States, Canada, and England, (New York: The Haworth Press, 1983), and Alan M. Kraut, The Huddled Masses: The Immigrant in American Society, 1880-1921, (Arlington Heights, Illinois: Harlan Davidson, 1982).

Richard J. Meister, Race and Ethnicity in Modern America, (Lexington, Massachusetts: Head, 1979); Jamshid A. Momeni, Demography of Racial and Ethnic Minorities in the United States, (Westport, Connecticut: Greenwood Press, 1984); James Stuart Olson, The Ethnic Dimension in American History, (New York: St. Martin's Press, 1979); Benjamin B. Ringer, 'We the People' and Others: Duality and America's Treatment of its Racial Minorities, (New York and London: Tavistock Publications, 1983); Maxine Seller, To Seek America: A History of Ethnic Life in the United States, (Englewood, New Jersey: Jerome S. Ozer, 1977); J.P. Shalloo and Donald Young, "Minority Peoples in a Nation at War," The Annals, CCXXIII (September, 1942); Thomas Sowell, Ethnic America: A History, (New York: Basic Books, 1981); Charles V. Willie, ed., Black/Brown/White Relations: Race Relations in the 1970s, (New Brunswick, New Jersey: Transaction Books, 1977), and David M. Zielonka, The Eager Immigrants: A Survey of the Life and Americanization of Jewish Immigrants to the United States, (Champaign, Illinois,: Stripes Publishing Co., 1972).

Several other publications will provide further background for those interested in the question of nationalism and conformity in American life. They are Seymour Martin Lipset, The First New Nation, (New York: Basic Books, Inc., 1963); Will Herberg, "Religion and Education in America," in James Ward Smith and A. Leland Jamison, Religion in American Life, volume two, Religious Perspectives in American Culture, (Princeton, New Jersey: Princeton University Press, 1961); Robert N. Bellah, "Civil Religion in America," Daedalus, XLVI (Winter, 1967), pp.1-21, and David Brion Davis, "Some Themes of Counter-Subversion: An Analysis of Anti-Masonic,

Anti-Catholic, and Anti-Mormon Literature," The Mississippi Valley Historical Review, XLVII (September, 1960), pp.205-224. Lipset attempted to build a sociological model of twentieth century nation-building based on his conception of the eighteenth century U.S. approach. While historians might question the parallels he suggested, he did give considerable background on the politics and economics of nation-building that provided insights into the development of an American identity. Herberg had some philosophical doubts about the wisdom of inculcating the civic religion. Even so, he expressed fears strikingly similar to those of Horace Mann and the other Americanizers in wanting the public schools to create unity out of what he saw as an "ethnically, racially, and religiously heterogeneous society...." Davis discussed nativism as a psychological phenomenon of a rootless society swept by social change. He dramatically showed how Americans' fear of nonconformity could be more important than the nature of that nonconformity. Even the anti-Catholicism of the Masons and Mormons, for example, was insufficient to gain their acceptance during the nineteenth century by the equally anti-Catholic mainstream of U.S. society. "Strange" ceremonies or rejection of prevailing customs could bring persecution to non-Catholics just as quickly as it did to Catholics.

Also of value in this study were three other books. One was Robert H. Wiebe, The Search for Order, 1877-1920, (New York: Hill and Wang, 1967), which traced the development of middle class thought in America from the post-Civil War period through World War I. The other two were Edward A. Krug, Salient Dates in American Education, 1635-1964, (New York: Harper and Row, 1966), and the U.S. Bureau of the Census, Historical Statistics of the United States, Colonial Times to 1957, (Washington, D.C.: U.S. Government Printing Office, 1960).

The introduction to The Americanization Syndrome utilized only a few sources that will not be acknowledged later in this essay. Russell B. Nye, This Almost Chosen People, (East Lansing: Michigan State University Press, 1966), provided insights into America's sense of mission. The Wisconsin State Journal, Madison, Wisconsin, February 8, 1968, p.1., was among the many U.S. newspapers carrying the story of a "Mekong Delta Town 'Destroyed to Save It.'" Johathan Schell, The Vil-

Bibliographical Essay

lage of Ben Suc, (New York: Random House, Vintage Book, 1968), tended to reinforce the picture of a continuing U.S. mission. Sir William A. Craigie and James R. Hulbert, eds., A Dictionary of American English on Historical Principles, (Chicago: University of Chicago Press, 1938), p.45, designated the eighteenth century beginnings of the concept of Americanization. Norman Podhoretz, Making It, (New York: Random House, 1967), helped to corroborate the interpretation of the unfair exchange. He termed the situation in the 1940s between a middle class, Anglo-Saxon teacher and himself, a teen-aged son of lower class Eastern European Jews, "The Brutal Bargain."

CHAPTER ONE

The most helpful sources for understanding the Puritans were the writings of these early colonists themselves and their contemporary critics. Cotton Mather, Magnalia Christi Americana, (Hartford: Silas Andrus, 1820), two volumes; James Kendall Hosmer, ed., Winthrop's Journal, 1630-1649, (New York: Charles Scribner's Sons, 1908), two volumes; Charles H. Lincoln, ed., Narratives of the Indian Wars, 1675-1699, (New York: Barnes and Noble, Inc., 1952), and Paul Leicester Ford, ed., The New England Primer, (New York: Teachers College, Columbia University, 1962), were the major works relied upon in preparing this chapter. Perry Miller and Thomas H. Johnson, The Puritans, (New York, Evanston, and London: Harper and Row Torchbook, 1963), Volume One, provided an introduction and a selection of Puritan writings that gave additional insight into the thought of these early New Englanders.

Four secondary sources influenced the interpretation of the Puritan phase of Americanization. They were Perry Miller, Errand Into the Wilderness, (New York: Harper and Row Torchbook, 1964); Edmund S. Morgan, The Puritan Dilemma: The Story of John Winthrop, (Boston and Toronto: Little, Brown, and Co., 1958); Thomas Jefferson Wertenbaker, The Puritan Oligarchy, (New York: Charles Scribner's Sons, 1947), and George M. Waller, ed., Puritanism in Early America, (Boston: D.C. Heath and Co., 1950). The Morgan book was especially useful in its interpretation of John Winthrop's activities as intended to bind the Puritan commonwealth together at all costs. The Waller compilation was a handy, con-

Bibliographical Essay

densed overview of the varying interpretations historians have presented of the New England Puritans. Other secondary sources aiding in the study of the Puritans were Charles M. Andrews, Our Earliest Colonial Settlements, (Ithaca, New York: Cornell University Press, 1962); Edmund S. Morgan, Visible Saints: The History of a Puritan Idea, (New York: New York University Press, 1963), and Wallace Notestein, The English People on the Eve of Colonization, (New York, Evanston, and London: Harper and Row Torchbook, 1962).

In writing about the American Indian, the expertise of William T. Hagan was indispensable. Major reliance was placed on his American Indians, (Chicago and London: The University of Chicago Press, 1966), but some use was also made of his brief overview, The Indian in American History, (Washington, D.C.: The American Historical Association, 1966).

CHAPTER TWO

Benjamin Franklin was an artful politician who kept his contemporaries and later historians guessing regarding his goals and motivations. Studying Franklin as an Americanizer provided a new dimension for viewing this early U.S. statesman. In developing the picture of Franklin described here reliance was placed mostly on his own writings but also on the exciting and controversial book by Paul W. Conner, Poor Richard's Politicks: Benjamin Franklin and His New American Order, (New York: Oxford University Press, 1965). Conner tended to make a bit too much of Franklin as having a preconceived operational plan for creating a harmonious community in America. None the less, Franklin's activities and his reaction to events indicated a pattern of thought consistent with Conner's interpretation even if Franklin had no consciously formed master plan until quite late in his life.

Many of the primary documents cited may be found in Albert Henry Smyth, ed., The Writings of Benjamin Franklin, (New York: The Macmillan Co., 1905-1907), ten volumes, or in the more recent compilation by Leonard W. Labaree, ed., The Papers of Benjamin Franklin, (New Haven and London: Yale University Press, 1959-1968), twelve volumes. Among the most important of Frankin's writings that related to his role as an Americanizer were "Plain

Bibliographical Essay

Truth or Serious Considerations on the Present State of the City of Philadelphia, and Province of Pennsylvania," 1747; "Observations Concerning the Increase of Mankind, Peopling of Countries, etc.," 1751; Letter to Richard Jackson, 1753; "Reasons Against Partial Unions," 1754; "A Dialogue Between X, Y, and Z, Concerning the Present State of Affairs in Pennsylvania," 1755; Letter to Lord Henry Home of Kames, London, January 3, 1760; "The Interest of Great Britain Considered with Regard to Her Colonies and the Acquisitions of Canada and Guadaloupe," 1760; "A Narrative of the Late Massacres in Lancaster County," 1764; Letter to Sir William Johnson, London, September 12, 1766; Letter to Anthony Benezet, London, August 22, 1772; "An Account of Negotiations in London for Effecting a Reconciliation Between Great Britain and the American Colonies," March 22, 1775; "An Address to the Public," 1789, and Letter to John Wright, 1789.

Several other sources also proved helpful. Benjamin Franklin, "A Memorial of the Case of the German Emigrants Settled in Pennsylvania," (London, 1754), was extremely important, as was L. Jesse Lemisch, ed., Benjamin Franklin: The Autobiography and Other Writings, (New York: The New American Library, Signet Classic, 1961). Other secondary sources consulted were Verner W. Crane, Benjamin Franklin and a Rising People, (Boston: Little, Brown, and Co., 1954); Crane's Benjamin Franklin: Englishman and American, (Providence, Rhode Island: Brown University, 1936); Gerald Stourzh, Benjamin Franklin and American Foreign Policy, (Chicago: University of Chicago Press, 1954), and William S. Hanna, Benjamin Franklin and Pennsylvania Politics, (Stanford, California: Stanford University Press, 1964).

John Woolman, A Journal and Other Writings, (Dublin: R. Jackson, 1778), provided the basis for the picture presented of this eighteenth century Quaker although several secondary sources were also consulted regarding Woolman. These were the major biography of him by Janet Whitney, John Woolman: American Quaker, (Boston: Little, Brown, and Co., 1942), and Edwin H. Cady, John Woolman: The Mind of the Quaker Saint, (New York: Washington Square Press, Inc., 1966).

Further background on the times and the issues then current was drawn from Adam Smith, "Of Colonies," The Nature and Causes of the Wealth of Nations, (Aalen: Otto Zellner, 1963), Volume Three,

Bibliographical Essay

pp.343-485; Frederick B. Tolles, James Logan and the Culture of Provincial America, (Boston: Little, Brown, and Co., 1957); Edwin B. Bronner, William Penn's "Holy Experiment," (New York: Temple University Publications, 1962); Rufus M. Jones, The Quakers in the American Colonies, (London: Macmillan and Co., 1911); "Isaac Sharpless: Colonial Pennsylvania: The Quest for Non-violence," in Mulford Q. Sibley, ed., The Quiet Battle: Writings on the Theory and Practice of Non-violent Resistance, (Garden City, New York: Anchor Books, Doubleday and Co., 1963); David Hawke, The Colonial Experience, (Indianapolis: The Bobbs-Merrill Co., 1966); Louis B. Wright, The Cultural Life of the American Colonies, (New York: Harper and Row Torchbook, 1962), and William Appleman Williams, The Contours of American History, (Chicago: Quadrangle Books, 1966).

CHAPTER THREE

The Special Collections Section of Butler Library at Columbia University was a fruitful source of old American textbooks. It also provided Jedediah Morse's "A Sermon Exhibiting the Present Dangers, and Consequent Duties of the Citizens of the United States of America," (Charlestown, Massachusetts: Samuel Etheridge, 1799). Other primary sources related to old textbooks were Noah Webster, Noah Webster's American Spelling Book, (New York: Teachers College, Columbia University, 1962), and William Holmes McGuffey, McGuffey's Fifth Eclectic Reader, (New York: The New American Library, Signet Classic, 1962).

Other primary sources: Charles Francis Adams, ed., The Works of John Adams, (Boston: Charles C. Little and James Brown, 1851), ten volumes; William J. Chute, The American Scene: 1600-1860, Contemporary Views of Life and Society, (New York; Bantam Books, 1964); Hector St. John de Crèvecoeur, Letters from an American Farmer, (New York: The New American Library, Signet Classic, 1963); Congressman John Page of Virginia in Joseph Gales, Sr., ed., The Debates and Proceedings in the Congress of the United States, (Washington: Gales and Seaton, 1834), pp.1148 and 1149; Benjamin Rush, An Account of the Manners of the German Inhabitants of Pennsylvania, (Philadelphia: Samuel P. Town, 1875), and Noah Webster, "The Reforming of Spelling," Leaflet

156

Bibliographical Essay

196 in Old South Leaflets, (New York: Burt Franklin, no date), Volume Three.

Lawrence A. Cremin, ed., The Republic and the School: Horace Mann on the Education of Free Men, (New York: Teachers College, Columbia University, 1957); Pope Gregory XVI, Epistola Encyclica, (Rome: The Vatican, 1832); the Reverend Peter Guilday, ed., The National Pastorals of the American Hierarchy, 1792-1919, (Westminster, Maryland: The Newman Press, 1954); Lawrence Kehoe, ed., Complete Works of the Most Rev. John Hughes, D.D., (New York: The Catholic Publication House, 1864), two volumes; Mary Tyler Peabody Mann and George C. Mann, eds., Life and Works of Horace Mann, (Boston: Lee and Shepard, 1891), two volumes; Joy Elmer Morgan, ed., Horace Mann: His Ideas and Ideals, (Washington, D.C.: National Home Library Foundation, 1936); Samuel F.B. Morse, "Imminent Dangers to the Free Institutions of the United States through Foreign Immigration and the Present State of the Naturalization Laws," (New York: John F. Trow, 1854 version), and R.W. Thompson, The Papacy and the Civil Power, (New York: Harper and Brothers, 1876).

A number of secondary publications were utilized regarding textbooks and schooling in America. Ruth Miller Elson, Guardians of Tradition: American Schoolbooks of the Nineteenth Century, (Lincoln, Nebraska: University of Nebraska Press, 1964), was an exhaustive and relatively impartial analysis of U.S. school books through the years. Sister Marie Léonore Fell, The Foundations of Nativism In American Textbooks, 1783-1860, (Washington, D.C.: The Catholic University of America Press, 1941), was an extensive listing of old textbook passages unfriendly to Roman Catholicism by an author unfriendly to the traditional pattern of U.S. public education. Contributing a number of facts about the history of schooling were R. Freeman Butts and Lawrence A. Cremin, A History of Education in American Culture, (New York: Holt, Rinehart, and Winston, 1953); Lawrence A. Cremin, The American Common School, (New York: Teachers College, Columbia University, 1951); Raymond B. Culver, Horace Mann and Religion in the Massachusetts Public Schools, (New Haven: Yale University Press, 1929); Peter Vincent Lannie, "Archbishop John Hughes and the Common School Controversy, 1840-1842," (Unpublished Ph.D. dissertation, Columbia University, 1963); Timothy L. Smith, "Protes-

Bibliographical Essay

tant Schooling and American Nationality, 1800-1850," The Journal of American History, LIII (March, 1967), pp.679-695; David Tyack, "Forming the National Character," Harvard Educational Review, XXXVI (Winter, 1966), pp.29-41, and David Tyack, "The Kingdom of God and the Common School," Harvard Educational Review, XXXVI (Fall, 1966), pp.447-469.
Other important secondary sources consulted included Ray Allen Billington, The Protestant Crusade, 1800-1860, (New York: Rinehart and Co., 1952 edition), the standard source on Protestant-Roman Catholic antagonisms in this period; Merle Curti, The Roots of American Loyalty, (New York: Columbia University Press, 1946); John Tracy Ellis, Catholics in Colonial America, (Baltimore and Dublin: Helicon, 1965); Oscar Handlin, Boston's Immigrants, (Cambridge, Massachusetts: Harvard University Press, 1959); Oscar Handlin, The Uprooted, (Boston: Little, Brown, and Co., 1951), chapter five, "Religion as a Way of Life;" Donald L. Kinzer, An Episode in Anti-Catholicism: The American Protective Association, (Seattle: University of Washington Press, 1964); Russel Blaine Nye, The Cultural Life of the New Nation, (New York: Harper and Row Torchbook, 1963), and William Warren Sweet, Religion in the Development of American Culture, 1765-1840, (New York: Charles Scribner's Sons, 1952).

CHAPTER FOUR

Primary sources: Roy P. Basler, ed., Abraham Lincoln: His Speeches and Writings, (New York: Grosset and Dunlap, 1962); Daniel Calhoun, ed., The Educating of Americans: A Documentary History, (Boston: Houghton Mifflin Co., 1969); James Russell Lowell, "The Seward-Johnson Reaction," North American Review, CIII (October, 1866), pp.520-549; Eric L. McKitrick, ed., Slavery Defended: The Views of the Old South, (Englewood Cliffs, New Jersey: Prentice-Hall, Inc., 1963); F.B. Sanborn, Recollections of Seventy Years, (Boston: Richard G. Badger, 1909), two volumes; Harriet Beecher Stowe, Uncle Tom's Cabin, (New York: Collier Books, 1962), and John L. Thomas, ed., Slavery Attacked: The Abolitionist Crusade, (Englewood Cliffs, New Jersey: Prentice-Hall, Inc., 1965).
    Henry Steele Commager, ed., The Struggle for Racial Equality: A Documentary Record, (New York:

Bibliographical Essay

Harper and Row Torchbook, 1967); Congressional Record, 55th Cong., 3rd Session, Volume XXXII, pp.1-2938 and appendix, regarding Chinese exclusion; W.E. Burghardt DuBois, The Souls of Black Folk, (Greenwich, Connecticut: Fawcett Publications, Inc., 1961); Richard Henry Pratt, Battlefield and Classroom, (New Haven and London: Yale University Press, 1964); John Anthony Scott, ed., Living Documents in American History, (New York: Washington Square Press, 1969), Volume Two; the Reverend Josiah Strong, Our Country: Its Possible Future and Its Present Crisis, (New York: The Baker and Taylor Co. for the American Home Missionary Society, 1885), and William Appleman Williams, ed., The Shaping of American Diplomacy, (Chicago: Rand McNally and Co., 1956), two volumes.

Secondary sources that gave insight into the activities and motivations of the abolitionists were John L. Thomas, The Liberator, (Boston: Little, Brown, and Co., 1963), an incisive biography of William Lloyd Garrison that exposed the New England roots of abolitionism; Richard O. Curry, ed., The Abolitionists: Reformers or Fanatics, (New York: Holt, Rinehart, and Winston, 1965), and Hugh Hawkins, The Abolitionists, (Boston: D.C. Heath and Co., 1964), which included excerpts from the writings of some of the abolitionists as well as interpretations of them by later historians.

Four secondary sources were extremely important in the preparation of this chapter. Edwin C. Rozwenc, ed., Slavery as a Cause of the Civil War, (Boston: D.C. Heath and Co., 1949), provided a succinct compilation of historical interpretations of this subject. Paul H. Buck, The Road to Reunion, 1865-1900, (Boston: Little, Brown, and Co., 1938), was an invaluable aid in developing the interpretation of the narrowing of the national ideology in the aftermath of the Civil War. Dorothea R. Muller, "Josiah Strong and American Nationalism: A Reevaluation," The Journal of American History, LIII (December, 1966), pp.487-503, effectively reinterpreted this nationalist's interest in U.S. world influence as the purification of the American example rather than military conquest. Elmer Clarence Sandmeyer, The Anti-Chinese Movement in California, (Urbana, Illinois: The University of Illinois Press, 1939), gave a brief but effective picture of the drive for exclusion of Oriental immigration in California and other parts of the West.

Bibliographical Essay

Other secondary sources were relevant to this chapter. They included Ray Stannard Baker, Following the Color Line, (New York: Harper and Row Torchbook, 1964); Willard W. Beatty, Education for Cultural Change, (Chilocco, Oklahoma: U.S. Department of the Interior Bureau of Indian Affairs, 1953); Robert L. Beisner, Twelve Against Empire: The Anti-Imperialists, 1898-1900, (New York: McGraw-Hill Book Co., 1968); Lerone Bennett, Jr., "Was Abe Lincoln a White Supremacist?" Ebony, XXIII (February, 1968), p.35ff.; Henry Blumenthal, "Woodrow Wilson and the Race Question," The Journal of Negro History, XLVIII (January, 1963), pp.1-21; Henry Allen Bullock, A History of Negro Education in the South, (Cambridge, Massachusetts: Harvard University Press, 1967); Roger Butterfield, The American Past, (New York: Simon and Schuster, 1966); Avery Craven, Reconstruction: The Ending of the Civil War, (New York: Holt, Rinehart, and Winston, 1969); Gavan Daws, Shoal of Time: A History of the Hawaiian Islands, (New York: The Macmillan Co., 1968); Philip Foner and Josephine F. Pacheco, Three Who Dared: Prudence Crandall, Margaret Douglass, Myrtilla Miner - Champions of Antebellum Black Education, (Westport, Connecticut: Greenwood Press, 1984); John Hope Franklin, From Slavery to Freedom: A History of Negro Americans, (New York: Knopf, 1980), and Paxton Hibben, Henry Ward Beecher: An American Portrait, (New York: The Press of the Readers Club, 1942).

Sister Mary Lane, "A Critical Study of the Contemporary Theory and Policy of the Indian Bureau with Regard to American Indian Education," (Unpublished Ph.D. dissertation, The Catholic University of America, 1962); Gilbert Osofsky, "The Enduring Ghetto," The Journal of American History, LV (September, 1968), pp.243-255; Julius W. Pratt, A History of United States Foreign Policy, (Englewood Cliffs, New Jersey: Prentice-Hall, Inc., 1965); Thomas J. Pressly, Americans Interpret Their Civil War, (New York: The Free Press, 1962); Elliott M. Rudwick, Race Riot at East St. Louis, July 2, 1917, (Cleveland and New York: The World Publishing Co., Meridian Book, 1966); David A. Shannon, Twentieth Century America: The United States Since the 1890's, (Chicago: Rand McNally and Co., 1963); Jean R. Soderlund, Quakers and Slavery: A Divided Spirit, (Princeton, New Jersey: Princeton University Press, 1985); Samuel R. Spencer, Jr., Booker T. Washington and the Negro's Place in American Life, (Boston:

Bibliographical Essay

Little, Brown, and Co., 1955); David Tyack and Robert Lowe, "The Constitutional Moment: Reconstruction and Black Education in the South," American Journal of Education, XCIV (February, 1986), pp.236-256, and C. Vann Woodward, The Strange Career of Jim Crow, (New York: Oxford University Press, 1957).

CHAPTER FIVE

Primary source documents for this chapter came largely from the Jane Addams papers of the Swarthmore College Peace Collection, the Gino Speranza papers of the New York Public Library, the Lizzie Black Kander papers of the Wisconsin State Historical Society, the Social Welfare History Archives and the Immigrant Archives of the University of Minnesota, and from books and articles by the various humanitarian Americanizers. Most of the articles were by Jane Addams, including "A New Impulse to an Old Gospel," The Forum, XIV (November, 1892), pp.345-358; "Foreign-Born Children in the Primary Grades," Journal of Proceedings and Addresses of the National Education Association, 36th Annual Meeting, Milwaukee, Wisconsin, July 6-9, 1897, pp.104-112; "The Subtle Problems of Charity," The Atlantic Monthly, LXXXIII (February, 1899), pp.163-178; "A Function of the Social Settlement," Annals of the American Academy of Political and Social Science, XIII (May, 1899), pp.33-55; "Recent Immigration: A Field Neglected by the Scholar," Educational Review, XXIX (March, 1905), pp.245-263; "The Chicago Settlements and Social Unrest," Charities and The Commons, XX (May 2, 1908), pp.155-166, and "The Public School and the Immigrant Child," Journal of Proceedings and Addresses of the National Education Association, 46th Annual Meeting, Cleveland, Ohio, June 29-July 3, 1908, pp.99-102. Another helpful article was by John Dewey, "The School As Social Center," Journal of Proceedings and Addresses of the National Education Association, 41st Annual Meeting, Minneapolis, Minnesota, July 7-11, 1902, pp.373-383.

Primary source books were Jane Addams, Twenty Years at Hull-House, (New York: The New American Library, Signet Classic, 1961); Mary Antin, The Promised Land, (Cambridge, Massachusetts: The Riverside Press, 1955); Irving King, Social Aspects of Education, (New York: The Macmillan Co.,

1912); Constantine M. Panunzio, The Soul of an Immigrant, (New York: The Macmillan Co., 1934); Robert A. Woods and Albert J. Kennedy, The Settlement Horizon, (New York: Russell Sage Foundation, 1922), and three books by Edward A. Steiner, On the Trail of the Immigrant, (New York: Fleming H. Revell Co., 1906); The Immigrant Tide: Its Ebb and Flow, (New York: Fleming H. Revell Co., 1909), and From Alien to Citizen: The Story of My Life in America, (New York: Fleming H. Revell Co., 1914).

The most important secondary sources for this chapter were Allen F. Davis, Spearheads for Reform, (New York: Oxford University Press, 1967), an outstanding study of the settlement movement that perhaps glorified Jane Addams a bit; Marion McKenna, "Some Catholic Churchmen as Americanizers," in Harold M. Hyman and Leonard W. Levy, Freedom and Reform, (New York: Harper and Row, 1967); John W. Higham, Strangers in the Land, (New Brunswick, New Jersey: Rutgers University Press, 1955); John Higham, "Anti-Semitism in the Gilded Age: A Reinterpretation," The Mississippi Valley Historical Review, XLIII (March, 1957), pp.559-578; Edward George Hartmann, The Movement to Americanize the Immigrant, (New York: Columbia University, 1948; reprinted in 1967 by AMS Press, Inc., of New York), and Edward A. Krug, The Shaping of the American High School, (New York, Evanston, and London: Harper and Row, 1964). Other secondary sources were Oscar Handlin, Adventures in Freedom, (New York, Toronto, and London: McGraw-Hill Book Co., Inc., 1954), chapter seven, "Americanization: 1880-1920;" Staughton Lynd, "Jane Addams and the Radical Impulse," Commentary, XXXII (July, 1961), pp.54-59, and Louise C. Wade, "The Educational Dimension of the Early Chicago Settlements," Adult Education, XVII (Spring, 1967), pp.166-178.

The interpretation of Jane Addams presented in this chapter took a middle road between the usual adulation and the more recent efforts to debunk her as a psychologically driven "do-gooder." Christopher Lasch, The New Radicalism in America, (New York: Alfred A. Knopf, 1965), is representative of the latter school of thought. He pictured her as possessed of an unhealthy "veneration" of a "stern, remote, and even forbidding" father and committed "to live up to his demanding standard of rectitude." Lasch argued, too, that Miss Addams experienced a morbid fascination over her inability to have children. He attributed her life of service

Bibliographical Essay

less to a desire to help others than to a need to compensate for having no children, to live up to her father's expectations, and to express her revulsion toward her stepmother's life of cultured ease. Perhaps Mary Antin's reaction to the anthropologists early in the twentieth century could apply equally well to Christopher Lasch. Let him psychoanalyze his subject at his leisure. It could be a most interesting intellectual pasttime. But, whatever his interpretations, don't let them becloud the crucial issue. In the case of Jane Addams, her influence on Americanization education was one of compassion and moderation. It was an important and much needed influence. Even if Lasch could prove that she was driven by the devil himself, or perhaps motivated by his surrogate, it should not detract from her works or her influence.

CHAPTER SIX

The story of the immigration restrictionists was pieced together largely from primary sources although six secondary writings proved useful. Richard Hofstadter, The Age of Reform, (New York: Random House, Vintage Book, 1955), provided a thoughtful interpretation of Progressivism in America. Arthur S. Link, Woodrow Wilson and the Progressive Era, 1910-1917, (New York: Harper Torchbook, 1954), looked at the political role of President Woodrow Wilson in the period up to the entry of the United States into World War I. Mark H. Haller, Eugenics: Hereditarian Attitudes in American Thought, (New Brunswick, New Jersey: Rutgers University Press, 1963); Oscar Handlin, Race and Nationality in American Life, (Garden City, New York: Doubleday and Co., Inc., Anchor Book, 1957); Barbara Miller Solomon, Ancestors and Immigrants, (New York: John Wiley and Sons, 1956), and Julius Weinberg, "E.A. Ross: The Progessive as Nativist," Wisconsin Magazine of History, L (Spring, 1967), pp.242-253, contributed to the development of an interpretation of racism as a major motivation for immigration restriction in the early part of the twentieth century.

The papers of E.A. Ross in the Wisconsin State Historical Society, together with an important school book he read over and over, his autobiography, and his writings on Eastern and Southern

163

Bibliographical Essay

European immigrants, provided a good picture of this early sociologist. Seventy Years of It, (New York and London: D. Appleton-Century Co., 1936), gave his version of his life story. The Old World in the New, (New York: The Century Co., 1914), and "The Value Rank of the American People," The Independent, LVII (November 10, 1904), pp.1061-1064, were his major attempts to convince the public of the weaknesses of the "new immigration." Joel Dorman Steele, A Brief History of the United States, (New York and Chicago: A.S. Barnes and Co., 1855), a school book Ross used continually as a child, painted a rosy picture of the U.S. as a happy and homogeneous nation.

Other restrictionist writings included John R. Commons, Races and Immigrants in America, (New York: The Macmillan Co., 1907); Prescott F. Hall, Immigration and Its Effects Upon the United States, (New York: Henry Holt and Co., 1906); Immigration Commission, Abstracts of Reports of the Immigration Commission, U.S. Senate Document 747, 61st Cong., 3rd Session, (Washington, D.C.: U.S. Government Printing Office, 1911), first two volumes of the forty-two volume report of the Immigration Commission; Henry Cabot Lodge, "A Million Immigrants a Year: Efforts to Restrict Undesirable Immigration," The Century Magazine, LXVII (January, 1904), pp. 466-469; John Mitchell, "Protect the Workman," The Outlook, XCIII (September 11, 1909), pp.65-69; William Z. Ripley, The Races of Europe, (London: Kegan Paul, Trench, Trübner, and Co., circa 1900); Richmond Mayo-Smith, Emigration and Immigration, (New York: Charles Scribner's Sons, 1908), and Walter Weyl, The New Democracy, (New York: The Macmillan Co., 1913).

Among the writings of antirestrictionists were Jane Addams, "America's Treatment of Immigrants," The Ladies Home Journal, XXX (May, 1913), p.27; Mary Antin, They Who Knock at Our Gates, (Boston and New York: Houghton Mifflin Co., 1914); Franz Boas, The Mind of Primitive Man, (New York: The Macmillan Co., 1921), and Edward A. Steiner, From Alien to Citizen, (New York: Fleming H. Revell Co., 1914).

Several other publications were of use. One of these was Richard Hofstadter, ed., The Progressive Movement, 1900-1915, (Englewood Cliffs, New Jersey: Prentice-Hall, Spectrum Book, 1963). Several books provided insight into the work of the journalists Theodore Roosevelt dubbed the "muckrakers."

Bibliographical Essay

They were Lincoln Steffens, The Shame of the Cities, (New York: Sagamore Press, Inc., 1904); Harvey Swados, ed., Years of Conscience: The Muckrakers, (Cleveland and New York: The World Publishing Co., Meridian Book, 1962), and Ida Tarbell, The History of Standard Oil Company, (New York: The Macmillan Co., 1904).

CHAPTER SEVEN

Frances Kellor was a prolific writer of articles and reports by which she tried to influence the development of Americanization education in the United States. A small but convenient packet of these materials was located in New York City at the American Arbitration Association, an organization with which Miss Kellor was associated later in her life. Others of her publications that helped in the preparation of this chapter were "Who Is Responsible for the Immigrant?" The Outlook, CVI (April 25, 1914), pp.912-917; "Americanization by Industry," Immigrants in America Review, II (April, 1916), pp.15-26, and "What Is Americanization?" Yale Review, VIII (January, 1919), pp.282-299.
Other writers, too, urged a more effective Americanization education. They included George B. Hodge, Association Educational Work for Men and Boys, (New York: Association Press, 1912); Gregory Mason, "Americans First," The Outlook, CXIV (September 27, 1916), pp.193-201; Gregory Mason, "An Americanization Factory," The Outlook, CXII (February 23, 1916), pp.439-448; Peter Roberts, The New Immigration, (New York: The Macmillan Co., 1912), and the many colleagues and associates of Miss Kellor who wrote in Volumes One and Two of her Immigrants In America Review.
The most important primary sources consulted regarding Americanization and the public schools were: Leonard P. Ayres, Laggards in Our Schools, (New York: Charities Publication Committee, Russell Sage Foundation, 1909); Frederic Ernest Farrington, Public Facilities for Educating the Alien, Department of the Interior Bureau of Education Bulletin No. 18, (Washington, D.C.: U.S. Government Printing Office, 1916); Immigration Commission, Abstract of the Report on "The Children of Immigrants in Schools," Abstracts of Reports of the Immigration Commission, Volume Two, U.S. Senate Document 747, 61st Cong., 3rd Session, (Washington, D.C.: U.S.

Government Printing Office, 1911), pp.5-86; M. Catherine Mahy, "The Differentiation of English Classes in the High School," Education, XXXVI (May, 1916), pp.575-580; William Hughes Mearns, "Our Medieval High Schools," Saturday Evening Post, (March 2, 1912), pp.18 and 19, and Henry C. Morrison, "Vocational Training and Industrial Education," Educational Review, XXXVI (October, 1908), pp.242-254.

A number of articles in several periodicals gave an impression of the state of the art of education at the time, the trends and issues in the field, and the pressures exerted by lobbyists for changes in methods of Americanization education. These publications included Education, the Journal of Proceedings and Addresses of the National Education Association, and the Patriotic League's Our Country, Volumes One to Six, 1895-1898, especially the article by Charles F. Dole, "Religion in the Schools: The Religion of Citizenship," IV (January, 1897), pp.278-281. Among the NEA articles were: Clifford B. Connelley, "Citizenship in Industrial Education," 50th Annual Meeting, 1912, pp.899-907; Margaret E. Schallenberger, "The Function of the School in Training for Right Conduct," 46th Annual Meeting, 1908, pp.232-246, and Richard Welling, "Pupil Self-Government as a Training for Citizenship," 49th Annual Meeting, 1911, pp.1005-1009.

Among helpful articles in Education were C.F. Crehore, "Influence of Race Upon Educational Methods," VII (February, 1887), p.403; William H. Dooley, "Evening Elementary Schools," XXXVI (February, 1916), pp.357-361; Editorial, VII (March, 1877), p.515; Charles A. Ellwood, "The Sociological Basis of Education," XXXII (November, 1911), pp.133-140; S.E. Forman, "A Neglected Problem of Education," XXV (October, 1904), pp.104-111; William A. Mowry, "The Promotion of Patriotism," IX (November, 1888), pp.197-200; Winthrop D. Sheldon, "The Ethical Function of the School," XXV (February, 1905), pp.321-332; Charles R. Skinner, "Moral Instruction in Our Schools," XXIII (October, 1902), pp.75-82; George Stuart, "The Raison D'Etre of the Public High School," VIII (January, 1888), pp.291-295, and E.E. White, "Moral Training in the Public School," VII (December, 1886), pp.223-233.

Secondary sources provided background for many areas covered in this chapter. Agha Ashraf Ali, "Theories of Americanization: Operative in Gary

Bibliographical Essay

Schools, 1907-1917," (Unpublished Ph.D. dissertation, Ball State Teachers College, August, 1964), presented a great deal of material regarding the work of William Wirt. Ali's favorable and uncritical view of Wirt and Americanization was effectively countered by Raymond E. Callahan, Education and the Cult of Efficiency, (Chicago: The University of Chicago Press, Phoenix Book, 1964), and by Edward A. Krug, The Shaping of the American High School, (New York, Evanston, and London: Harper and Row, 1964). John Hardin Best, "A History of the Development of the Concept of Citizenship Education in America," (Unpublished Ph.D. dissertation, the University of North Carolina, 1961), gave a broad overview of Americanization education as articulated by schoolmen through the years, showing how it shifted from individual "moral" education to a more group-centered citizenship education during the twentieth century.

Gerd Korman, Industrialization, Immigrants and Americanizers: The View from Milwaukee, 1866-1921, (Madison, Wisconsin: The State Historical Society of Wisconsin, 1967), presented as a part of his study a general survey of industrial Americanization in the U.S. in which he dealt effectively with Frances Kellor as a leading figure. Edward Corsi, "Frances A. Kellor Sponsored New State Policy Toward Immigrant," Industrial Bulletin, Monthly News Magazine of the New York State Department of Labor, March, 1952, drew a highly favorable sketch of Miss Kellor.

Other studies that were helpful were George Edward Hartmann, The Movement to Americanize the Immigrant, (New York: Columbia University, 1948; reprinted in 1967 by AMS Press, Inc., of New York); John W. Higham, Strangers in the Land, (New Brunswick, New Jersey: Rutgers University Press, 1955); Christopher Lasch, The New Radicalism in America, (New York: Alfred A. Knopf, 1965); Timothy L. Smith, "School and Community: The Quest of Equal Opportunity, 1910-1921," mimeographed article in Immigrant Archives, University of Minnesota, and Barbara Miller Solomon, Ancestors and Immigrants, (New York: John Wiley and Sons, Inc., 1965).

CHAPTER EIGHT

Americanizers published many articles and other materials in behalf of their crusade during this

Bibliographical Essay

period. University Extension provided an institutional base for some of their work. Lillian Gay Berry, "The Americanization of America," Bulletin of the Extension Division, Indiana University, Bloomington, Indiana, Volume Four, July, 1919, and A Course on Americanization, University of North Carolina Extension Leaflet, Volume Two, April, 1919, were examples of this Extension activity. A book by Royal Dixon, Americanization, (New York: The Macmillan Co., 1916), came out of Frances Kellor's own organizational structure by which Dixon was employed. Miss Kellor also issued quantities of material from her office, including "National Americanization Day - July 4th," Immigrants in America Review, I (September, 1915), pp.18-29; Straight America, A Call to National Service, (New York: The Macmillan Co., 1916); "Welfare or Manpower Engineering," National Efficiency Quarterly, November, 1918 (in American Arbitration Association archives packet on Miss Kellor); "What Is Americanization?" Yale Review, VIII (January, 1919), pp.282-299, and Immigration and the Future, (New York: George H. Doran Co., 1920).

Pressures to learn English to make immigrants efficient and loyal came from many sources. These could be seen in the Journal of Proceedings and Addresses of the National Education Association, 57th Annual Meeting, Milwaukee, Wisconsin, June 28-July 5, 1919, especially pp.22-29; "Necessary to Industrial Efficiency," Americanization, I (January 1, 1919), p.5; "One Language in Church," Americanization, I (February 1, 1919), p.5, "State Programs of Immigrant Education," The Survey, XLVI (July 16, 1921), pp.516-518, and two articles by Winthrop Talbot, "Americanization in Industry," Industrial Management, LVI (December, 1918), pp.510 and 511, and "The One Language Industrial Plant," Industrial Management, LVIII (October, 1919), pp.313-320.

The above were just a few of the primary sources indicating the growing support of Americanization education by public and voluntary organizations in U.S. society. Others included "Americanization by the Public Library," The Survey, XLI (January 18, 1919), pp.537-538; "Americanization Notes," The Survey, XLVI (July 16, 1921), p.519; Mary Clark Barnes, "The New Day in Christian Americanization," The Missionary Review of the World, XLII (January, 1919), pp.57-59; Anthony Beck, "Promotion of Citizenship," The Catholic World, CIX (September, 1919), pp.735-743; The Chicago Associa-

Bibliographical Essay

tion of Commerce, "Americanization, 1919," Annual Report, reprint, 1920; Council of National Defense, Ohio Branch, A Practical Americanization Program for Ohio Cities, Americanization Bulletin No. 2, circa 1918-1920.
Eleanor E. Ledbetter, Americanization Through the Public Library, Americanization Bulletin No. 4, (Columbus, Ohio: Council of National Defense, circa 1918-1920); Mayor's Advisory War Board, Report of the Work of the Cleveland Americanization Committee, July, 1917-July 1918; Anne Rhodes, "Americanization Through Women's Organizations," Immigrants in America Review, II (April, 1916), pp.71-73; Frank Trumbull, "Report of the Committee on Immigration of the Chamber of Commerce of the United States of America," Immigrants In America Review, II (April, 1916), pp.32-34, and "Wanted: Traveling Representatives," The Survey, XLIII (February 21, 1920), p.598.

A series of articles in Education helped to show the kind of thought prevailing in the educational establishment during World War I. Mary Gove Smith, "The Foreign Child and the Teacher," XXXVIII (March, 1918), pp.504-507, reflected the traditional U.S. view that American democracy was the best form of government yet devised. Henry Lincoln Clapp, "Pupil Self-Government," XXXVIII (April, 1918), pp.593-609, was among those differentiating between the "new immigration" and "the steadygoing descendants of the old New England stock who understand what our institutions and laws signify." Robert J. Aley, "The War and Secondary Schools," XXXVIII (May, 1918), pp.628-634, expressed fears of "near" treasonous activities by some teachers and advocated rewriting the history books to show that "the best things in our government and our institutions are of English origin."

"American Notes - Editorial," XXXVIII (May, 1918), p.731, showed that the National Education Association was calling for all public and private school instruction to be in English. Lewis S. Mills, "Purposes, Sources and Methods in the Teaching of Citizenship," XXXVIII (June, 1918), pp.755-766, heard the "alarum of Bolshevick echoes across our New England hills...."

Serious questioning of Americanization education set in during the 1920s from several different points of view. Representative of these attacks were "Americanizing Americanization," The Survey, XLVI (July 16, 1921), p.521; "Americanski," Satur-

169

day Evening Post, CXCIII (May 14, 1921), p.20; Isaac B. Berkson, Theories of Americanization: A Critical Study, (New York: Teachers College, Columbia University, 1920); Charles Scott Berry, "Some Problems of Americanization As Seen by an Army Psychologist," School and Society, XIII (January 22, 1921), pp.97-104; Edward Hale Bierstadt, "Pseudo-Americanization," The New Republic, XXVI and XXVII (May 25 and June 1, 1921), pp.371-373 and pp.19-23; Allen T. Burns, "American Americanization," address to Americanization workers by the director of the Carnegie Corporation Americanization study, January 9, 1920, and Henry Pratt Fairchild, The Melting-Pot Mistake, (Boston: Little Brown, and Co., 1926). Several works by Horace M. Kallen were useful in this study. They were "Democracy Versus the Melting-Pot," The Nation, C (February 18 and 25, 1915), pp.190-194 and pp.217-220; "The Meaning of Americanism," Immigrants in America Review, I (January, 1916), pp.12-19, and Culture and Democracy in the United States, (New York: Boni and Liveright, 1924).

John J. Mahoney, Americanization in the United States, U.S. Bureau of Education Bulletin No. 31, (Washington, D.C.: U.S. Government Printing Office, 1923); M.E. Ravage, "The Immigrant's Burden," The New Republic, XIX (June 14, 1919), pp.209-211; Gino Speranza papers in the New York Public Library; Gino Speranza, "The Immigration Peril," The World's Work, XLVII and XLVIII (November, 1923, through May, 1924); Gino Speranza, Race or Nation, (Indianapolis: The Bobbs-Merrill Co., 1923); Harold E. Stearns, ed., Civilization in the United States, (New York: Harcourt, Brace, and Co., 1922); Lothrop Stoddard, The Revolt Against Civilization, the Menace of the Under Man, (New York: Charles Scribner's Sons, 1922); Lothrop Stoddard, Re-Forging America, the Story of Our Nationhood, (New York: Charles Scribner's Sons, 1927); Frank V. Thompson, Schooling of the Immigrant, (New York: Harper and Brothers, 1920), and Anzia Yezierska, "Soap and Water and the Immigrant," The New Republic, XVIII (February 22, 1919), pp.117-119.

Other primary sources that aided in the writing of this chapter were Jane Addams, Forty Years at Hull-House, (New York: The Macmillan Co., 1935), Volume Two; "'Americanization' - Just What Do We Mean By It," The Evening Post, New York, August 9, 1918; "Efficiency and Patriotic Duty," Americanization, I (February 1, 1919), p.13, and John J.

Bibliographical Essay

Mahoney, Training Teachers For Americanization, U.S. Bureau of Education Bulletin No. 12, (Washington, D.C.: U.S. Government Printing Office, 1920). A few secondary sources, all of which have been listed for earlier chapters, were important enough in the development of this chapter to list them here again: Edward Corsi, "Frances A. Kellor Sponsored New State Policy Toward Immigrant," Industrial Bulletin, New York State Department of Labor, March, 1952 (American Arbitration Association archives); Mark H. Haller, Eugenics: Hereditarian Attitudes in American Thought, (New Brunswick, New Jersey: Rutgers University Press, 1963); John W. Higham, Strangers in the Land, (New Brunswick, New Jersey: Rutgers University Press, 1955); Gerd Korman, Industrialization, Immigrants and Americanizers: The View from Milwaukee, 1866-1921, (Madison, Wisconsin: The State Historical Society of Wisconsin, 1967); Edward A. Krug, The Shaping of the American High School, (New York: Harper and Row, 1964), and David A. Shannon, Twentieth Century America: The United States Since the 1890's, (Chicago: Rand McNally and Co., 1963).

CHAPTER NINE

The continuing drive for homogeneity was documented in this chapter by reference to a number of primary and secondary sources. Newspaper articles consulted included Charles Bartlett, "Job Corps Program Faces Many Problems," Capital Times, Madison, Wisconsin, September 2, 1966, p.34; Homer Bigart, "McNamara Plans to Draft Rejects," New York Times, August 24, 1966, pp.1 and 18; Rod Currie, "Fear, Prejudice Strike Responsive Chord for Wallace," Star-Phoenix, Saskatoon, Saskatchewan, October 16, 1968, p.48, and John Edgar Hoover, "Vicious Crimes, Civil Protests Worry Hoover," Free Press, Mankato, Minnesota, November 27, 1967, pp.1 and 11. Magazine articles were Stewart Alsop, "The Anti-Honky War," Newsweek, LXXII (December 16, 1968), p.116; Arthur P. (Jack) Crabtree, "The Americanization of the Native Born," Adult Leadership, II (May, 1962), p.2ff.; I.M. Greenberg, "Project 100,000: The Training of Former Rejectees," Phi Delta Kappan, L (June, 1969), pp.570-574; Glenn Jensen and Frederick A. Goranson, "Adult Education - To Be Or Not To Be!" Adult Leadership, XIV (November, 1965), p.157ff.; "New Role for Adult Education in Washing-

Bibliographical Essay

ton Planning," Washington Newsletter on Adult Education, I (October, 1969), p.1, and William Randel, "KKK Seed Bed," The Progressive, XXXII (March, 1968), pp.45 and 46.

Helpful books, articles, reports, studies, and conferences related to the drive for conformity were James B. Conant, Slums and Suburbs, (New York: The New American Library, Signet Book, 1964); Terry Ferrer, "Conant Revisited," Saturday Review, L (March 18, 1967), pp.56, 57, and 73; attendance at and program of 1969 Galaxy Conference on Adult Education, Washington, D.C., December 6-10, 1969; Will Herberg, Protestant-Catholic-Jew: An Essay in American Religious Sociology, (Garden City, New York: Doubleday and Co., Anchor Book, 1960); J. Edgar Hoover, J. Edgar Hoover on Communism, (New York: Random House, 1969), J. Edgar Hoover, Masters of Deceit, (New York: Henry Holt and Co., 1958); Thomas F. Jones, "An Administrator Looks at Continuing Education," speech at Galaxy Conference on Adult Education, Washington, D.C., December 6-10, 1969; William Heard Kilpatrick, Education and the Social Crisis, (New York: Liveright, Inc., 1932); Robert S. Lynd and Helen Merrell Lynd, Middletown: A Study in Contemporary American Culture, (New York: Harcourt, Brace, and Co., 1929); National Advisory Commission on Civil Disorders, U.S. Riot Commission Report, (New York: Bantam Books, 1968); Caroline A. Whipple, Education for Citizenship, (Albany, New York: New York State Education Department Bureau of Adult Education, 1953), and David S. Wyman, Paper Walls: America and the Refugee Crisis, 1938-1941, (Amherst, Massachusetts: The University of Massachusetts Press, 1968).

Articles, papers and books challenging the concept of Americanization in the 1960s were Warner Bloomberg, Jr., "Continuing Education Among the Poor," paper prepared for the Summer Adult Education Conference, University of Wisconsin, Madison, Wisconsin, Summer, 1965; "The Gadfly of the Poverty War," Newsweek, LXVI (September 13, 1965), pp.30-32; Malcolm X, The Autobiography of Malcolm X, (New York, Grove Press, Inc., 1966), and James Ridgeway, "Saul Alinsky in Smugtown," The New Republic, CLII (June 26, 1965), pp.15-17.

Other published material important to this study were Frank Adams, Unearthing Seeds of Fire: The Idea of Highlander, (Winston-Salem, North Carolina: John F. Blair, 1975); "The Black Panthers and

Bibliographical Essay

the Law," Newsweek, LXXV (February 23, 1970), pp.26-30; "The Black Panther Toll Is Now 28," New York Times, December 7, 1969, p.4; Oscar Handlin, Adventures in Freedom, (New York, Toronto, and London: McGraw-Hill Book Co., Inc., 1954), chapter eight, "Anti-Semitism: 1890-1941;" Oscar Handlin, The Newcomers, (Cambridge, Massachusetts: Harvard University Press, 1959); Rosemary Kendrick, "Chicago Pastor Fears Era of 'Civil Agony,'" Capital Times, Madison, Wisconsin, August 3, 1968, p.11, and Martin Luther King, Where Do We Go From Here?, (New York: Bantam Books, 1968).

Herbert Kohl, 36 Children, (New York: The New American Library, Signet Book, 1968); Jonathan Kozol, Death at an Early Age, (New York: Bantam Books, 1968); "C. Eric Lincoln and Martin Luther King, Jr.: Non-violence and the American Negro," in Mulford Q. Sibley, ed., The Quiet Battle: Writings on the Theory and Practice of Non-violent Resistance, (Garden City, New York: Anchor Book, Doubleday and Co., 1963), Bernard Nossiter, "Panthers Winning Backing from Negro Moderates," Free Press, Winnipeg, Manitoba, December 16, 1969, p.12; Talcott Parsons and Kenneth B. Clark, eds., The Negro American, (Boston: Beacon Press, 1967); Kathleen Teltsch, "Priest Sees Need for Ethnic Study," New York Times, June 21, 1968, p.24, and "U.S. Civil War Anticipated," Star-Phoenix, Saskatoon, Saskatchewan, November 18, 1968, p.3.

More recent books and news articles provided updated information and varied interpretations regarding the efforts and outcomes of the black civil rights movement. They included the eminently readable, autobiographical retrospective of Southern white newspaper editor Harry S. Ashmore, Hearts and Minds: The Anatomy of Racism from Roosevelt to Reagan, (New York: McGraw-Hill Book Co., 1982); "Going Back to the Back of the Bus", editorial in the New York Times, November 10, 1985, p.26E; William Johnson, "The Heart of Dixie," The Globe and Mail, Toronto, Ontario, August 9, 1986, pp.A1 and A2; William Johnson, "Segregation Endures: Change Comes Slowly in Georgia Town, But Signs Are There," The Globe and Mail, Toronto, Ontario, August 21, 1986, pp.A1 and A4; William Johnson, "Vote Divides Civil-Rights Heroes," The Globe and Mail, Toronto, Ontario, August 12, 1986, p.A9; Michele Landsberg, "Lifelines Being Hauled In As Economy Drowns the Black Poor," The Globe and Mail, Toronto, Ontario, March 1, 1986, p.A2;

Bibliographical Essay

Manning Marable, Black American Politics: From the Washington Marches to Jesse Jackson, (London: Verso, 1985); Thomas Sowell, Civil Rights: Rhetoric or Reality, (New York: William Morrow, 1984); Special Report, Maclean's, XCIX (January 20, 1986), pp.14-22, and Lena Williams, "Blacks Debating a Greater Stress on Self-Reliance Instead of Aid," New York Times, June 15, 1986, pp.1 and 24.

Recent publications related to education included Jacques Barzun's attack on the "perpetuation of dialects," including black English, in Language and Life, (Washington, D.C.: U.S.ENGLISH, no date but circa 1984); Ezra Bowen, "Dramatic Drop for Minorities," Time, CXXVI (November 11, 1985), p.84; Paul Egly, "The Fate of School Desegregation: The Los Angeles Experience," The Center Magazine, XV (July/ August, 1982), pp.6-17, including introduction by the editor, Donald McDonald; Allan Fotheringham, "Black Americans' Educational Plight," Star-Phoenix, Saskatoon, Saskatchewan, September 13, 1985, p.A5. Meyer Weinberg's angry, one-sided A Chance to Learn: The History of Race and Education in the United States, (New York and London: Cambridge University Press, 1977), presented an idealized view of the purpose of the public school as the provider of equal opportunity for all American children, whatever their race, religion, ethnic origin, or social class. Robert A. Carlson, "Abusing History: A Presentist Picture of the Historical Purpose of American Public Schooling," History of Education Quarterly, XVIII (Fall, 1978), pp.341-347, offered a critique of the Weinberg book and a necessary context for understanding the purposes of public schooling in the United States.

CHAPTER TEN

Chapter ten discussed the struggle of the Americanizers of the 1980s against the new threat they perceived to national unity, the possibility that Spanish might come to rival English as the language of general usage in the country. It also provided a summary of the history of the various Hispanic groups in the United States as a context for assessing both the reality of the danger alleged by the Americanizers and the merits of their proposed solutions.

The most valuable source of information regarding the positions of the Americanizers and their

Bibliographical Essay

adversaries was the national headquarters of U.S. ENGLISH, Suite 201, 1424 16th St. N.W., Washington, D.C. Newspaper clippings, published reprints of articles related to the work of U.S.ENGLISH, and a complete set of the organization's regular newsletter, Up date, Volume I, No. 1 (Spring, 1963) through Volume IV, No. 3 (May-June, 1986), were made available. Among the article reprints were several by Executive Director Gerda Bikales: "Make English Official By Passing New Laws," U.S.A. Today, April 10, 1985; "'Temporary' Bilingual Education Lives On," The Washington Times, no date, and "You'd Be a Nobody If They Didn't Make You Learn English," The Christian Science Monitor, no date.

Other materials from the files of U.S.ENGLISH were its form letter to the editor, signed by S.I. Hayakawa, describing the background and purposes of the organization and a series of newspaper clippings from around the country: Brandon Bailey, "Bilingual Education Failing Hispanics, Hayakawa Declares," San Jose Mercury-News, San Jose, California, circa March 1, 1986; Stephen Chapman, "Make English the National Tongue," Chicago Tribune, circa February 22, 1985; "English-Only Ballots," The San Diego Union, San Diego, California, circa March 25, 1984, p.C-2; "Hayakawa Plan Finds Receptive Audience," Anaheim Bulletin, Anaheim, California, circa 1986; "Membership Card," Santa Barbara News-Press, Santa Barbara, California, circa June 22, 1984, and Raul Yzaguirre, "English-Only Movement Is Out of Control," Corpus Christi Caller Times, Corpus Christi, Texas, circa May 3, 1986, p.15A.

Sources providing the best insights into the background and thinking of Gerda Bikales were a personal interview with her in Washington, D.C., on June 5, 1986, and a tape-recording of her comments on a radio talk show broadcast by KOA-Denver on May 8, 1986. She was also the co-author with Gary Imhoff of a pamphlet, A Kind of Discordant Harmony: Issues in Assimilation, (Washington, D.C.: U.S. ENGLISH, July, 1985), that succinctly and effectively argued her case. John Kolesar, "Bilingual Advocates Speak with Forked Tongues," The Record of Bergen/Passaic/Hudson Counties, New Jersey, August 4, 1983, provided valuable personal information about Ms. Bikales and a well written account faithful to her position.

Other documents that contributed to the writing of this part of the chapter on the new Americanizers were Peter Applebome, "Surge of Illegal Aliens Taxes Southwest Towns' Resources," New York Times, March 9, 1986, pp.1 and 30; Peter W. Barnes, "Spanish-Language TV Faces Big Changes," Wall Street Journal, April 24, 1986, p.6; "English Isn't the Only Language We Speak," letters to the editor from Julio Barreto, Jr., and Adán A. González III, The Washington Post, August 9, 1986, p.A19; "English Spoken Here, Please," Newsweek, CIII (January 9, 1984), pp.24 and 25; Harold Evans, "Melting Pot - or Salad Bowl?" U.S. News and World Report, C (March 31, 1986), p.76; FAIR, "How Many Immigrants?" (Washington, D.C.: Federation for American Immigration Reform, circa 1984; Herb Michelson interview with S.I. Hayakawa, "An English-Only Crusade," Maclean's, XCVII (October 8, 1984), pp.8 and 10; "Spanish-Language Stations to Be Sold to Settle Suit," Wall Street Journal, May 13, 1986, p.14; P.J. Wingate, "U.S.English? Geez, Yawl Musn't Be Like Serious, Podner," Wall Street Journal, June 24, 1986, p.30; Steve Workings, government relations associate for U.S.ENGLISH, "Pretty Terrible Stuff," letter to the editor, The Washington Post, August 16, 1986, p.A21, and Jonathan Yardley, "Bilingualism and the Backlash," The Washington Post, July 28, 1986, p.D2.

For the portion of the chapter devoted to the history of the Hispanics in the U.S. this study relied heavily on the information provided by Raymond Carr, Puerto Rico: A Colonial Experiment, (New York: Vintage Books, 1984); Matt S. Meier and Feliciano Rivera, The Chicanos: A History of Mexican Americans, (New York: Hill and Wang, 1972), and Joan Moore and Harry Pachon, Hispanics in the United States, (Englewood Cliffs, New Jersey: Prentice-Hall, Inc., 1985). Helpful background on Hispanic American civil rights activities in the early 1970s can be found in the archives of the Wisconsin State Historical Society in the files of Concilio Mujeres, an organization formed in 1970 by a group of Hispanic women attending San Francisco State College. Adam Smith's Money World television program broadcast by PBS, Detroit, on Saturday, July 5, 1986, provided an excellent overview of the current economic situation in Mexico. "Now One American in 14 Is Hispanic," Free Press, Mankato, Minnesota, January 28, 1986, p.3, and an interview with Domingo Gonzalez and Primitivo Rodriguez, staff members of the American Friends Service Committee, Philadelphia, Pennsylvania, June 13, 1986,

Bibliographical Essay

furnished demographic and social background. Publications consulted regarding Mexican Americans were: Mario Barrera, Race and Class in the Southwest, (Notre Dame, Indiana: University of Notre Dame Press, 1979); "Braceros," Americas, I (March, 1949), pp.14-17 and 41; Peter G. Brown and Henry Shue, The Border that Joins: Mexican Migrants and U.S. Responsibility, (Totowa, New Jersey: Rowman and Littlefield, 1983); John H. Burma, Spanish-Speaking Groups in the United States, (Durham, North Carolina: Duke University Press, 1954); Albert Camarillo, Chicanos in a Changing Society, (Cambridge, Massachusetts: Harvard University Press, 1979); John R. Chávez, The Lost Land: The Chicano Image of the Southwest, (Albuquerque, New Mexico: University of New Mexico Press, 1984); Richard Craig, The Bracero Program, (Austin, Texas: University of Texas Press, 1971); R.H. Dana, Jr., Two Years Before the Mast and Twenty-Four Years After, (New York: P.F. Collier and Son, 1909), and Livie Isauro Duran and H. Russell Bernard, eds., Introduction to Chicano Studies, (New York: Macmillan Publishing Co., Inc., 1982).

Ernesto Galarza, Merchants of Labor: The Mexican Bracero Story, (Charlotte, North Carolina and Santa Barbara, California: McNally and Loftin, 1964); Manuel Gamio, The Mexican Immigrant: His Life-Story, (Chicago: University of Chicago Press, 1931); Manuel Gamio, Mexican Immigration to the United States: A Study of Human Migration and Adjustment, (Chicago: University of Chicago Press, 1930); Richard A. Garcia, ed., The Chicanos in America, 1540-1974: A Chronology and Fact Book, (Dobbs Ferry, New York: Oceana Publications, 1977); Beatrice W. Griffith, "Viva Roybal - Viva America," Common Ground, X (Autumn, 1949), pp.61-70; Max Sylvius Handman, "Economic Reasons for the Coming of the Mexican Immigrant," The American Journal of Sociology, XXXV (January, 1930), pp.601-611; Richard C. Hedke, "Simpático at Dowagiac," The Rotarian, LXVIII (January, 1946), pp.28-30; Robert F. Heizer and Alan F. Almquist, The Other Californians: Prejudice and Discrimination Under Spain, Mexico, and the United States to 1920, (Berkeley, California: University of California Press, 1971); A.J. Jaffe, et al., The Changing Demography of Spanish Americans, (New York: Academic Press, 1980); Oakah L. Jones, Jr., Los Paisanos: Spanish Settlers on the Northern Frontier of New Spain, (Norman, Oklahoma: University of Oklahoma Press,

1979); Richard C. Jones, ed., Patterns of Undocumented Migration: Mexico and the United States, (Totowa, New Jersey: Rowman and Allanheld, 1984), and Paul Kutsche and John R. Van Ness, Cañones: Values, Crisis, and Survival in a Northern New Mexico Village, (Albuquerque, New Mexico: University of New Mexico Press, 1981). Ruth Laughlin, "Coronado's Country and Its People," Survey Graphic, XXIX (May, 1940), pp.277-282; Art Leibson, "The Wetback Invasion," Common Ground, X (Autumn, 1949), pp.11-19; Robert N. McLean, "Goodbye, Vicente!" The Survey, LXVI (May 1, 1931), pp.182 and 183; Carey McWilliams, "America's Disadvantaged Minorities: Mexican-Americans," The Journal of Negro Education, XX:3 (1951), pp.301-309; Carey McWilliams, Brothers Under the Skin, (Boston: Little, Brown, and Co., 1964); Carey McWilliams, "The Forgotten Mexican," Common Ground, III:3 (1943), pp.65-78; "The Mexican Wetbacks," Newsweek, XXXII (October 25, 1948), pp.80 and 81; Joan W. Moore with Alfredo Cuéllar, Mexican Americans, (Englewood Cliffs, New Jersey: Prentice-Hall, Inc., 1970); Joan W. Moore, "Social Class, Assimilation and Acculturation," in June Helm, ed., Spanish-Speaking People in the United States, Proceedings of the 1968 Annual Spring Meeting of the American Ethnological Society, 1968, pp.19-27; Dale L. Morgan and James R. Scobie, eds., William Perkins' Journal of Life at Sonora, 1849-1852, (Berkeley, California: University of California Press, 1964), Joe West Neal, "The Policy of the United States Toward Immigration from Mexico," (Unpublished Master of Arts thesis, University of Texas, 1941); Leonard Pitt, The Decline of the Californios, (Berkeley, California: University of California Press, 1966), and Enrique L. Prado, "Sinarquism in the United States," The New Republic, CIX (July 29, 1943), pp.97-102.

Milo Milton Quaife, ed., The Southwestern Expedition of Zebulon M. Pike, (Chicago: R.R. Donnelley and Sons, 1925); Barbara J. and J. Cordell Robinson, The Mexican American: A Critical Guide to Research Aids, (Greenwich, Connecticut: Jai Press, Inc., 1980); Arnold R. Rojas, The Vaquero, (Charlotte, North Carolina and Santa Barbara, California: McNally and Loftin, 1964); George I. Sanchez, Forgotten People: A Study of New Mexicans, (Albuquerque, New Mexico: The University of New Mexico Press, 1940); Stan Steiner, La Raza: The Mexican Americans, (New York: Harper and Row, 1969); Jay S.

Bibliographical Essay

Stowell, The Near Side of the Mexican Question, (New York: George H. Doran Company, 1921); David J. Weber, The Mexican Frontier, 1821-1846: The American Southwest Under Mexico, (Albuquerque, New Mexico: University of New Mexico Press, 1982); "Wetbacks in Middle of Border War," Business Week, No. 1260 (October 24, 1953), pp.62-66; Hensley C. Woodbridge, "Mexico and U.S. Racism: How Mexicans View Our Treatment of Minorities," The Commonweal, LXII (June 22, 1945), pp.234-237, and "Zoot Suits and Service Stripes: Race Tension Behind the Riots," Newsweek, XXI (June 21, 1943), pp.35-40.

A number of other publications were utilized in developing an understanding of Puerto Ricans, of recent immigrants to the U.S. from Cuba, and of the sanctuary movement and its tie to John Woolman. PUERTO RICO: An outstanding study was Charles J. Beirne, The Problem of Americanization in the Catholic Schools of Puerto Rico, (Editorial Universitaria, Universidad de Puerto Rico, 1975). This priest and principal of a high school in Puerto Rico, admitting he could not prove that Americanization by Roman Catholic private schools was unplanned and non-deliberate, made an effective case for what he called their "latent" promotion of American values. Lydia Chavez, "Striving But Still Lagging, Puerto Ricans Seek Reasons," New York Times, June 5, 1986, pp.B1 and B15, summarized the economic and social situation of Puerto Ricans on the mainland in mid-1986. Jesus Colon, A Puerto Rican in New York and Other Sketches, (New York: Mainstream Publishers, 1961), presented a powerful series of often autobiographical essays showing how experience of a Puerto Rican with American life and institutions could logically lead where it led Colon, to advocacy of Puerto Rican independence from the United States: "Independence and socialism. Socialism and independence."

Joseph P. Fitzpatrick, "The Adjustment of Puerto Ricans to New York City," in Milton L. Barron, ed., Minorities in a Changing World, (New York: Alfred A. Knopf, 1967); Joseph P. Fitzpatrick, Puerto Rican Americans: The Meaning of Migration to the Mainland, (Englewood Cliffs, New Jersey: Prentice-Hall, Inc., 1971); Oscar Lewis, La Vida: A Puerto Rican Family in the Culture of Poverty - San Juan and New York, (New York: Random House, 1965); C. Wright Mills, et al., The Puerto Rican Journey: New York's Newest Migrants, (New York: Harper and Brothers, 1950), and Stan Steiner, The Islands: The

Bibliographical Essay

Worlds of the Puerto Ricans, (New York: Harper and Row, 1974).
CUBA: "Cuba, U.S. to Discuss Immigration Agreement," Star-Phoenix, Saskatoon, Saskatchewan, July 4, 1986, p.A8; Roger Lowenstein, "Cuban Arrivals of 1980 Hit Miami Very Hard But Assimilated Well," Wall Street Journal, November 13, 1985, pp.1 and 22; Jon Nordheimer, "Miami Runoff Candidates Hunt Pivotal Black Vote," New York Times, November 12, 1985, p.10; "Refugee Is Miami's First Cuban-American Mayor", Star and Tribune, Minneapolis, Minnesota, November 15, 1985, p.3; Dan Sewell, "Ethnic Tensions Threaten Miami's Future," Star and Tribune, Minneapolis, Minnesota, November 18, 1985, p.3A, and "Voting Is Close In Miami Race for Mayor Post," New York Times, November 13, 1985, p.12.
SANCTUARY: Pilar Celaya, "The Celaya Family Testimony" Friends Journal, XXXI (October 1, 1985), p.5, explained why a family from El Salvador took sanctuary in 1985 in the Ann Arbor, Michigan, Friends Meetinghouse. Jim Corbett, "Sanctuary as a Quaker Testimony," Excerpts of an Address to Philadelphia Yearly Meeting of Friends presented March 22, 1986, Philadelphia Yearly Meeting News, June, 1986, p.3, presented a Quaker rationale for participating in sanctuary; Claudia Dreifus, "Women of the Sanctuary Movement," Glamour, LXXXIII (September, 1985), pp.356, 357, and 418-423; "In Search of Sanctuary," Friends Journal, XXX (August 1/15, 1984), pp.1-10; "Liberty Ambiguous in Sanctuary Case," The Globe and Mail, Toronto, Ontario, July 7, 1986, p.A8, and Richard N. Ostling, "A Defeat for Sanctuary," Time. CXXVII (May 12, 1986), pp.50 and 51.

This study made use of a considerable amount of material regarding bilingual education and the schooling of Hispanics in the U.S. The listing will be divided into three parts: the early background, selected publications describing bilingual education, and the current political argument over bilingualism.
THE EARLY BACKGROUND: Price Richard Ashton, "The Fourteenth Amendment and the Education of Latin-American Children in Texas," (Unpublished M.Ed. thesis, University of Texas, 1949); Carlos E. Castaneda, "Some of Our Earliest Americans Await the 'Magic Touch,'" The Texas Outlook, XXXVII (January, 1953), pp.22, 23, and 35; W. Henry Cooke, "The Segregation of Mexican-American School Children in Southern California" School and Society,

Bibliographical Essay

LXVII (June 5, 1948), pp.417-421; Don T. Delmet, "A Study of the Mental and Scholastic Abilities of Mexican Children in the Elementary School," Journal of Juvenile Research, XIV (October, 1930), pp.267-279; Marvin Ferdinand Doerr, "Problem of the Elimination of Mexican Pupils from School," (Unpublished M.Ed. thesis, University of Texas, 1938); Editorial, The Nation, CLXIV (May 3, 1947), p.503; "Federal Judge Outlaws Segregation in Public Schools," Common Ground, VIII (Winter, 1947), pp.102 and 103, and Thomas R. Garth and Harper D. Johnson, "The Intelligence and Achievement of Mexican Children in the United States," The Journal of Abnormal and Social Psychology, XXIX (July-September, 1934), pp.222-229.

Ennis Hall Gilbert, "Some Legal Aspects of the Education of Spanish-Speaking Children in Texas," (Unpublished M.Ed. thesis, University of Texas, 1947); Shirley E. Greene, The Education of Migrant Children, (Washington, D.C.: Department of Rural Education of the National Education Association, 1954); A.H. Hughey, "Speaking English at School," The Texas Outlook, XXVIII (November, 1944), p.36; Roberta Muriel Johnson, "History of the Education of Spanish-Speaking Children in Texas," (Unpublished M.A. thesis, University of Texas, 1932); Albert Turner Kaderli, "The Educational Problem in the Americanization of the Spanish-Speaking Pupils of Sugarland, Texas," (Unpublished M.A. thesis, University of Texas, 1940), especially chapter V, "Americanization of These Children;" Carey McWilliams, "Is Your Name Gonzales?" The Nation, CLXIV (March 15, 1947), pp.302-304; Herschel T. Manuel, The Education of Mexican and Spanish-Speaking Children in Texas, (Austin, Texas: The Fund for Research in the Social Sciences, University of Texas, 1930), and Herschel T. Manuel, "The Spanish-Speaking Child," The Texas Outlook, XIV (January, 1930), pp.21 and 47.

Laura Frances Murphy, "An Experiment in Americanization," The Texas Outlook, XXIII (November, 1939), pp.23 and 24; Ruby Payne, "Learning to Say 'Good Morning' As Well as 'Buenos Dias,'" NEA Journal, XLI (March, 1952), p.165; Lester H. Phillips, "Segregation in Education: A California Case Study," Phylon, X:4 (1949), pp.407-413; George I. Sánchez and Howard Putnam, Materials Relating to the Education of Spanish-Speaking People in the United States, (Westport, Connecticut: Greenwood Press, 1971); George I. Sanchez, "Pachucos in the

181

Making," Common Ground, IV:1 (1943), pp.13-20; George I. Sánchez, "Spanish-Speaking People in the Southwest - A Brief Historical Review," California Journal of Elementary Education, XXII (November, 1953), pp. 106-111; Luisa G.G. Sanchez, "The 'Latin American' of the Southwest - Backgrounds and Curricular Implications," (Unpublished Ph.D dissertation, University of Texas, 1954), and Donovan Senter and Florence Hawley, "The Grammar School as the Basic Acculturating Influence for Native New Mexicans," Social Forces, XXIV (May, 1946), pp.398-407.
  BILINGUAL EDUCATION: Andrew D. Cohen, A Sociolinguistic Approach to Bilingual Education: Experiments in the American Southwest, (Rowley, Massachusetts: Newbury House Publishers, Inc., 1975); Joshua A. Fishman, Bilingual Education: An International Sociological Perspective, (Rowley, Massachusetts: Newbury House Publishers, Inc., 1976); A. Bruce Gaarder, Bilingual Schooling and the Survival of Spanish in the United States, (Rowley, Massachusetts: Newbury House Publishers, Inc., 1977); William F. Mackey, et al., The Bilingual Education Movement: Essays on Its Progress, (El Paso, Texas: Texas Western Press, 1977); William F. Mackey and Von Nieda Beebe, Bilingual Schools for a Bicultural Community: Miami's Adaptation to the Cuban Refugees, (Rowley, Massachusetts: Newbury House Publishers, Inc., 1977); Judith Socolov, ed., Early Childhood Bilingual Education, (New York: The Modern Language Association of America, 1971); Bernard Spolsky, ed., The Language Education of Minority Children, (Rowley, Massachusetts: Newbury House Publishers, Inc., 1972), and L.S. Tireman, Teaching Spanish-Speaking Children, (Albuquerque, New Mexico: The University of New Mexico Press, 1951).
  CURRENT POLITICAL ARGUMENT: Tomás A. Arciniega, "Bilingual Education in the Eighties: One Hispanic's Perspective," Education Research Quarterly, VI (Fall, 1981), pp.25-31; Gaynor Cohen, "The Politics of Bilingual Education," Oxford Review of Education, X (June, 1984), pp.225-241; "The Controversy Over Bilingual Education in America's Schools," New York Times, November 10, 1985, Section 12, pp.1 and 46-63; Manuel R. Gomez, "Officials Pound Bilingualism," The Miami News, Miami, Florida, no date but circa 1986, no page number (clipping in files of U.S.ENGLISH, Washington, D.C.); Rosalie P. Porter, "It's Time to Restructure Bilingual Education," The Boston Globe, Boston,

182

Bibliographical Essay

Massachusetts, circa April 2, 1986, no page number (clipping in files of U.S.ENGLISH, Washington, D.C.); Max Rafferty, "Bilingual Education: Hoax of the '80s," American Legion Magazine, CX (March, 1981), pp.14-15 and 38-40; Keith B. Richburg, "Secretary Bennett Defends His Plan to Change Bilingual-Education Law," The Washington Post, June 6, 1986, p.A9; Iris C. Rotberg, "Bilingual Education Policy in the United States," Prospects, XIV:1 (1984), pp.133-147; Lucia Solorzano with Muriel Dobbin, et al, "Educating the Melting Pot," U.S. News and World Report, C (March 31, 1986), pp.20 and 21; John H. Tanton, "Bilingual Education: Is It Threatening to Divide the United States Along Language Lines?" Vital Issues, XXXIII (November, 1984), and U.S. Commission on Civil Rights, Mexican-American Education Study, (Washington, D.C.: Superintendent of Documents, 1971-1974), six volumes.

CONCLUSION

In the wake of passage of the 1965 immigration law that took effect in 1968, the contemporary observer could get a feeling of watching an old movie from somewhere between 1914 and 1919, color tinted in the current fashion of TV reruns. The similarities are stiking enough to provide further corroboration of the Americanization syndrome. They also suggest that historical perspective may offer insight for practical solutions to temper or avoid the needless suffering imposed upon outsiders by an unwelcoming established population, an oft-repeated tragedy in American history that quickly gets beclouded and romanticized in people's minds.

This chapter outlined the growing struggle in the American body politic over· what is once again being called the "new immigration." A number of individuals and organizations are supporting solutions consistent with cultural pluralism. The work of the American Friends Service Committee was emphasized because of its long-time work with Hispanics and Asians and because it can trace its own heritage directly to the pluralistic values of eighteenth century American Quaker John Woolman. Several pamphlets describing current AFSC programs directed toward undocumented immigrants were utilized. They were "Eyes on the Border: The AFSC U.S.-Mexico Program in Southern California,"

Bibliographical Essay

"Justice for the Harvesters: A Program of the American Friends Service Committee in Florida," and "Seeking Safe Haven in Florida," (Philadelphia, Pennsylvania: American Friends Service Committee, all produced circa 1985). Especially helpful was the interview on June 13, 1986, with AFSC national staff members Domingo Gonzalez and Primitivo Rodriguez at the organization's national office at 1501 Cherry Street in Philadelphia, Pennsylvania.
Among others providing background and compassionate positions on the question of Hispanic immigration were Tony Bonilla and Louis B. Casagrande. Bonilla, chairman of the National Hispanic Leadership Conference, was part of a panel representing different sides of the issue on a Phil Donahue television program, "Illegal Immigrants," circa 1984, Donahue Transcript 09165. Casagrande, associated with the Department of Anthropology at the Science Museum of Minnesota, succinctly put the situation into perspective in a letter to the editor of the Star and Tribune, Minneapolis, Minnesota, January 4, 1986, p.11A. Among his salient comments: "...In the great majority of cases, those [Mexicans] who go north are risk-takers who have earned the ante to play the hand, who have the guts to put their lives in jeopardy, who know how to move through networks of friends and relatives to find work and avoid capture in an officially hostile land."
Advocates of further restrictions on immigration to the U.S. whose views were emphasized in The Americanization Syndrome were Richard Lamm, Roger Conner, and the organization Conner served as executive director, the Federation for American Immigration Reform (FAIR) located at 1424 16th St. N.W., Room 701, Washington, D.C. One of Conner's letters to the editor was published by the Star and Tribune, Minneapolis, Minnesota, March 13, 1986, p.14A, giving insight into his thinking. Publications of FAIR reviewed for this book included "FAIR: What They're Saying," "How Many Immigrants?," "Illegal Aliens - A 'Free Lunch' Myth," "Immigration Helped Build This Country. But Immigration That Is Out of Control Could Destroy It," "Public Opinion on Immigration," "Questions You Should Ask About Sanctuary," "Take a Short, Hard Quiz on Immigration," and "U.S. Immigration, 1965-1985," (Washington, D.C.: Federation for American Immigration Reform, circa 1983-1985). Governor Richard D. Lamm and Gary Imhoff, The Immigration

184

Bibliographical Essay

Time Bomb: The Fragmenting of America, (New York: Truman Talley Books, E.P. Dutton, 1985), became scripture for the new restrictionists. The Lamm book caught the attention of journalists around the nation. An editorial, "Taking Control of U.S. Immigration Policy," *Star and Tribune*, Minneapolis, Minnesota, January 3, 1986, p.10A, announced that the book would be published during the week of January 6, 1986. Two black columnists soon came out in support of parts of Lamm's program. William Raspberry, columnist for *The Washington Post*, mentioned the Lamm book in agreeing that the U.S. should avoid an oversupply of workers in the country in "Illegal Aliens and American Jobs," *Star and Tribune*, Minneapolis, Minnesota, March 6, 1986. Syndicated journalist Carl Rowan published a column, "America Must Retake Control of Her Borders," *Star-Phoenix*, Saskatoon, Saskatchewan, January 28, 1986, p.A4, shortly after the Lamm book appeared. Rowan complained about a recommendation by fruit and vegetable growers, supported by the President's Council of Economic Advisers, to resist efforts to pass a law punishing employers for hiring undocumented workers. He warned that slave labor and terrorists could be entering America across its allegedly uncontrolled southern border. In "Mexico Major Problem for U.S.," *Star-Phoenix*, Saskatoon, Saskatchewan, June 19, 1986, p.A4, Rowan recommended establishment of an aid plan aimed at Mexico. "I don't know that any U.S. 'Marshall Plan' can be big enough, or successful enough, to convince Mexicans to stay in woefully overcrowded Mexico City, or even Acapulco or Cancun. I do know that the price of illegal immigration in terms of welfare, education, crime and other factors will be as great as any aid plan the U.S. Congress is likely to approve."

Two collections of more scholarly opinions regarding the most recent "new immigration" were consulted for this study. One was Demetrios G. Papademetriou and Mark J. Miller, eds. *The Unavoidable Issue: U.S. Immigration Policy in the 1980s*, (Philadelphia, Pennsylvania: Institute for the Study of Human Issues, 1983). The other was Nathan Glazer, ed., *Clamor at the Gates: The New American Immigration*, (San Francisco, California: Institute for Contemporary Studies, 1985).

Newspaper and magazine articles that provided useful perspective were: Peter Applebome, "Surge of Illegal Aliens Taxes Southwest Towns' Resources,"

185

Bibliographical Essay

New York Times, March 9, 1986, pp.1 and 30; "Immigrants: The Changing Face of America," Time, CXXVI (July 8, 1985), pp.24-101; Matt Moffett, "Guarding the Gates: Fear of Terrorists Directs New Attention to Illegal Immigrants," Wall Street Journal, May 14, 1986, pp.1 and 19; Robert Reinhold, "Flow of 3d World Immigrants Alters Weave of U.S. Society," New York Times, June 30, 1986, pp. A1 and B5, and "Whites to Lose Majority in California," Associated Press dispatch, Free Press, Mankato, Minnesota, November 19, 1985, p.36.

Materials utilized in describing the so-called Liberty Weekend of 1986 and the poll of American opinion on immigration taken about the same time included Henry Steele Commager, "Standing Tall," Modern Maturity, XXIX (February-March, 1986), pp.33-39; Samuel G. Freedman, "While Liberty Fete Nears, 219 Aliens in City Face Expulsion," New York Times, July 1, 1986, pp.B1 and B4; Robert Pear, "Rising Public Support for Limits on Immigration Is Found in Poll," New York Times, July 1, 1986, pp.A1 and A21; Ronald Reagan, speech from New York Harbor televised nationally, July 3, 1986; "Sweet Land of Liberty," special edition of Newsweek, CVII (Summer, 1986), and "Two Killed By Slasher on N.Y. Ferry," Reuter dispatch, The Globe and Mail, Toronto, Ontario, July 8, 1986, p.A8.

Contributing to the discussion of the language issue in this chapter were "English Speaking Amendment," Phil Donahue television program, circa 1984, Transcript 02076, Governor Richard D. Lamm, "Diversity, Except in Language," Star and Tribune, Minneapolis, Minnesota, July 2, 1986, p.19A, and Jonathan Yardley, "Bilingualism and the Backlash," The Washington Post, July 28, 1986, p.D2. Lamm wrote, "America must make sure the melting pot continues to melt; immigrants must become Americans." Yardley added: "When in America one must do as the Americans do, and the Americans speak English." Julio Barreto, Jr., and Adán A. González III, in letters to the editor, pointed out to Yardley, "English Isn't the Only Language We Speak," The Washington Post, August 9, 1986, p.A19.

David Carlin, Jr., "Charm and the English Language Amendment," The Christian Century, CI (September 12-19, 1984), pp.822 and 823, presented the views of this state senator from Rhode Island. He favored linguistic uniformity in English in the U.S. but sought it through "magnetism," not compulsion. "It is, I suspect, no accident that this

Bibliographical Essay

attempt - conceived especially with Latin American immigrants in mind - to make English prevail by compulsion, not attraction, should surface at a time when we have in Washington an administration which believes that it can make American political values prevail by compulsion, not attraction, in Latin America. The United States, I fear, is losing faith in its own charm."
An important piece of scholarship on the language question was a ponderous tome by Calvin Veltman of Montreal. In the hands of David F. Marshall, a scholar with a more felicitous writing style, Veltman's data had the potential for putting U.S.ENGLISH out of business. It would go to its burial with its corporate visage wreathed in smiles, for Veltman's data indicated that the fears of the Americanizers were unfounded, that Hispanics were indeed learning English. See Calvin Veltman, Language Shift in the United States, (Berlin, Germany: Mouton, 1983), and David F. Marshall, "An Endangered Language?" English Today, No. 6 (April, 1986), pp.21-24.
A series of articles, starting in 1983, was useful in describing developments in the Roman Catholic Church in the U.S. favorable to Hispanics. The articles were Ari L. Goldman, "Fulfilling a Promise, Arzobispo O'Connor Says a Special Mass," New York Times, August 27, 1984, pp.A1 and B3; Ari Goldman, "New York's Controversial Archbishop," New York Times Magazine, October 14, 1984, p.38ff; Cecilio J. Morales, "The Bishops' Pastoral on Hispanic Ministry," America, CXLIX (July 2, 1983), pp.7-9; "New York's Archbishop O'Connor Skeptical About Bilingual Education," Up·date, II (September-October, 1984), probably p.3 but no number indicated; "O'Connor Off to Puerto Rico," New York Times, August 7, 1984, p.B4; "Pressures to Assimilate Decried," Up·date, I (Winter, 1983), unnumbered p.6; Jesus Rangel, "Hispanic Priests Seek Influence in the Church," New York Times, November 9, 1985, p.50; Thomas J. Reese, "American Bishops and Their Agenda," America, CXLIX (December 17, 1983), pp.393 and 394, and "Twenty Million Hispanics," America, CL (February 18, 1984), p.102.
Materials of value in reflecting upon some of the economic and social changes that will have to be grappled with by Americans now and in the future: Paul Hawken, The Next Economy, (New York: Ballantine Books, 1983). Robert Kuttner, The Economic Illusion: False Choices Between Prosperity

187

Bibliographical Essay

and Social Justice, (Boston: Houghton Mifflin Co., 1984). Joyce Purnick, "Moynihan Warns City of a Deep Rift," New York Times, November 9, 1985, p.29, reported Daniel Moynihan's assessment that a basic premise of his Beyond the Melting Pot was wrong. He now believed that different groups in New York City were not adapting socially and economically in U.S. society. He warned that, in New York City at least, Benjamin Franklin's dream of a "happy mediocrity" was turning into the American nightmare of "two cities" divided between the extremely wealthy and an economic underclass.
"Race or Class," colloquy between Carl Gershman and Kenneth B. Clark, Current, No. 227 (November, 1980), pp.20-45. "Rich Get Richer: U.S. Poor Losing Share of Wealth," The Globe and Mail, Toronto, Ontario, July 26, 1986, pp.A1 and A2. Stuart M. Speiser, "We Can Redistribute Income Without Taxes or Tears," New Options, No. 29 (June 30, 1986), pp.1, 2, and 6. Robert Theobald, An Alternative Future for America's Third Century, (Chicago: The Swallow Press, 1976). Roberto Vargas, "Adult Education for Empowerment and Social Change: Conversation with Roberto Vargas," tape recorded conference session, University Extension, University of Regina, November 12, 1985. Roberto Vargas, Provida Leadership: A Guide to Human/Social Transformation, (Oakland, California: Razagente Associates, 1985). And Roberto Vargas and Samuel C. Martinez, Razalogia: Community Learning for a New Society, (Oakland, California: Razagente Associates, 1984).
Other items of assistance in the writing of this chapter were Gerda Bikales and Francois Grosjean, Debate on the issue of multilingualism, Miami News, Miami, Florida, January 2, 1986, p.13A, reprinted in Up·date, IV (January-February, 1986), unnumbered pp.4 and 5; Joel Brinkley, "U.S. Preparing Drug Drive Along the Mexican Border," New York Times, June 5, 1986, p.A16; David Broder, "GOP Appeal to Hispanics?" Free Press, Mankato, Minnesota, January 15, 1986, p.4; César Chávez, tape recording of his talk at the Union Centre, Saskatoon, Saskatchewan, September 29, 1985; "A Florida First," Up·date, III (September-October, 1985), unnumbered p.5; Theodore M. Hesburgh, "Enough Delay on Immigration," New York Times, March 20, 1986, p.A27; "Hispanics Meet to Examine How U.S. Churches Respond to Them," Christianity Today, XXVIII (September 21, 1984), pp.79 and 80; Dolores Huerta,

Bibliographical Essay

"Reflections on the UFW Experience," The Center Magazine XVIII (July/August, 1985), pp.2-8; Ann Landers, "Blaming Growing Crime on 'Illegal Aliens' Unfair," Star-Phoenix, Saskatoon, Saskatchewan, September 16, 1985, p.B4, and Jay Mathews, "Immigrant Dominance Spurring a Backlash," The Washington Post, reprint in office of U.S.ENGLISH, hand-dated May 10, 1986.
Constanza Montana, "Papago Indians' Gate Admits Illegal Aliens, Narcotics and Liquor," Wall Street Journal, June 9, 1986, p.1; "Profile: Jeb Bush," Star and Tribune, Minneapolis, Minnesota, August 5, 1986, p.3A; Robert Reinhold, "Mexican Official Sees Harm in U.S. Bill on Aliens," New York Times, February 16, 1986, p.44; Royal Commission on Bilingualism and Biculturalism, General Introduction and Book I, The Official Languages, (Ottawa, Ontario: Queen's Printer, October 8, 1967); Royal Commission on Bilingualism and Biculturalism, A Preliminary Report, (Ottawa, Ontario: Queen's Printer, February 1, 1965); "Stop Bullying Mexico," New York Times, June 5, 1986, p.A26, and William H. Truesdale, Jr., "Organizational Schizophrenia in the I.N.S.," New York Times, November 12, 1985, p.26.

INDEX

abolitionists 26, 47-8
Adams, John 31, 33
Addams, Jane 8, 60-6, 71, 79, 83, 90, 95
adult education, profession of 5
AFSC 131-5. See also American Friends Service Committee (Quakers)
Aldrich, Thomas Bailey 76
Alien and Sedition Acts (1798) 35
Alinksy, Saul 106
Alsop, Stewart 105
Amalgamated Meat Cutters and Butcher Workmen 65
American Bible Society 34
American Colonization Society 48
American Friends Service Committee (Quakers) 111, 131. See also AFSC
American Party 41
American Protective Association 41
American Protective League 93
American Slavery As It Is 48
American Tract Society 34
Americanization, passim
 as syndrome 11, 12, 103, 108, 110, 125, 129, 131, 138
 by environment 6, 7, 12, 33-4, 73, 102, 131, 134
 of the English language 32

Americanization education, passim
Americanization of 97
 as citizenship management 82
 as "cultural tyranny" 96, 106
 as scientific profession 82-4
 as social science 82-3, 89, 93-4
 by abolitionists 47-8
 by academicians 74
 by blacks 8, 53
 by industry 93
 by Jewish Americans 67-70
 by parochial schools 43, 69
 by professional people 74
 by Protestant clergy 32-3
 by public schools 36-7, 73
 by Radical Republicans 50-1
 by Roman Catholic Church 43, 68-9, 119, 134
 by school book writers 32-3
 by settlement workers 60-6, 73
 definition of 1-5
 for efficient society 89
 for righteous society 89
 for Southern whites and Negroes 50-1
 of blacks 8, 10-11, 50-1, 104-6
 of Indians 55-6
 of native born Caucasian adults 95

190

Index

professionalization of 97-8, 101
World War I campaign of 92
Americans-first program, Detroit (1915) 86-7
Anglicans 15
Anglification 27,114
Anglo-Saxonism 2, 5, 53, 56-7, 59, 77-8, 99-100, 115, 125
Annenberg, Walter 9, 113
Antin, Mary 69-70, 79
antipoverty program 106
antislavery societies 47
Antonovich, Mike 128
Armour, J. Ogden 65
Aryan superiority 103
Asians 9, 125-6, 130-1, 135
asylum, America as 35, 41, 77, 80, 98, 121
Atkinson, George 37
Ayres, Leonard P. 89

Baldwin, Theron 37
Bancroft, George 49
banishment 9, 10, 12, 15, 19-20, 54, 56, 59, 116, 129. See also deportation
Barzun, Jacques 9, 113
Beecher, Henry Ward 48
Bemis, Edward 76
Bettelheim, Bruno 9, 113
Beveridge, Albert 57
Bierstadt, Edward Hale 96
Bikales, Gerda 9, 112
Bilingual Education Act 121-2
bilingualism
  in business 112, 123
  in education 112, 121-2, 127
  in French and English (Canada) 137
  in public services 112
  in Puerto Rico 120
  in Spanish and English 137-8
  in U.S. society 112, 124, 127
bilingualism and biculturalism policy
  in Canada 127, 137-8
  in the U.S. 124, 138
blacks 8, 10-11, 26, 45-54, 58-9, 101, 103-10
"Black Codes" of 1865, 1866 50
Black Muslims 107
Black Panthers 107
Board of Land Commissioners (California) 116
Boas, Franz 76
Bonilla, Tony 133, 135
Border Patrol, U.S. 111, 131-2
Breckinridge, Robert 37, 49
Brookings Institution 105
Brown, Rap 107
Brumbaugh, Martin S. 118
Bureau of Education, U.S. 83, 88, 97
Burroughs, George 20

Cadillac Company 87
Calvinism 3
Canada 28, 112, 137-8
Caribbean 11, 57-8, 118, 120
Carlisle Indian School 56
Carmichael, Stokely 107
Carnegie Corporation 98
Carver, Thomas N. 76
Central America 132
Chamber of Commerce, U.S. 85
Channing, William Ellery 48
Cháves, César 130
Chicanos 117, 136. See also Mexican Americans
Chickatabot 16
"chosen people" 1, 11, 14, 16, 28, 57, 129
citizenship education 5, 11, 89, 101
"citizenship management" 85
citizenship plants, schools as 88
"City on a Hill" 13, 19, 38, 129
civic religion, American 4, 6, 11, 29, 33-4, 36-7, 43, 50, 60, 64, 70, 78, 84, 90, 92, 98, 101-3, 105, 107
  adoption of 6
  definition of 4
Civil Rights Act of 1875 51-2

Index

civil rights movement 103-4, 107, 109, 113, 122, 137
Civil War 4-5, 50-1, 59
Clamor at the Gates 126
Class Book of American Literature 33
Clinton, DeWitt 36
Colgate, Florence 99
Commission on Civil Rights, U.S. 117
Committee for Immigrants in America 83, 86
Committee on Public Information 93
Commons, John 75, 80
Communists 1, 95
Compromise of 1877 52, 116
Conant, James 105
Congregationalists 41
Congressional Hispanic Caucus 114, 130
conscience, right of 43
conspiracy 28, 38-41, 49, 92, 95
  Catholic 38-41
  "Rumanian" 95
  slaveholder 49
containment policy, British 4
Continental Congress, First 29
Cooke, Alistair 113
Coolidge, President Calvin 100
Cordova, Robert 123
Corrada, Baltasar 114
Cotton, John 15
Council of National Defense 93
Cousins, Norman 113
Crary, Isaac 37
Crèvecoeur, Hector St. John de 7, 36, 71
Cronkite, Walter 113
cuisine, ethnic 103
cultural genocide 12, 59
cultural pluralism 10, 12, 97, 99, 130-1, 133-5, 137-8

Dana, Richard Henry, Jr. 115
democracy 2, 92

Department of Immigrant Education (NEA) 98
deportation 49, 117-18, 129. See also banishment
Detroit, Americanization campaign of 86-7, 110
Dewey, John 66, 90
Dey, Alex 118
Dictionary of Races 77
Dixon, Royal 95
Dole, Charles 89
Dred Scott Decision (1858) 49
DuBois, W. E. B. 53-4
Dudley, Thomas 15
Duke, Angier Biddle 9, 113
Dumke, Glenn 126-7

Eastern Orthodoxy, acceptance of 102
Easton, John 19
Eliot, John 16
Ely, Richard T. 61, 76
English, as official language 9, 111-12
English Language Amendment (ELA) 9, 112, 114, 137
Episcopalians 34
ethnic associations 94

Fairchild, Henry Pratt 97
Farmer, James 103
Federalist Party 34-5
Federation for American Immigration Reform (FAIR) 112, 127, 130
Ferré, Luis 120
Ferre, Maurice 123
Ford Motor Company 87
"foreignisms" 5
foreign-language press 94
Franklin, Benjamin 3-4, 8, 22-9, 31-2, 35, 41-2, 69, 86, 107, 110, 114
French and Indian War 23
French Canadians 28, 113
Friends, Religious Society of 10, 15, 22-6, 34. See also Quakers
Frost, John 33
Fugitive Slave Act (1850) 47

Index

Galloway, Samuel 37, 48
Garcia, Robert 128
Garrison, William Lloyd 46-8, 50
Garza, Kika de la 128
Gonzales, Henry B. 128
genocide 12, 19-20, 129
  cultural 12, 59
  of Indians 9-10, 19
Geography Made Easy 33
German language, removal from curriculum 93
Germans 26-7, 35, 110, 114
Giddings, Franklin 76
Giddings, Joshua 47, 49
Goodrich, Charles 32
Green, Beriah 47
Guadalupe Hidalgo, Treaty of 115
"happy mediocrity" 3, 27-9, 31, 42
Harding, President Warren G. 96
Hartwell, S. C. 88
Hawaii 11, 57, 125
Hayakawa, S. I. 9, 112-14, 121-2, 126, 137
Hayes, President Rutherford B. 52
Helton, Aurora 123
Highlander 104
Hispanics 9-11, 110-14, 118-23, 125-8, 130-5, 137
Hope Street School, Providence, R.I. 89-90
Horton, Myles 104
Huerta, Dolores 130
Hughes, John 39-40, 107
Hull-House 61-3, 66, 95
Hutchinson, Anne 16

Illich, Ivan 119
Immigrant Education, Division of 83
immigrants, passim
  Asian 9, 135
  Central American 121
  Chinese 54-5
  Cuban 120, 127, 129
  Eastern European 8, 61, 67, 69, 77, 99-104
  English 114
  German 26-7, 35-8, 46, 53, 77-8, 94
  Greek Orthodox 61
  Hispanic 9, 127, 135
  Irish 35, 38, 46, 49, 53, 77-8
  Italian 7, 62-3, 70-1
  Japanese 55
  Jewish 8, 65, 69-70
  Mariel 120, 127, 129
  Mexican 117
  Roman Catholic 36, 61
  Scandinavian 53, 77-8
  South American 121
  South European 61, 67, 77, 99-104
  Spanish-speaking 111
Immigrants in America Review 83
immigration, passim
  free 35
  restriction 10, 12, 15, 20, 38, 55, 75-6, 79-80, 98, 100, 117, 129-31
  to Mexico from U.S. 114-15
Immigration and Naturalization Service (INS) 120, 131
Immigration Commission 77, 79
Immigration Restriction League 77, 80
Immigration Time Bomb, The 127
Indians, American 1, 3, 9-10, 14, 16-19, 22-5, 55-6, 110
  Conestoga 24
  genocide of 9-10, 19
  Moravian 24
  Pennsylvania 10
  Pequot 16-18
Indian Bureau 56
Industrial Workers of the World 79
Institute for Contemporary Studies 126
integration of blacks 107
International Monetary Fund 132

193

Index

Inter-Racial Council 96
Ireland, John 8, 69, 110, 119
Irish, as "Americanizers" 54

Jay, John 4
Jefferson, Thomas 35
Jenks, Jeremiah 77, 79
Jews, acceptance of 101-2
Jim Crow laws 104
Jive (black English) 108
Job Corps 106, 108
Johnson, President Andrew 50
Johnson, President Lyndon 121
Jones, Thomas F. 106

Kallen, Horace M. 97
Kander, Mrs. Simon 8, 69
Kanjobal Indians 131
Keely, Charles B. 132
Kellogg, Paul 80
Kellor, Frances 8, 82-97, 110, 112
Kilpatrick, William Heard 102
King Charles II 19
King James Bible, use of 15, 40, 42
King, Martin Luther, Jr. 103-4, 107-8
Krome Detention Center 120
Ku Klux Klan 52, 103

Lamm, Richard D. 127-8
Lane, Franklin K. 83
Language Shift in the United States 137
League of United Latin American Citizens (LULAC) 114, 123, 128
Leipziger, Henry 67
Leopoldine Society 38
Letters from an American Farmer 36
Lewis, Samuel 37, 48
Liberator 47
Lincoln, President Abraham 49-50
Lodge, Henry Cabot 77
Lovett, Robert Morss 96
Lowell, James Russell 51
Lutherans 34, 37

Lynd, Robert and Helen 102

McDowell, Mary 65
McGuffey, William Holmes 33
McKinley, President William 58
Magnalia Christi Americana 13, 16-20
Mahoney, John J. 97
Mahy, M. Catherine 89-90
Mann, Horace 8, 36, 41-3, 48, 60, 66, 88, 105
Marshall, David F. 137
Marshall Plan 135
Mason, Gregory 86
Massachusetts Bay Colony 1, 10, 13-16, 20
Massasoit 17
Mather, Cotton 1, 8, 13, 16-20
Mayo-Smith, Richmond 75-6
"melting pot" 7, 36, 71
Mexican American Legal Defense and Education Fund 122, 128
Mexican Americans 10, 114-18, 121, 130-1. See also Chicanos
Mexican War 47, 115
Mexico 111, 114-15, 117-18, 128, 131-3
middle class society 3-4, 28
Middletown 102
Miller, Stephen D. 46
Mills, Caleb 37
Morse, Jedediah 33, 38
Morse, Samuel F. B. 38-9, 81
Morton, Oliver P. 54
"muckrakers" 73

National Americanization Day Committee 93
National Conference of Catholic Bishops 133
National Council of La Raza 114, 128
National Education Association 96, 98
National Hispanic Leadership Conference 133

194

Index

National Origins Act 100
National Security League 93
National Spanish Television Network 123
nativism 7, 113
Negroes 10, 26, 48-9, 58, 106. See also blacks
New Democracy, The 80
"new education" 66-7
New England 3, 10, 13-16, 20, 22, 36-8, 43, 46-8, 51, 56, 76, 115
"new immigration" 60, 64, 67, 73, 77-9, 90
North American Civic League 79, 83
North American Review 51
Northway Motor and Manufacturing Company 87
Northwest Territory 45

O'Connell, William 89
O'Connor, John 134
Obledo, Mario 123
"old immigration" 77
Old World in the New 79
"On the Canon and the Feudal Law" 31
Operation Wetback 118
Our Country 56
Outlook, The 86

pacifism, Quaker 22-7
Packard Motor Company 87
Page, John 35
Page, Thomas Nelson 52
Page-Detroit Company 87
Palmer, Mitchell 96
Panunzio, Constantine 68
parochial schools 37, 43-4, 69
Patriotic League 89
Peabody, Francis 61
Pennsylvania 22-7, 34, 114-15
Pentecostals 134
Philippine Islands 11, 57-8
Pierce, John D. 37
pietists, German 22
"Plain Truth" 23
"platoon school", Gary, Ind. 88
pluralism 10, 20, 22
Plymouth Plantation 17
Podhoretz, Norman 113
Poland, Addison B. 91
Pope Gregory XVI 39, 49
  as antirepublican 49
Pope Pius IX, as antirepublican 49
Population Council 132
Population Reference Bureau 126
Pratt, Richard Henry 56
Presbyterians 3, 22-4, 36-7
Progressives 74-6, 83
Project 100,000 106
Protestant Reformation 31, 38
Protestantism 29, 32-4, 46, 100
public schools 4-5, 36-7, 40-4, 51-2, 66-7, 101-2, 104, 106, 113, 116-17, 119-20
Puritans 1-3, 13-22, 30-2, 57, 81, 110, 125
  education by 14-15, 20-1

Quakers 10, 15, 22-6, 34, 48. See also Friends
Quebec Act 28-9
Quebecization 127, 137
Québecois 137

racism 5, 7, 53-9, 75-9, 81, 90, 103, 113, 116, 125
  Anglo-Saxon 53, 56-7, 59, 77-9, 116, 125
  of social scientists 75-6
Radical Republicans 50-1
Randolph, A. Philip 103
Razagente Associates 130
Reagan, President Ronald 109, 122, 128-9, 134
Reconstruction 4, 50, 52, 75, 116
Reformed Church 34
"Republican machines" 32, 35, 38
Republican Party, opposition to slavery 48

195

Index

Republicanism 33, 45-6
Rhode Island 10, 16
Ripley, William Z. 76
Roberts, Peter 85-7, 110
Roman Catholic Church 8, 34, 37, 42-3, 68-9, 119, 134
Roman Catholicism 8, 15, 28, 33-4, 37-44, 56, 70
Roosevelt, President Theodore 55
Ross, Edward A. 78-81
Roybal, Edward 128, 130
Rush, Benjamin 32, 35
Russell Sage Foundation 89

sanctuary movement 121
Saur, Christopher 27
Saxon Motor Company 87
Schlegel, Frederick 38
schools 4, 26-7, 36-7, 40-6, 51-2, 66-7, 69, 73, 87-91, 93-4, 101-2, 104, 106, 113, 116-17, 119-20
Schurz, Carl 52, 56
Scots-Irish frontiersmen 22-4, 115
secession of the South (1861) 50
segregation 10, 19, 58-9, 116, 125
separatism 37, 43, 107
settlement house movement 60-6
"Shame of the Cities, The" 73
slaveholders 45, 48, 50
slavery 25-7, 44-52
Smith, Adam 28
Snedden, David 89
Society for the Protection of Italian Immigrants 70-1, 85-6
Spanish-American War 57, 118
Spanish language 110-11, 116-17, 119-20, 123, 131, 133
Spellman, Francis 119
Speranza, Gino 7-8, 70-2, 85, 99-100
Squanto 17
Stanton, Henry 47
Starr, Ellen Gates 50, 62

Statue of Liberty 129
Steffens, Lincoln 73
Steiner, Edward A. 68, 79
Stevens, Thaddeus 8, 50
Stoddard, Lothrop 97
Stone, John 16-17
Stowe, Calvin 37, 48
Stowe, Harriet Beecher 48
Strong, Josiah 56-7
Suares, Xavier, 120
Sunday School Union 34
Swett, John 37

Talbot, Winthrop 93
Tanton, John 112, 127, 130
Taylor, Joseph S. 88
Texas, annexation of (1845) 115
Texas Rangers 116
Torres, Arnoldo 114
Trumbull, Frank 85

Uncle Tom's Cabin 48
"underground railroad" 47, 121
"unfair exchange" 5, 29, 39, 52, 56, 60, 69-70, 84, 106, 110, 113, 122
Unitarians 41
United Farm Workers 136
U.S.ENGLISH 9, 112-14, 122-5, 127, 130, 134, 136
"Value Rank of the American People" 78
Vargas, Roberto 130
Veltman, Calvin 137
Vidal, Gore 113
vocational education 11, 53, 66, 90-1

Wald, Lillian 66
Walker, Francis A. 76
Walling, William English 62
Ward, Robert De C. 80
Washington, Booker T. 8, 53, 56
Webster, Noah 4, 8, 32
Weld, Theodore 47
"welfare colonialism" 106

196

Index

Weyl, Walter 80
Wheelwright, John 16
Williams, Roger 10, 15-16,
Wilson, President Woodrow 92
Winthrop, John 8, 14-17
Woods, Robert 60, 80
Woolman, John 10, 24-5, 48, 111, 131
World's Work, The 99
Wright, Elizur 47
Wussausmon (John Sausaman) 18, 68, 110

Young Men's Christian Association 5, 85-6
Yzaguirre, Raul 114